CAPTURING IDENTITY

Quantitative and Qualitative Methods

Edited by

Meike Watzlawik
Aristi Born

University Press of America,® Inc.
Lanham · Boulder · New York · Toronto · Plymouth, UK

Copyright © 2007 by
University Press of America,® Inc.
4501 Forbes Boulevard
Suite 200
Lanham, Maryland 20706
UPA Acquisitions Department (301) 459-3366

Estover Road
Plymouth PL6 7PY
United Kingdom

Library of Congress Control Number: 2007922242
ISBN-13: 978-0-7618-3734-3 (clothbound : alk. paper)
ISBN-10: 0-7618-3734-5 (clothbound : alk. paper)
ISBN-13: 978-0-7618-3735-0 (paperback : alk. paper)
ISBN-10: 0-7618-3735-3 (paperback : alk. paper)

♾™The paper used in this publication meets the minimum
requirements of American National Standard for Information
Sciences—Permanence of Paper for Printed Library Materials,
ANSI Z39.48—1984

Table of Contents

Preface

In February 2004, Meike Watzlawik and her research team from the Technical University of Braunschweig (Germany) met with Aristi Born and her colleagues at the Otto-von-Guericke University of Magdeburg (Germany). Purpose of this meeting was to exchange experiences of quantitative and qualitative methods used by each research team to measure identity and to develop meaningful procedures for future projects. Expanding on the content of the initial meeting, the group decided to draw thoughts and experience from a larger pool of research scientists in this field by co-organizing an International Conference on "Identity Development: Toward an Integration of Quantitative and Qualitative Methods". This conference took place from November 4-6, 2005 in Braunschweig (Germany) and was funded with a grant from the German Research Foundation. Scientists from six countries, well known for their work in the field of identity research, presented their perspectives by explaining and commenting on methodological approaches to identity. We would like to share the findings on the different methodological approaches to identity gathered at this conference with a wider audience and promote international methodological and theoretical exchange in the field of identity research.

This book concentrates on qualitative methods such as narrative identity analysis or semi-structured interviewing techniques to determine identity statuses as well as on the quantitative method of using questionnaires, discussing the advantages and disadvantages of these methods and their future integration –where possible and reasonable. We would like to invite the reader to explore qualitative and quantitative research and discover the similarities and differences of understanding identity, which depends on research having its methodological roots in one or the other field, or in both. The book begins by comparing results of research rooted in the qualitative and then quantitative methodology of understanding identity and its development throughout life.

James E. Marcia, Founder of the Identity Status Approach, has paved the way for obtaining empirical access to personal identity development. The key words "identity status" produce 730 hits in the International Psychological Database "PsycINFO online" (search conducted on October 6th, 2006). Marcia is actively involved in the further development and discussion of his approach and joined the conference from West Canada. The reader is invited to study his latest thoughts and experiences with regard to the identity status concept and especially the Identity Status Interview (ISI) as a method to obtain empirical access to ego identity development. Karl Haußer from Germany's most Northern University, the University of Flensburg, developed the FISI (Flensburg Identity Status Interview), a variation of Marcia's ISI, which emphasizes the relative subjective meaningfulness of the identity domains education/work/ professional activity, political orientation, friendships/relationships and home/regional identity in relationship to each other. Wolfgang Kraus from Munich (Germany) is designing a long view on identity development focusing on identity capital as a basic ingredient to construct identity through self-narratives. He presents a longitudinal qualitative project of East and West Germany, which started in 1989 in line with the opening of the Berlin Wall, and studied identity in adolescents' lifeworlds. Alejandro Iborra from Alcalá (Spain) describes a qualitative approach using categorical and holistic content analyses of narratives of people who have experienced ritualized transitions. He explores how these content analyses can help to describe the person's meaning-making process and shows the differences between those who express identity changes and those who do not. Günter Mey from Berlin (Germany) presents a case study from his project "Adolescence, Identity, Narration" based on problem-centered interviews, and the specific interviewing, transcription and data analysis procedures utilized. He explores subjective meaning and identifies construction processes of personal life plans over time and expands on the micro-narration, -presentation and -construction logics of adolescents' stories. Mechthild Kiegelmann from Tübingen (Germany) introduces the Voice Approach, a qualitatively oriented research methodology, developed by Carol Gilligan, Lyn Brown and their colleagues, that can be applied to identity research. Especially one feature of this research technique offers insight on identity: the analysis of the "Voice of Self" via interview transcripts. In this paper, Mechthild Kiegelmann illustrates with an empirical example how the concept of the "Voice of Self" can provide insight on identity development. Werner Deutsch and Christina Börges from the hosting University of Braunschweig present an explorative study of pictorial representations of life courses. Combined with a biographical interview, they may offer a new approach to identity formation processes in different periods of life. In this chapter, case studies illustrate other depictions of life courses like stars of life, a street of life and a rock of life that deviate from the staircase tradition, which has been the most popular symbol for more than 450 years in the history of art.

"Statistics are like a bikini. What they reveal is suggestive, but what they conceal is vital", said Alejandro Iborra, citing Aaaron Levenstein, at the conference once we switched the focus to the quantitative approaches. Following this perspective, Luc Goossens and Koen Luyckx from Leuven (Belgium) present their results, which are mainly based on questionnaires offering a broad range of data analyses. The Belgium research team followed identity development in college students via variable-centered and person-centered analyses, which were appropriate methods for them to get answers in addressing two specific research questions in what was referred to as a model of identity formation. Meike Watzlawik introduces a German version of the modified Dutch Utrecht-Groningen Identity Development Scales II (U-GIDS) for adolescents (10 to 12 years of age), who were interviewed to examine commitment and exploration in the life domains siblings, best friend, intimate friend, school and hobby. She discusses if the dimensional approach (examining exploration and commitment) is appropriate for the examined age group. Wim Meeus, the author of the U-GIDS, and Minet de Wied from Utrecht (Netherlands) offer an overview of 25 years of research on relationships with parents and identity in adolescence. The main conclusion from their review of 35 studies, in which a variation of quantitative self-report data were used, and of only two studies which made use of qualitative data, is that parent-adolescent relationships are not linked to identity development in adolescence. They discuss how well the subtleties of parent-adolescent relations and identity formation can be captured with quantitative and qualitative methods. Aristi Born presents an attempt to construct a questionnaire that should differentiate between the four subgroups of Identity Diffusion (Disturbed Diffusion, Carefree Diffusion, Developmental Diffusion, Culturally Adaptive Diffusion) discorvered by James Marcia and colleagues. She reports the quality of the questionnaire and discusses, based on the correlations of identity diffusion with self-efficacy, self-esteem and the subjective well-being, if it is possible for emerging adults to be "well-diffused". The German-American author quartett Olaf Reis (Rostock, Germany), James Youniss and Hugh McIntosh (both Washington D.C., USA) as well as Jens Eisermann (Berlin, Germany) review three studies, each using a person-oriented analysis to find developmental trajectories in U.S. high school students as described by the identity scale of the Erikson Psychosocial Stage Inventory (EPSI). They underline the need to study developmental changes and continuity in identity and their underlying causes to capture the mechanisms of identity development. Jane Kroger from Tromsø (Norway) concentrates on the integrative benefit of quantitative and qualitative approaches. In her presentation she focuses on what qualitative and quantitative methods can contribute to identity development in midlife adulthood, using both methods with the same data set. The quantitative methods show the most common paths of identity transitions, whereas the qualitative in-depth interview produces information on the transitions of a particular individual. In his closing statement, Werner Deutsch invites the readers to continue the dialogue about the possibilities and limitations of qualitative and quantitative methods to capture identity. Both methods are important for future identity research, and sometimes a combination of qualitative and quantitative methods can be the most appropriate way.

We hope that our readers will follow the invitation and continue the dialogue on methodology and remain open minded for new ways to capture identity. Whichever method you prefer as the most appropriate way in your work, remember that there are researchers to share with and reflect on your findings on different methodological approaches to identity.

Acknowledgements

We thank all research scientists who attended the conference and who contributed to this book; the personal assistants, Sandrine Clodius, Susanne Wiedau, Marion Seifert, Julia Kobs, Johannes Kleikamp, and Christina Börges, who looked after the invited speakers in Braunschweig, Christine Riedel, who gave the book its "face", Jèrôme Ehring, who volunteered for the identity status interview, and Jennifer Fröhlich as well as all other native speakers and copy editors, who embellished the English of our contributors, who did not speak English as their first language.

Holger von der Lippe thankfully wrote a conference report for the Forum for Qualitative Research (FQS), that offers an excellent overview of our meeting and is available in the web:

Von der Lippe, Holger (2006, March). On Snowflakes and Gardens: Multiple Methods in the Field of Psychological Research on Identity Development. Conference Essay: International Conference: "Identity Development – Towards an Integration of Quantitative and Qualitative Methods". Forum Qualitative Sozialforschung / Forum: Qualitative Social Research [Online Journal], 7(2), Art. 46. Available at http://www.qualitative-research.net/fqs-texte/2-06/06-2-46-d.htm.

Enjoy reading the book!

Aristi Born & Meike Watzlawik

Chapter 1

Theory and Measure: The Identity Status Interview

James E. Marcia
Simon Fraser University
Burnaby, Canada

What should the relationship be between a theoretical construct and the form its measurement takes? Need a measure be complex simply because the construct in question is complex? What should be the balance between reliability and validity, between expediency and thoroughness? These are questions we faced at the inception of research on Erik Erikson's concept of ego identity. The measure we arrived at, and the one that I, my students, and some of my colleagues have been using for forty years, the Identity Status Interview (ISI), arose out of consideration of these issues. In order to understand both the nature and context of the identity construct, it is necessary to discuss its theoretical origins. I shall begin my essay with theory, move on to a description of various initial measurement options, discuss some of the advantages and disadvantages of the ISI, note briefly the current "status" of the identity statuses, and conclude with general comments on the choice of measures for complex constructs like identity, as well as a personal note.

1.1   Theoretical origins of the identity statuses

Erikson's psychosocial developmental theory

Erikson's concept of ego identity (1959; 1963; 1968) arose out of ego psycho-analytic theory as articulated by theorists such as Rapaport (1960), Hartmann (1958), and Anna Freud (1936). Ego psychoanalytic theory is an extension of, not an alternative to, Freud's classical psychoanalytic theory (1923/1961). It places a greater emphasis on adaptation to the environment than does classical Freudian theory which is more concerned with inner dynamics and the uncon-scious. Especially as articulated by Erikson, ego psychoanalytic theory places the individual *within* a more or less nurturing social context, as contrast with the more confrontative view of classical theory wherein the individual is seen more as *contesting* society (Freud, 1930). However, one must acknowledge that not all social contexts are nurturing and the psychoanalytic sense of growth through conflict is retained in Erikson's use of the term "versus" to describe the resolu-tion of the psychosocial stages (e.g., Basic Trust *vs.* Mistrust, Identity *vs.* Iden-tity Diffusion). "Versus", here, refers to turning-points in development when the individual faces the risky possibilities of gain or loss, advancement or decline. Ego psychoanalytic theory is "optimistic" only to the extent that the social con-text is considered as the necessary milieu within which individual development takes place –a milieu that has adapted cultural institutions which provide, more or less, for individual growth throughout the lifespan.

A further addition to classical analytic theory furnished by Erikson is the description of eight psychosocial stages of ego development which parallel the first five Freudian psychosexual stages, and then move beyond these to encom-pass the whole life cycle (see figure 1.1). Different tasks in ego growth are as-sumed to arise at different chronological periods. The successful resolution of each issue is assumed to be important for the resolution of succeeding issues. This epigenetic developmental chart assumes that given an "average expectable environment", growth will be continuous and cumulative over the life cycle. Each stage is marked by a somatic-societal mutuality: what an individual *can* do meshes with what a society *requires*; and what the individual *needs* corresponds to what a society *provides*. As one peruses the chart, one sees that there are sixty-four, not just eight, stages. Each stage has contributions from preceding stages and makes contributions to succeeding ones. Furthermore, each psycho-social issue arises, in some form, at every chronological age, so that at, say, young adulthood, when the primary issue is Intimacy vs. Isolation, the person is also dealing with the resolution or re-resolution of seven other psychosocial stages. A discussion of some of the psychotherapeutic implications of this epi-genetic model is found in Marcia, 1994. In addition, a fuller discussion of Erikson's psychosocial developmental outline is also found in Marcia, 1998.

Chronological Age

Identity issue at Integrity Stage

Chronological Age	1	2	3	4	5	6	7	8
VIII OLD AGE	T-M Intg.	A-S, D Intg.	I-G Intg.	Ind-I Intg.	Id-ID Intg.	Int-Is Intg.	G-S Intg.	Integrity and Dispair
VII ADULTHOOD	T-M G.	A-S, D G.	I-G G.	Ind-I G.	Id-ID G.	Int-Is G.	Generativity and Stagnation, Self-absorption	Inty-D G.
VI YOUNG ADULTHOOD ■ Mature intrusion-inclusion	T-M Int.	A-S, D Int.	I-G Int.	Ind-I Int.	Id-ID Int.	Intimacy and Isolation	G-S Int.	Inty-D Int.
V ADOLESCENCE ▲ Genital	T-M Id.	A-S, D Id.	I-G Id.	Ind-I Id.	Identity and Identity Diffusion	Int-Is Id.	G-S Id.	Inty-D Id.
IV SCHOOL AGE ▲ Latent	T-M Ind.	A-S, D Ind.	I-G Ind.	Industry and Inferiority	Id-ID Ind.	Int-Is Ind.	G-S Ind.	Inty-D Ind.
III PLAY AGE ▲ Phallic (oedipal) ■ intrusion-inclusion ● Individuation	T-M I.	A-S, D I.	Initiative and Guilt	Ind-I I.	Id-ID I.	Int-Is I.	G-S I.	Inty-D I.
II EARLY CHILDHOOD ▲ Anal ■ eliminative-retentive ● Practising	T-M A.	Autonomy and Shame, Doubt	I-G A.	Ind-I A.	Id-ID A.	Int-Is A.	G-S A.	Inty-D A.
I INFANCY ▲ Oral ■ Passiv-Active Incorporative ● Attachment	Basic Trust and Basic Mistrust	A-S, D T.	I-G T.	Ind-I T.	Id-ID T.	Int-Is T.	G-S T.	Inty-D T.

Autonomy at Trust Stage

Figure 1.1 *Psychosocial Stages*　(▲ = Psychosexual zone;　■ = Related behavioural modality;　● = Object relational phase)

Identity and adolescence. The development of an identity is focused on adolescence because this is the first time that the necessary individual and social ingredients are present. On the individual's side are sexual maturation, cognitive development, and a growing desire for autonomy. On society's side are expectations that the adolescent will begin to consider occupational alternatives, take some steps toward becoming an informed adult, and the provision of some latitude for exploration. Essentially, what is required of the adolescent is the relinquishing of the childhood position of one-who-is given-to and the gradual adoption of the stance of one-who-is-to-give-to-others, a change from being a recipient to being a provider. This necessitates a change in a view of oneself in the world. Hence, for this reason, as well as pubertal changes, adolescence is a normal de-structuring period –an ideal time for the re-structuring that will culminate in an initial identity. At late adolescence, an individual experiences his/her abilities, needs, and beliefs within a perceived social context of demands, available alternatives, and expectable rewards. All of these become synthesized into a new personality structure an identity –that provides a sense of continuity with one's past, meaning for one's present, and direction for one's future.

1.2   Measuring the unmeasurable: How to assess identity?

Initial methodological considerations

Identity is a concept derived not just from psychoanalytic theory, but from the process of psychoanalysis itself. This was Erikson's primary "research" method. In addition, he conducted field studies of non-technological societies and made several psycho-biographical explorations. For us, however, a psychoanalysis of each individual subject was not a feasible way to conduct empirical research. We wanted generalizeable measures that would allow for individual expression. Initially, we were confronted with questions of relevance to theory and degree of structure. We required sufficient structure in our measure to permit objective scoring without sacrificing fidelity to the complexity of the identity construct. We knew that increasing structure would increase reliability of scoring, yet would risk decreasing face validity. Decreasing structure would decrease scoring reliability, while likely increasing face validity.

In the beginning of the identity research there was no "we" as there later came to be, so the decisions about measures were ones that I, alone, had to make. Some early candidates for measuring identity and their reasons for rejection were:

Rorschach test. It might be possible to look at the organization and quality of percepts. This could give a guide to the inner state of the individual and to the more unconscious aspects of identity. However, identity was an elusive enough concept without attempting, at this stage, to look at the even more elusive unconscious aspects of it.

Thematic Apperception Test. One could assess certainty of goals and commitments to life directions within an imaginative interpersonal context. Stories told about others could be assumed to be projections of oneself. Again, it was thought to be too much of a conceptual leap to go from stories constructed about other persons to an assessment of a subject's own identity.

Kelly's Role Repertory Test. This measure could give a sense of the individual's way of construing the interpersonal world. One could determine tightness and looseness, permeability and impermeability, general organization, and complexity of an individual's personal construct system. This measure, however, seemed too theoretically distant from Erikson's theory and necessitated too many theoretical assumptions in order to construct the conceptual bridge.

All three of the above were considered to be too conceptually distant from the identity construct. I felt that I needed something closer to the content of Erikson's own description of identity. Perhaps the above measures could be used later as dependent, rather than as defining, variables.

What I arrived at were the following:

A semi-structured interview (The Identity Status Interview-ISI). Erikson (1968) had identified the content areas of occupation and ideology (religion + politics) as being crucial for adolescent identity development, so these were the initial topic areas. The process variable of commitment was to be determined within these domains. Exploration, as a second process variable, was added later after pilot interviews suggested that commitments could be arrived at by different avenues. Criteria for determining commitment (and, later, exploration), as well as examples of subjects' statements, were contained in a scoring manual. Using the two criteria of exploration and commitment I was able, eventually, to formulate the four identity statuses to be described below. Today, we can use the ISI to locate categorically subjects in an identity status (an excerpt of the interview is shown in figure 1.2). Because these identity status categories can be weighted relative to each other within a particular interview content area, we can obtain separate scores for each status as well as an overall status designation. This allows for both parametric and non-parametric data analysis as well as the use of percentage of agreement or alpha coefficients for inter-scorer reliability estimates.

The Ego Identity Incomplete Sentences Blank (EI-ISB). Stems were constructed that could elicit responses relevant to Erikson's ideas about identity development. Each stem is scored on a 1-3 scale reflecting degree of correspondence to Erikson's ideas about characteristics of identity formation. As with the ISI, scoring criteria and examples were contained in a scoring manual, one considerably shorter than that for the ISI.

Occupation (college)

How did you decide to come to ____ (name college or university)?

What are you majoring in?

How did you come to decide upon ____?

What do you plan to do with ____?

What seems attractive to you about ____ (either the major area of study, the future application of the area, or both, if appropriate)?

What other things have you considered besides ____?
When did that occur?
Tell me about how that was for you?

How do you feel about your current position with respect to ____?

Most parents have plans for their children, things they'd like them to do or go into. Did yours have any plans like that for you?

How do your parents feel about what you're doing now? About your future plans?

How willing do you think you'd be to change doing or going into ____ if something better came along? (If S responds: "What do you mean by better?") –Well, what might be better in your terms?

On a 5 point scale, how important do you see your occupation as being to you in your life? 5 means extremely important and 1 means not at all important.

Figure 1.2 *Occupation Part of the Ego Identity Status Interview: Late Adolescent*

The semi-structured interview (ISI) was capable of yielding identity statuses, whereas the Ego Identity Incomplete Sentences Blank gave only high-low scores on overall identity. The scoring criteria for the EI-ISB were drawn directly from all of Erikson's theoretical writings on identity. The criteria for the ISI, based upon process variables of extent of exploration and solidity of commitments, were abstracted from Erikson's writing as central identity-defining principles. As expected, these two measures were found to be significantly positively correlated.

Assumptions underlying the ISI and EI-ISB. Because identity is assumed to be, as Erikson stated, "an inner configuration," it is not amenable to direct observation. What can be observed are behaviors, i.e., statements of thoughts and self-reflections, that should be present if an underlying identity is present. Because such self-reflections may not be readily available to some participants, eliciting them may require the kind of focused and sometimes probing conversation possible with the ISI. The EI-ISB, by contrast, is a form of projective test that is less flexible (given that the stems are fixed), more indirect in its apparent aims, and more "subject-determined" (responses are freer), than the ISI. Hence, I initially approached the measurement of identity with two measures: a direct, semi-structured interview, and an indirect sentence completion test. Both measures were drawn directly from Erikson's theory.

Summary. The four identity statuses arose as an empirical tool to test the validity of Erikson's concept of identity. They are not considered to be a direct measure of the hypothesized identity structure, but, rather, an *indicator* of it. The question posed was: "What can we observe that will tell us something significant about this particular inner state (identity) of a person?" Drawing from Erikson's writings, an obvious criterion was the presence of *commitments* in significant life areas such as occupation and ideology. After interviewing a sample of college students in a pilot study, it became clear that if such commitments existed, they could be arrived at by different means. Hence, *exploration* became a second criterion for identity status. Research in ensuing years has expanded the significant life areas to include topics such as sexuality, sex roles, relationships, etc. The four identity statuses based upon the dual criteria of exploration and commitment are: *Identity Achievement* –has undergone exploration and is currently committed; *Moratorium* –is presently *in* an exploratory period and commitments are vague; *Foreclosure* –has not explored, but rather adopted, alternatives, and commitments are present; *Identity Diffusion* –has undergone only cursory exploration at most, and is not committed. A more extensive discussion of the identity statuses may be found in Marcia, Waterman, Matteson, Archer, & Orlofsky, 1993.

1.3 Identity statuses today

Forty years of research have established the construct validity of the identity statuses. From being simply an empirical tool to validate Erikson's theory, they have taken on a theoretical quality themselves. Some of the ways in which the identity statuses are currently considered are:

- Their original meaning as categories reflecting modes of adolescent identity resolution.
- Differing ways of thinking about the world, differing methods of information-processing. An example of this is Berzonsky's (1989) "identity styles".

- Epistemological modes –within a Piagetian framework, persons in different identity statuses may be described as primarily "assimilators or accommodators". (cp. Whitbourne, 1996)
- Differing approaches to experience –primarily "open" or "closed". (cp. Stephen, Fraser, & Marcia, 1992)
- Different existential positions –characteristic ways of being-in-the-world. (cp. Josselson, 1987 and Kroger, 1993)

Although the identity statuses have been remarkably productive in terms of research generated and explanatory power, it is well to bear in mind some reservations. The first is that usefulness is not equivalent to truth. The second is that longevity does not equal reality. The identity statuses are ways we social scientists have of labeling our experience of others' experience of themselves. They are revisable and discardable when more useful ways of labeling these experiences are invented. The identity statuses (Achievement, Moratorium, Foreclosure, and Diffusion) are essentially research constructs that have become habits of speech. And it is worth remembering that even within the paradigm, any individual is an admixture of these statuses, not solely one.

1.4   Methodological issues in measuring identity

Depth vs. surface. Identity, as construed within the ego psychoanalytic theory from which it was derived, consists of both conscious and unconscious aspects. Some of the roots of identity are found in the deepest levels of the personality structure. Hence, any measure seeking to assess this construct either has to tap these levels or to explore thoroughly those surface aspects that can be tied accurately to these probably unobservable levels. Most researchers on identity have chosen to forget or ignore the construct's theoretical origin and have opted for its consideration as a "social psychological" variable. That certainly makes matters less complex and methodologically "messy". However, the rather lengthy Identity Status Interview, scored with a fairly complex manual, is more consistent with the psychodynamic theoretical origins of the identity construct. A social psychological view, by contrast, can consider identity just an endorsement of questionnaire items covering exploration and commitment (and, sometimes, only commitment). One of the considerations, then, of the measurement one chooses has to do with one's theoretical construal of the construct, and the importance of theory, in general.

Accuracy vs. approximation. If one has access to a large pool of subjects, one can "waste" subjects more easily (i.e. absorb protocols that either inaccurately or insufficiently estimate subjects' identity statuses) than if one has a more limited pool. Those not meeting cut-off points on certain questionnaire measures can simply be dropped from the sample, or as is the case with the Extended Objective Measure of Ego Identity Status (EOM-EIS), put into a kind of wastebasket category, e.g., "low-profile Moratoriums". The problem with this strategy is that if a label is to be given to a group of subjects, then some construct validity should be demonstrated for persons with that common label. I don't know of any studies demonstrating the construct validity of "low-profile Moratoriums". By contrast, very few subjects are "wasted" when using the interview. A rough estimate is that about 5 out of 100 have to be dropped because they are unclassifiable using the scoring manual. In addition, the interview gives the opportunity to probe subjects' responses until the interviewer is satisfied that an accurate assessment has been made. Marks made upon a questionnaire form cannot be queried.

"Validity" vs. "reliability". I have put these words into quotation marks to indicate that I do not intend them only in their strict statistical sense wherein validity is contingent upon reliability. Rather, by validity I mean an assessment that is as accurate as possible with respect to an individual subject. Because of the complex nature of the identity construct (at least, as I see it), this takes time and questioning from a number of different vantages –sometimes even requiring a departure from the standard interview protocol. By reliability, I mean inter-scorer convergence. This poses no problem with questionnaire measures: a checkmark is a checkmark, and only in the most egregious cases of experimenter bias could inter-scorer reliability be low using this technique. However, inter-scorer reliability is a major issue with the interview measure. Even the best-trained scorers hover around 85%, including moderately high Kappas, in their reliability of scoring. This is an acceptable level of inter-scorer reliability, but one that does introduce a margin of error. What has been encouraging is that even with the error introduced by some inter-scorer variability, there is a very large body of significant and meaningful findings with respect to predictive validity of the identity statuses determined by the interview method (see, for example, Marcia et al., 1993).

Thoroughness vs. expediency. There would probably be little disagreement that an identity status interview yields a more complete picture of an individual than does a questionnaire measure. However, there is also no doubt that the number of person/hours it takes to administer and score an ISI is considerable as compared with a questionnaire. Even disregarding the time taken to train interviewers and scorers, just interviewing and rating one subject can, on average, consume about 2-3 person/hours. In that amount of time, if subjects are administered computer-scorable questionnaire measures, as many subjects can be run as there are questionnaires available. Of course, one is much less likely to find out anything *new* about a group of subjects using an inflexible questionnaire. It is almost impossible to generate new hypotheses based upon observations of subjects, given that the observations are constrained by pre-formulated, unvarying questionnaire items. By contrast, individual interviews permit the researcher to enter the personal worlds of subjects and perhaps to find out such things as variations upon the four identity statuses, or even new statuses. For example, had we used a questionnaire in the initial identity status research, we would not have discovered the importance of exploration as a defining criterion. We would have remained with only commitment and, hence, would not have discriminated Achievements from Foreclosures. As well, an interview can lead one to question the validity of the interview domains for a particular subject sample. For example, it may be that occupation and ideology are *not* the most important issues for some populations. All of these situations of uncovering new directions and ideas have occurred in the course of giving identity status interviews. Whatever form of measurement is used, it is important to remember that any instrument purporting to yield identity statuses *must* include a temporal perspective. Where an individual's commitments came from, their present state, and their behavioral implications for the future are important developmental defining characteristics of the identity statuses. "Exploration" alone, "commitment" alone, or even these two combined, outside the context of a temporal perspective, do not validly yield identity statuses

Idiographic vs. nomothetic. Some of the above issues boil down to the old distinction between studying individuals versus studying groups. Clearly, if one wants to sample very large populations, the time taken to administer and score ISI's is prohibitive. Still, individual interviews can be aggregated to yield group scores, but questionnaire measures give only an abbreviated portrait of any one individual. To stretch a metaphor, "slow cooking" may yield tastier and more nutritious meals, but "fast food" is sometimes the only viable alternative for researchers who are pressed for time. Before one disparages questionnaires as "McMeasures", one has to determine just how much time one wants to spend in the assessment kitchen. A more detailed discussion of the use of semi-structured interviews in psychological research may be found in Bartholomew, Henderson, and Marcia, 2000.

1.5   Choice of methods

In choosing a method for measuring identity and the identity statuses, some of the factors to be taken into consideration are the problem being addressed, pressure on investigators, available resources, and aesthetic preferences.

Problem being addressed. If one is concerned with obtaining as accurate and estimate as possible of an individual participant's identity status, or in describing the experience of individual subjects, then the interview method is preferable. However, if one is interested primarily in gathering large-scale data on a national or regional sample, one can easily sacrifice the validity of measures of single individuals and use questionnaire measures. Whether or not a questionnaire assesses accurately this or that person will not be crucial because the effects of measurement error will likely be reduced as scores are aggregated. In any case, I think that it would be wise for any investigator setting out to use the identity statuses as an experimental variable to administer several ISIs to some selected persons from the subject population. This will give the researcher a feel for his sample population as well as first-hand knowledge of the construct that is being investigated with the more abbreviated measure. Most research projects fall somewhere between the nomothetic and ideographic approaches. My opinion is that if N <100 and fairly specific hypotheses are being made, the interview will give a more accurate indication of subjects' identity status and almost all subjects will be useable.

Available resources. Resources can be considered in terms of the availability of time, subjects, finances, and available interviewer/scorers. For some researchers, large samples are not available and fewer available subjects means that the accuracy of each measurement counts; hence, the interview is preferable. For other investigators with access to large numbers of potential subjects, giving so many interviews would be prohibitive. Because so much identity research (and psychological research, in general) occurs within an academic setting, there is a way in which the interviewer/scorer problem can be addressed with added educational benefits. I have taught a number of upper level undergraduate seminars on Eriksonian theory and identity. Teaching students in those seminars to administer and rate identity status interviews both gives them firsthand experience with the constructs as well as providing them with insights into Erikson's theory. In addition, they can also administer measures of dependent variables. By this means, they become active participants and contributors in the general scientific endeavor and learn theory and research design in the process.

Pressure on investigators. As noted above, most research takes place within an academic setting, for better or worse. Because doing research is such a major part of the academic's job, and because of the ever-increasing emphasis on publication output, researchers can hardly be blamed for wanting to get as many articles published in as short a time as possible. Paychecks, promotion, and tenure (and, of course, narcissistic gratification) depend upon it. This may be one of the reasons why so many journal articles are so uninteresting to many of us. However, publication pressure is an inescapable fact of academic life. One can obtain publishable data on, say, 100 subjects in 2-4 hours using a questionnaire. That same data would "cost" the researcher about 230 person/hours using the interview, allowing for administration, scoring, and a reliability check. Whether or not the more "fine-grained" interview method is worth the extra time must be each researcher's decision.

Aesthetics. Some researchers prefer teasing out nuances in an interview: asking just the right questions, pursuing the genuineness of an individual's exploratory period, determining the depth of a participant's commitment, arriving at an overall identity status formulation taking into account all of the person's responses. Other researchers prefer playing with the statistics of large data sets, applying the newest, shiniest analytic procedures to a multitude of observations. It is likely that the methods favored by these two admittedly stereotypically described investigators are as much a function of their personality characteristics and aesthetic preferences as they are of the ultimate validity of either method. One is unlikely to persuade a therapeutically-oriented clinical psychologist that there is any substitute for in-depth assessment of single individuals. As well, one is unlikely to persuade a researcher working for a nationally-funded institute that there is any substitute for gathering a large number of relatively quick (sometimes less valid) measures on a large number of subjects and letting the statistics tell the empirical story. Most of us engaged in identity research fall somewhere between these two extremes. My preference has been for individual interviews, which, I believe, give a more accurate assessment of individuals' identity status, and then aggregating those individuals to furnish group data. Of necessity, that means that most of the identity studies that I and my students have conducted have involved about 100 participants per study, a reasonably large sample, but not large enough for some statistical analyses requiring a very large N. Generally, the larger the N, the smaller the value needed to obtain statistical significance, making it more likely for large versus small studies to find effects that are, indeed, present. On the other hand, smaller studies that repeatedly do find similar significant effects suggest that the effect is notable. Ultimately, there is room for everyone, I suppose, so long as we are each aware of the limitations of our techniques and the goals to be served.

A personal note

In response to a request from the editors of this volume I have appended a more personal description concerning the initiation of the identity research and the identity status interview. In 1963-64 I was undertaking my internship at Massachusetts Mental Health Center-Harvard Medical School (MMHC) as part of the requirements for my Ph.D. in clinical psychology at Ohio State University. I was assigned to do a psychodiagnostic work-up on a young man who was admitted to the hospital with a tentative diagnosis of acute schizophrenia. My supervisor, Dr. David Guttmann, and I concurred that all of the tests I administered to this patient were consistent with the diagnosis. Several months later, the young man was released from the hospital, in complete remission. This was not what either of us expected and we re-visited our diagnosis. Dave, at that time, was a Teaching Assistant for Erikson at Harvard. He asked me to read Erikson's monograph, "Identity and the Life Cycle". We then came to understand our young man's difficulty, not as a schizophrenic process, but as a temporary thought disorder accompanying an identity crisis. More important than a belatedly accurate diagnosis was the impression that Erikson's writings made on me.

I had come from a learning theory background (Hull, Skinner, etc.) at Ohio State. However, my immersion in psychoanalytic theory at MMHC had left me with a great deal of respect for this approach to treatment. Yet, I was frustrated by the distance between the sometimes arcane theoretical language (à Fenichel) and my actual experience of patients. Erikson ego psychoanalytic theory bridged the gap. Not only that, he provided a schedule for development throughout the life-span, different from the classical psychoanalytic one that ended primarily around the Oedipal period. On an aesthetic level, I was also impressed with the vividness of Erikson's writing style.

I knew that I would have to complete a dissertation upon my return to Ohio State. I could think of no more meaningful topic than Erikson's primary construct, Identity. My professors at Ohio State had persuaded me that the method of construct validity would permit testing of the most complex ideas, providing that they could be defined operationally and measured. So, I began the task of developing a measure of Identity and establishing construct validity for it. While the results are now obvious in the literature, the venture was not nearly so auspicious in the beginning. I underwent a good deal of criticism (*most* of it constructive), ranging from comments about the folly of embarking on such a complex project to repeated suggestions regarding an adequate methodology. Even after I came up with a workable proposal, one of my best graduate school friends took me aside and said, in essence, that while I'd proved such a thing could be done, I should now drop it and proceed to something more "practical", because even if the study came out positively, no one would be interested. Sometimes, one should not listen even to friends!

I never met Erikson. My work, and that of my students who have developed measures of other Eriksonian stages, has been based, not on personal contact, but solely upon his written work. Erikson was not fond of attempts to operationalize and measure his constructs. He felt that they would be trivialized. Hopefully, we have returned his necessarily abbreviated ideas back to him enriched them with even more meaning and empirical relevance than he anticipated.

My choice of an interview as the primary identity measure was not derived from my clinical orientation. I wanted the most flexible, subject-expressive, yet reliably scorable measure I could construct. Most of the early identity researchers were not clinicians, yet they found the interview relatively easy to administer and score. Of course, it was not as simple as a questionnaire and, given differences among interviewers, not so reliable. There would be far fewer identity status studies now if Gerald Adams and Hal Grotevant had not developed the Objective Measure of Ego Identity Status (OM-EIS).

Besides furnishing what I believe to be the most accurate measure of identity status, the interview has provided an opportunity for numerous advanced undergraduate and graduate students to learn first-hand what identity looks like in individuals. Teaching interested students to listen carefully to research participants' identity concerns has been a personally engaging activity of which I've never tired. Long though the identity status interview may be, and complex as it sometimes may be to score, helping people listen to each other is a project that is, in today's world of needless conflicts, an immensely worthwhile endeavor.

Acknowledgements

Thanks to Prof. Janet Strayer for her helpful comments on this manuscript.

References

Bartholomew, K., Henderson, A.J.Z., & Marcia, J.E. (2000). Coding Semi-Structured Interviews in Social Psychological Research. In H.T. Reis, & C.M. Judd (Eds.), *Handbook of Research Methods in Social and Personality Psychology*. New York: Cambridge University Press.

Berzonsky, M.D. (1989). Identity style: Conceptualization and measurement. *Journal of Adolescent Research, 4,* 268–282.

Erikson, E.H. (1959). *Identity and the life cycle*. New York: International Universities Press.

Erikson, E.H. (1963). *Childhood and Society* (2nd Edition). New York: Norton.

Erikson, E.H. (1968). *Identity: Youth and Crisis*. New York: Norton.

Freud, A. (1936). *The Ego and the Mechanisms of Defense*. New York: International Universities Press.

Freud, S. (1961). The ego and the id. In J. Strachey (Ed. and Trans.), *The standard edition of the complete psychological works of Sigmund Freud* (Vol. XIX, pp. 3–66). London: Hogarth. (Original work published 1923)

Freud, S. (1930). Civilization and its discontents. In J. Strachey (Ed. and Trans.), *The standard edition of the complete psychological works of Sigmund Freud* (Vol. XXI). London: Hogarth.

Hartmann, H. (1958). *Ego Psychology and the Problem of Adaptation*. New York: International Universities Press.

Josselson, R. (1987). *Finding Herself: Pathways to Identity Development in Women*. San Francisco: Jossey-Bass.

Kroger, J. (1993). On the nature of structural transition in the identity formation process. In J. Kroger (Ed.), *Discussions on Ego Identity*. Hillsdale, N.J.: Lawrence Erlbaum Associates.

Marcia, J.E. (1994). Identity and psychotherapy. In S.L. Archer (Ed.), *Interventions for Identity* (pp. 89–104). Newbury Park, CA: Sage.

Marcia, J.E. (1998). Optimal development from an Eriksonian psychosocial perspective. In H.S. Friedman (Ed.), *Encyclopedia of Mental Health* (Vol. 3) (pp. 29–39). San Diego, CA: Academic.

Marcia, J.E., Waterman, A.S., Matteson, D.R., Archer, S.L., & Orlofsky, J.L. (1993). *Ego Identity: A Handbook for Psychosocial Research*. New York: Springer.

Rapaport, D. (1960). *The structure of psychoanalytic theory: A systematizing attempt* (Psychological Issues, 2 (2), Monograph 6). New York: International Universities Press.

Stephen, J., Fraser, E., & Marcia, J.E. (1992). Moratorium-Achievement (MAMA) cycles in lifespan identity development: value orientations and reasoning system correlates. *Journal of Adolescence, 15,* 283–300.

Whitbourne, S.K. (1996). *The Aging Individual: Physical and Psychological Perspectives*. New York: Springer.

Chapter 2

Assessing Identity as the Meaningfulness of Meanings: The Flensburg Identity Status Interview (FISI)

Karl Haußer
University of Flensburg
Germany

In this article I would like to introduce the "Flensburg Identity Status Interview" (FISI), a variant and a further development of the Identity Status Interview (ISI) by James Marcia. The FISI differs somewhat from the ISI with regard to the interviewed identity domains, and it emphasizes the relative subjective meaningfulness of these identity domains in relationship to each other. I will begin with a discussion of "subjective meaningfulness" as an identity concept.

2.1   Subjective   meaningfulness   as   a   concept   of identity psychology

In psychological theory and concept formation, traditionally, one often speaks of "self-oriented" cognitions and emotions (e.g., Heckhausen, 1980, de Vol, 1982). There are difficulties, however, in determining a logically and psychologically appropriate complementary terminology. This is due to the fundamental social context, both implicit and explicit, of any given thought or feeling.

Certainly it is possible to divide the entire range of a persons cognitive experiences into two categories –the "self-model" and the "environment-model". Filipp takes this approach in her theoretical construction of an open system consisting of an "internal self-model" and an "internal environment-model" (Filipp, 1979). In this context, the counterpart to the term "self-referred" is "environment-referred". Epstein describes a similar dichotomy in his integrative personality theory, in which he differentiates between subjective self-theory and reality-theory (Epstein, 1979). Groschek draws a distinction between "self-consciousness" and "object-consciousness", between "self-concept" and "environment-concept" (Groschek, 1980).

I maintain that this model is inadequate for establishing a psychological identity theory (cf. Haußer, 1995). In this instance, self and environment are separated, isolated as static entities, when, by contrast, that which is relevant for identity consists in the relationship which exists between the two. In his oft-quoted article, Graumann speaks of the "problematic comma" in Lewin's well-known formula V=f(P,U), which postulates that behavior (V=Verhalten) is dependent upon the person (P) and his environment (U=Umwelt) (Graumann, 1975, 20f). The "problematic of the comma" refers to the influence which the person and the environment exert on each other.

Leontjew, in his activity theory, has developed the use of the term "object", or, more precisely, "object-relationship" to describe this connection (Leontjew, 1977, 18ff). According to Leontjew, the term "object" refers not only to things, but to persons, other living things, objects, changes, events, and relationships; in short, circumstances in the daily life of the subject. A person can have an object-relationship with his bicycle, his colleague at work, and even with his government.

In this sense Leontjew establishes a connection with Lewin, who speaks of the "valence" which a particular "object" has for a "subject". This means that a person's ability to satisfy needs and achieve goals is connected with his ability to deal with "objects". Through the "objectification" of needs and goals, an "object" takes on a very definite "valence" for a person, depending upon his experiences and expectations. Lewin defines "valence" as the perceived characteristics of an object which attract or repel a person with varying degrees of intensity. "I include in my definition the idea that the "valence" can vary considerably in its intensity: it may be impossible for the subject to resist, or it can have the character of a command, or of a request, or even of something less." (Lewin, 1982, 103 –my own translation).

With this background of object theory in mind, we can now move to the decisive question of subjective meaningfulness and attraction in an "object relationship". These two aspects, meaning and attraction, can be understood as the cognitive and the emotional sides of valence. Subjective meaningfulness is simply the perceived importance which an object has for a person (Haußer, 1995, Haußer, 1983, Frey & Haußer, 1987).

If one proceeds from Schiefele's meaning-profile with its selection and orientation functions (Schiefele, 1978, 140f), then "subjective meaningfulness" can be understood as *the meaningfulness of a person's various subjective meaning-themes* (e.g., attachment or lack of attachment in a relationship, career-orientation or satisfaction with an acquired job-position, political involvement or non-involvement, sensitivity or indifference to one's living conditions). If one considers, based on identity research and empirical surveys of individual meaning themes, that there are both high degrees and low degrees of "meaningfulness", one arrives at a *meaningfulness profile* that can be applied to individuals as well as groups.

From the point of view of identity psychology, *subjective meaningfulness* can be characterized as an instrument of organization and orientation. The subject thus determines the identity relevance of experiences (retrospectively) and of motivations (prospectively).

In social-psychological research one sometimes speaks of the related concept of *centrality* (Sherif, 1980, 2f). Even the occasionally observed differentiation between "core identity" and "subsidiaries" is simply a ranking of a person's "object-possessions" according to their subjective meaningfulness. The emotional counterparts to this process of ranking are attachment or involvement, and their opposite, indifference. When a person is deeply involved with a particular object-relationship, and absorbed in it, he needs other object-relationships which are less emotionally demanding in order to create a balance. Thus, object-relationships with high identity-relevance may come into the foreground without dominating and placing undue stress on an individual's mental/emotional capacity, or failing to take into consideration limitations of time and space.

2.2   The "Flensburg Identity Status Interview"

The *"Flensburg Identity Status Interview (FISI)"* presents a variant of the *"Identity Status Interview (ISI)"* by Marcia (Marcia, 1966, Marcia, 1993, Marcia, 2006). Two aspects are considered here by way of background. The first is that, in psychological identity research, only the person himself, as the actual possessor of identity, can provide information regarding his self-concept, self-esteem, and belief in control. The second is that this "self-information", as it relates to *subjective meanings and the meaningfulness of meanings*, can best be given in the form of free, open, self-formulated answers. For these reasons, it is recommended that the method used be a half-standardized identity interview. The *"Identity Status Interview (ISI)"* by Marcia compares with the "Methodological Questionnaire for Investigating Identity and Identity Development", established and developed by Haußer (Haußer, 1995, 129f).

Our *"Flensburg Identity Status Interview (FISI)"*, which is introduced below (see figure 2.1), presents a modification of the *ISI*. This modification is based on research in the field of identity psychology undertaken by Marcia, as well as on his evaluation strategy. The further development of the *FISI* differentiates it from the *ISI* in two essential characteristics: the selected identity domains (meanings), and the explicit consideration of the subjective meaningfulness of meanings.

Four identity domains: 1) Education/Work/Professional Activity, 2) Political Orientation, 3) Friendships/Relationships, 4) Home/Regional Identity. The identity domains "occupation", "religion", "politics", and "sex roles" (subsequently expanded) by Marcia seem to be rather narrow from the point of view of both theoretical rationale as well as my own extensive interview experiences (Marcia, 1966, Marcia, 2006). Two ideological categories, *religion and politics*, dominate, when, for many people, religious confession and political orientation have little or no influence upon their identity structure (see *subjective meaningfulness*). For this reason we limit ourselves in our interview schedule to the domain *political orientation*. We adopt the category *education/work/professional activity* because of its objective and societal importance, in the sense that material independence provides the basis for individual life-planning and identity development. Furthermore we adopt the domain *friendship/partnership* (*sex-roles*, as in the ISI, seems too narrowly conceived) as an important area of experience connected to friends and intimacy. The fourth and last identity domain addresses the question of *home* as an "object" of identity relating to socio-cultural origin, sense of belonging, and sense of community. This seems especially relevant in an era of economic globalization and individual mobility (Haußer, 2000).

How does *subjective meaningfulness* relate to the four identity domains? Even if there is a certain correlation between *objective meaning* and *subjective meaningfulness*, one cannot postulate a *subjective meaningfulness* which is applicable to every empirical study or to every individual. This is due, in part, to the fact that no individual, in the development of his own identity, can completely insulate himself from societal structures and expectations. Rather, it is more appropriate to examine the *meaningfulness of meanings* on a case by case basis. For this reason the interviewees are asked at the conclusion of the interview to rank the four identity domains in order of importance. In an effort to circumvent a cursory or superficial ranking, the interviewees are asked to evaluate the four identity domains on the basis of their interdependence, as well as their influence on the development of their identities.

Flensburg Identity Status Interview (FISI)
Version 2006 of Marcia's "Identity Status Interview"

Introduction
   (Guarantee of Anonymity/Procedure)
   Gender –Year of Birth and Age– Place of Birth and Places of Residence
   (Timeline in Calendar Years) –Education and Professional Status– Educa-
   tion and Professional Status of Parents (Family Background)

1. Education/Professional Activity
   - Present Educational/Professional Activity/Perspectives – When did you de-
     cide to pursue this education/profession? – Why? – What other opportunities
     existed? – When? – What did you find particulary interesting about
     this/these field(s)?
   - To what extent did your parents or other important persons influence your
     educational/professional pursuits?
   - What do your parents or other important persons think about your current
     educational/professional pursuits?
   - Would you be prepared to change your current educational/professional pur-
     suits if the opportunity presented itself?

2. Political Orientation
   - Do you have a definite political orientation?
   - When and how did your current political orientation come about? To what
     extent did your parents or other important persons influence your political
     orientation?
   - Were/Are you politically active? Have you worked for political organiza-
     tions, written letters, or participated in demonstrations?
   - Are there political issues which particularly concern you?
   - What would have to happen to cause you to change your political orienta-
     tion?

3. Friendships/Relationships
   - How many persons live in your household? How does this compare with
     your prior living situation?
   - Are you happy with your current situation (Single / Married / Partnership),
     or do you wish it were different? Why?
   - To what extent have your parents or other important persons influenced your
     ideas and the actual circumstances of your living arrangements?
   - What would have to happen to cause you to change your current living ar-
     rangement?

4. Home/Sense of Regional Identity
   - What does the expression "home" mean to you? Do you have a "home"?

Figure 2.1 *Flensburg Identity Status Interview (FISI)*

o   If yes: What does this "home" mean to you?
                What has this "home" meant to you?
                Have you previously had another "home"?
o   If no: Why does the expression "home" mean little or
                nothing to you? Did "home" ever have meaning for you?
- Do you feel you belong to a certain region/a certain group (of people)/a certain culture or language? To what extent?
- To what extent did your parents or other important persons influence your idea of "home"?
- What would have to happen to cause you to have a new "home"?

Meaningfulness of Identity Domains
You have provided information reflecting the meaning which you attach to the domains of
    o   education / professional activity,
    o   political orientation,
    o   friendships / relationships,
    o   home / regional identity
- How would you personally rank these four domains in order of importance? (What is most important to you? To what degree?)
- Is there overlap among the various four domains? (If yes, to what extent?)
- Think of an important change in your orientation to one of the four domains (describe the change). Did this have an influence on the other domains? Why? (To what extent?)

Thank you for this interview.

Figure 2.1 continued *Flensburg Identity Status Interview (FISI)*

The FISI has been practised until now in some hundred cases. Applying the interview schedule presented above takes about thirty minutes. The interpretation of the interview data follows the lines of the ISI: Each person is categorized in each of the four identity domains to one of the four identity statuses of Marcia with the wellknown dimensions exploration and commitment. As a further result in respect to the *meaningfulness of meanings* we get the ranking of the four identity domains according to subjective importance for each of the interviewees. The FISI is suitable for adults; interrater reliability has to be examined in future. Because of the different identity domains, a comparison but not a validation of FISI related to ISI seems to be adequate.

References

Epstein, S. (1979). Entwurf einer Integrativen Persönlichkeitstheorie [Approach to an Integrative Personality Theory]. In S.H. Filipp (Ed.), *Selbstkonzept-Forschung* (pp. 15–45). Stuttgart: Klett-Cotta.

Filipp, S.H. (1979) (Ed.). *Selbstkonzept-Forschung* [Self-Concept Research]. Stuttgart: Klett-Cotta.

Frey, H.P. & Haußer, K. (1987) (Eds.). *Identität. Entwicklungen psychologischer und soziologischer Forschung* [Identity. Development of Psychological and Sociological Research]. Stuttgart: Enke.

Graumann, C.F. (1975) Person und Situation [Person and Situation]. In U. Lehr & F.E. Weinert (Eds.), *Entwicklung und Persönlichkeit* (pp. 15–24). Stuttgart: Kohlhammer.

Groschek, W. (1980). Zur Dimensionierung des Selbstkonzepts [Dimensions of Self-Concept]. *Probleme und Ergebnisse der Psychologie, 75*, 39–57.

Haußer, K. (2000). Zur subjektiven Bedeutsamkeit und Bedeutung von Heimat als regionale Identität [On the Subjective Meaningfulness and Meaning of the Home as Regional Identity]. *Zeitschrift für Kultur- und Bildungswissenschaften, 10*, 17–23.

Haußer, K. (1995). *Identitätspsychologie* [Identity Psychology]. Berlin: Springer.

Haußer, K. (1983). *Identitätsentwicklung* [Identity Development]. Stuttgart: UTB.

Heckhausen, H. (1980). *Motivation und Handeln* [Motivation und Activity]. Berlin: Springer.

Leontjew, A.N. (1977). *Tätigkeit, Bewusstsein, Persönlichkeit* [Activity, Consciousness, Personality]. Stuttgart: Klett. (Original: Moscow, 1975)

Lewin, K. (1982). *Feldtheorie* [Field Theory]. Stuttgart: Huber.

Marcia, J.E. (2006). Theory and Measure: The Identity Status Interview. In M. Watzlawik, & A. Born (Eds.), *Capturing Identity – Quantitative and Qualitative Methods*. Lanham, MD: University Press of America.

Marcia, J.E. (1993). The Ego Identity Status Approach to Ego Identity. In J.E. Marcia, A.S. Waterman, D.R. Matteson, S.L. Archer, & J.L. Orlofsky (Eds.), *Ego Identity, A Handbook of Psycho-Social Research* (pp. 3–21). New York: Springer.

Marcia, J.E. (1966). Development and Validation of Ego-Identity Status. *Journal of Personality and Social Psychology, 3*, 551–558.

Schiefele, H. (1978). *Lernmotivation und Motivlernen* [Learning Motivation and Learning Motives] (2nd Edition). München: Ehrenwirth.

Sherif, C.W. (1980). Social Values, Attitudes, and Involvement of the Self. In M.M. Page (Ed.), *Nebraska Symposium on Motivation 1979* (pp. 1–64). Lincoln: University of Nebraska Press.

de Vol, D.M. (1982). *Selbstbezogene Kognitionen Jugendlicher in Abhängigkeit von der bereichsspezifischen Selbstwertrelevanz* [Self-Referring Cognitions of Adolescents Dependent on the Domain-Specific Self-Esteem Relevance]. Bochum: Brockmeyer.

Chapter 3

Designing the Long View: Lessons from a Qualitative Longitudinal Study on Identity Development.

Wolfgang Kraus
University of Munich
Germany

Given that identity development is about change over time, it would appear reasonable to take the long view and account for this process in the framework of a *longitudinal study*. If, furthermore, it can be argued that modes of identity processes have altered due to changes in the social construction of adolescence, then it makes sense to select a *qualitative* methodological approach in exploring the various aspects of these changes.

Such was our line of argument when we[1] began our longitudinal study on identity development back in 1989. Since then identity research has become a field characterised by a variety of approaches, which are more or less interrelated (table 3.1). Overall, it can be stated that identity as a research topic has left the domain of developmental psychology. It is no longer confined to research on adolescence, but also plays a central role in the discussion on "identity politics" and the post-modern condition. On the one hand, this broader view of identity is not without problems, in so far as it entails relating differing theoretical traditions with one another. On the other hand, however, it also brings to bear the very social dynamic which is engrained in the identity question and therefore stands for its actuality.

Table 3.1

Identity –basic theoretical questions and subfields

Identity question	Focusing on	e.g.
Who am I?	Individual, I –me, alterity, self-representation, self-	Personality, ascription by others
. . . in time. . .	Individual trajectories, personal experience, projects	Past, present, future
. . . through my beliefs . . .	Personal ideology, meaning making	Beliefs, moral standards, convictions
. . . as part of . . .	Community, Belonging, lifeworlds	Memberships as . . . (German, male, social psychologist)
. . . distinctive from . . .	Difference, power, boundary management, positioning, identity capital	The others: Nations, cultures, groups, gender roles, religions
. . . by expressing, talking and doing "identity"	Expressivity, narrativity, performativity	Works, stories, situations

3.1   Defining the question: Patchwork identity

The development in identity research is reflected in our research project on "patchwork identity". Its starting point consisted of a growing body of evidence surrounding the *changing state of adolescence*, widely discussed in social psychological and sociological literature in the 1980s. The changes were characterised as a substantial prolongation of adolescence (Cavalli & Galland, 1993)[2] and a destandardisation of the trajectories through adolescence (Münchmeier, 1998). Furthermore, it became obvious that in many western societies unemployment rates among adolescents and young adults were growing, leading to a more general debate on the role of work as a defining variable for identity in "late modernity" (Wagner, 1994; Baethge, 1988). Adolescent identity projects seemed to be endangered by the necessity of having to cope with a downward rather than an upward mobility.

The *sociological analysis* of these symptoms of change is marked by two discussions. The first concerns the process of *individualisation*, encompassing a multi-faceted change of individual development on many levels. The second, intimately related discussion, centres on the attempt to understand these changes on a more general level as indicating the arrival of a "late modern", "postmodern" or "reflexively modern" situation (cf. Beck, Giddens & Lash 1994; Gergen, 1991). Analysis of the subjective experience of change in late modernity is based on the notion of *disembedding* (Giddens, 1991). Here, dissociation is diagnosed as taking place between individual and collective patterns of life. Life trajectories are no longer standardised. Large social groups (classes, milieus, religious communities) are losing their defining power. Work as a basis for identity is becoming a scarce and unreliable resource as increasingly more people experience unemployment and are forced to change their profession or occupation at some point of their working-life. Moreover, gender roles are becoming blurred, adding yet another source of insecurity with regard to the identity-question. As the great ideologies and belief-systems relinquish their defining power, individual *meaning making* becomes more than ever a personal task (Bruner, 1990). The stages for this meaning making are to be found in the individual's various lifeworlds which, taken together, represent the resources of self-experience. These trends lead to a pluralisation of our way of life, and to *destandardised* personal biographies, which are less compatible with one another, thus complicating personal relationships and necessitating reflexive networking (Sampson, 1985). However, as the virtual world opens up completely novel means of self-exploration and -presentation, new possibilities in exploring the identity question also arise. Consequently, the identity question is more open than ever. Whether this is experienced as a chance or a menace depends on individuals' *identity capital*, i. e. personal, social, cultural and material resources as preconditions for the construction of identity (Coté & Levine, 2002).

From the point of view of *Eriksonian identity theory*, we addressed the question as to whether the identity model developed by Erik Erikson and others can still be considered appropriate when it comes to understanding the identity development task with which adolescents were faced at the end of the last millennium. Erikson himself emphasised that identity is not a private project, because it concerns, as he wrote "a process located in the core of the individual and yet also in the core of his communal culture, a process which establishes, in fact, the identity of those two identities" (Erikson, 1968, p. 22). The social thus plays a central role within identity development. Accordingly, fundamental changes in society have consequences at the level of individual identity development.

It was within the context of such an analysis of social change that we developed our concept of "patchwork identity". At the onset, this notion held, to use a notion from Herbert Blumer, the status of a "sensitising concept". Beginning with a critique of Erikson's identity model (Erikson, 1966), we posed the question, whether the openness of identity projects and the heterogeneity of various lifeworlds today might actually constitute characteristics of identity development. In late modernity, according to our line of argument, it may be more adaptive to refrain from an "achieved identity" and to maintain the status of moratorium or even identity diffusion.

Proceeding from a diagnosis of change in individual development, we subsequently contemplated whether Erikson's model of identity might have been influenced by the era in which he lived, i.e. the time of post-war prosperity, in which achievement and coherence was a goal to be striven for by a large majority of (white, male) adolescents. In contrast, identity at the end of the millennium appeared in our eyes destandardised and open-ended[3](see table 3.2).

Table 3.2

Patchwork identity –theses
Identity as an open, destandardised, and prolonged process,
…. taking place in individuals' lifeworlds,
…. in need of "identity capital",
…. as the construction of meaning an coherence through self-narratives.

Three ingredients thus contributed to the construction of our theses: findings concerning the changing face of adolescence, the general sociological debate on late modernity and Erikson's identity theory. Viewed from a *methodological point of view* the elaboration process of our research question can be generalised as follows.

- Development of a semantic and theoretical reference system relating to established theories.

While it is plausible that a research project requires a certain "identity" in its own right, it remains absolutely essential that the project is understood by others in the field. The most challenging task is therefore elucidating relationships to other theories, while simultaneously explicating the distinctiveness of one's own approach. This proved especially true in our case, due to the fact that we positioned ourselves outside of "traditional" developmental psychology, and relied heavily on sociological modernisation theory. Our project therefore demanded presentation in a language making sense to experts in both fields. This lead us, for instance, to commence our work with examinations of the main traditions of identity research in psychology and sociology, i.e. the Eriksonian theoretical context and the interactionist debate (Krappmann, 1997).

- Adaptation of new theoretical approaches.

A number of our ideas could be linked to new theoretical developments such as individualisation theory, post-modern approaches or constructivism. In these domains, the identity debate was also gaining force, although mainly within a sociological frame of reference. Further approaches emerged out of the "narrative turn" (Bruner, 1991; Gergen & Gergen, 1988). Hence, it was possible to share the effort of having to construct a plausible line of argument with neighbouring theoretical contexts.

- Use of available "under-explained" scientific results.

There were several puzzling results available, which strengthened our argument. One especially helpful finding, for instance, originated from an empirical study by James Marcia on the basis of his identity status approach. In his study, Marcia reported an increase of identity diffusion from 20% to 40 % between the 1960s and the 1980s (Marcia, 1989). In attempting to explain this development he proposed the distinction of four different types of identity diffusion, among them the *culturally adaptive identity diffusion*. The reasoning behind this type of diffusion was that remaining diffuse may, in certain social situations, constitute a good coping strategy for an individual, on account of society itself being in a diffuse situation. Within our project, Marcia's results –though only briefly discussed in his own work– appeared to make sense from the viewpoint of individualisation theory. This also provides an example of the way in which results accumulated in the context of a specific empirical approach over a period of time, can be compared with further approaches and thus lead to interesting new questions.

3.2   Selecting a methodology: Patchwork identity as a methodological question

The ideal method for monitoring an individual's experience of change across time would be a proper longitudinal study where the person is followed across a lengthy span of time –years or decades. Practical difficulties however mean that longitudinal studies will always be rare. Financial costs, maintaining a committed research team across years, [. . .] the difficulty of identifying suitable individuals for study at the onset and keeping the main respondents committed to the study involved over a span of years, all conspire to keep true longitudinal studies rare (Miller 2000, p. 109).

While Miller's statement continues to ring true today, recent publications nonetheless show that qualitative longitudinal studies in identity research have increased in frequency over the last decade (cf. Thomson, Plumridge, & Holland, 2003). This was not the case at the time when we were faced with the decision concerning the methodological approach to be taken for the project on "patchwork-identity". We were, however, able to build on a generalised concern, also existent at that time, surrounding the limits of quantitative methods in identity research (cf. Bourne, 1978). Karl Haußer, for instance, complained back then about the predominance of "ready-made, narrowly focused research instruments, which regularly fail to take into account the subjective importance of self experience, so important for identity development" (Haußer, 1983, p. 177). A further argument for qualitative methods was the general impression of change in our society; a change which appeared to be rather felt than analysed, more sensed than known. Qualitative methods had already gained a certain amount of credit for being appropriate for the exploration of changing social realities, even if only to prepare the way for subsequent quantitative research. A general change in the methodological climate was also clearly observable, induced by the rise of post-modern theory, the narrative turn and constructivist and deconstructivist approaches.

Deciding on a focus

Since then, this change in climate has gained ground in social science. Grant proposals today are usually not faced with an ideological battle with respect to methodology. The "simple" question is: Does the proposal make sense to the granting body? Is the choice of method plausible with regard to the research question? In line with our general decision to employ a qualitative approach, we developed a research design to be used in conjunction with our specific research questions (see table 3.3).

Focusing on "identity as an open process"

Given that identity development is not about a *result* which can be inspected, but rather about the long view, i.e. a construction work which cannot be terminated, then it is the characteristics of the *process* which come to the forefront of interest. These, in our view, are *not* to be assessed by "measurements" carried out at certain points in time, but by participating in discursive and situated self-construction. The process is to be organised as an interview bearing three temporal perspectives in mind: as a prospective, situative and retrospective self-positioning, each of which is to interactively take place during the interview. Emphasis is made upon this positioning in time, especially in the future, for two reasons, a theoretical and a methodological one. The theoretical argument centres on my conviction that the importance of a future time perspective is largely underestimated in psychology.

Table 3.3

Theses - focuses - tools

Theses	Methodological Focus	Tools
Identity as an open, destandardised, and prolonged process.	Dynamics and tensions, change in identity status	Identity status (change) per lifeworld, Change of I-positions across the three interviews
Identity development takes place in various lifeworlds, each accompanied by a different logic (complementary, antagonistic?)	Lifeworlds: characteristics, logic, relationship	Network-map, Life-event-questionnaire
Identity requires *"identity capital"*, i.e. personal, social, cultural and material resources as preconditions for the construction of identity	Resources: their functional role and their actual use	Network-map, Sociodemographic questionnaire, Interview questions
Construction of meaning and coherence by means of self-narratives	Self-narratives	Interview structure: Emphasis on narratives, Empathy, "normalisation", Story-line, Photos

Frederik Melges (1990) takes the same line of argument. He has coined the notion of "futuring", i.e. the capability to develop one's own personal future time perspective. He diagnoses a lack of futuring as time diffusion, a state which Erik Erikson considers to be a symptom of identity diffusion and which, in my view, concurs with Marcia's notion of "culturally adaptive identity diffusion" under the condition of post-modernity. From a methodological point of view on the other hand, the positioning in time constitutes an important interview strategy, promoting interviewees' reflexivity during the interviews.

Process orientation was to be realised by a longitudinal design consisting of three waves of interviews with an interval of approximately two years. The three interviews were designed to coincide with foreseeable major life events and situations of change. Research on adolescence has for example convincingly shown that the start of a professional career indeed represents a situation of immense change. It entails deciding on a profession, finding an apprenticeship, commencing training, and deciding on a professional project at the end of the apprenticeship. Accordingly, we planned to initially interview the adolescents at the *start of their apprenticeship* and for a second time upon *apprenticeship completion*. The third interview coincided with *no foreseeable external trigger* for change. It was assumed, however, that having completed their training and eventually having found a permanent job, our interviewees would take on other professional and private identity projects (e.g. leaving the family home and living on their own, starting an intimate relationship).

Focusing on "lifeworlds" as stages –and resources– for identity development

A methodology oriented towards various lifeworlds will lead to results which are more differentiated and "thicker" than methods which are far removed from everyday life (Geertz, 1973). Besides this, our focus on lifeworlds was also a consequence of individualisation theory, positing that individualised networks become the basis of experience for one's self-definition. In differentiating between various lifeworlds, we were able to build on methods and experiences from the Eriksonian tradition; primarily Marcia's Identity Status Interview (Marcia, 1966; 1993). While this interview distinguishes between the lifeworlds of work, family and peers, we insisted that subjects should also be free to introduce additional lifeworlds. The importance of this non-restriction rested in the awareness that "[. . .] an adolescent today is usually involved in a great number of everyday lives" (Ziehe, 1991, p. 64). We therefore aimed to cover the various lifeworlds not only as stages for the construction of partial identities, but also as identity capital for one another. Of interest was the question pertaining to how the dynamics of identity construction are related to the developmental dynamics in specific lifeworlds and further how these lifeworld dynamics are related to one another.

Focusing on identity capital as a precondition for identity development

Identity capital as the entirety of personal, social, cultural and material resources (Coté & Levine, 2002) is closely linked to lifeworlds and to the quality of the personal relationships within them. It is in these lifeworlds that the availability of these resources is decided upon. In order to gain information regarding the importance of various resources we differentiated our 150 interviewees into two groups of individuals. One group consisted of trainees in local authorities, a professional trajectory with a high degree of job security, the second group of youths with very poor school graduations, integrated in social projects designed to prepare them for the job market. This differentiation was carried out in order to bring systematic variation into our empirical design, concerning the question of individual resources.

Identity capital is not simply a matter of possessing resources but also of using them, i.e. a matter of the agentic role, an individual is able to attribute to him- or herself. To aid the exploration of this self-positioning as an "active subject", we aimed to create an interview situation enabling the interviewees to present themselves as competent designers of their own lives. This strategy was supposed to differentiate between different types of agentic self-positioning. The relevance of this differentiation again followed from our analysis of individualisation and a self-reflexive biography. Adolescence here is not conceptualised as a time which is to be passively lived through, where society –or biology– takes on the active role, but rather as a process, which is and can be influenced by an active subject. While this focus may nowadays seem trivial, it is actually a rather new theoretical accomplishment (Harré, 1995).

Focusing on identity as meaning making and the construction of coherence

Individualisation theory insists on the eminent task of self construction which is to be realised by individuals today. In the face of individuals' dissonant self-experiences, the question is whether the concept of coherence still carries meaning. Apart from answering this as a *theoretical question*, it also remained to be addressed as an empirical one. As pre-study interviews had shown, we were, methodologically speaking, facing a threefold dilemma of coherence: (a) The interaction in the interview forces interactive partners to demonstrate competence in displaying a plausible presentation of self, adequate for the given situation. Coherence is a central part of this. (b) As a normative expectation, coherence is woven into many methods and its acceptance by communication partners is thus called for. (c) Finally, the interviewers themselves are not free from subscribing to a coherency-focused identity model in their interviewing, even if they take a rather critical stance to it within their theoretical work. Their own subjective urge for coherence, their desire for a plausible individual story "with a beginning, a middle and an end", assures the validity of a paradigm in communication, which is theoretically questioned.

As can thus be seen, there are many factors which hamper the revelation of personal ambivalence or ruptures in self narratives. Yet such incoherence was exactly what we were looking for. Apart from a generally permissive atmosphere, in line with the proposals of Carl Rogers, several other strategies appeared to be of relevance. One was the offer of *changing I-positions*. The choice of a profession, for instance, can be discussed during the interview from various perspectives, including as a general topic for adolescents, as a child located within family opinion and tradition, as a peer group member, or as regional adherence. Parallel involvement in various social roles, is thus reflected in a sequence of interview topics which can be discussed one after the other. *Normalisation* is a further strategy allowing identity patchwork to show up during the interview. Here, it is underscored that people indeed have many lifeworlds and present different selves in different situations. "It is ok to be incoherent", was the subtext of this intervention; "You are not supposed to force your-self into narrating a coherent story, if you don't feel like it".

Tools

These theory-driven methodological focuses had to be translated into a toolbox, which contained the various adequately defined methods to be applied during the three interviews. Since several tools are of use for more than one focus, the presentation of the assorted tools will follow a different logic than that which was applied in introducing the research questions and methodological focuses. A short description of the various tools will thus follow, in order to provide the reader with insight into the empirical situation created for our interviewees.

As a framework for our empirical work we selected a qualitative interview as *problem-centred partially structured interview*, following Claes, who argued, that " [. . .] the systematic interview, centred on topics which have a central meaning for the development of the adolescent personality, obviously is the method of choice" (Claes, 1986, p. 186). Here, the interviewer does not play a passive role, but rather tries "[. . .] by confronting the narrated with information from other spheres or with contradictions during their interview, by focused in-quiries [. . .] to find out as precisely as possible that which the interviewee means". This must be undertaken without any form of evaluation on the part of the interviewer "accepting fully the interviewee as the only expert of his or her situation" (Krüger-Müller, 1990, p. 18). While confrontation was employed as one (!) interview strategy, a further consisted of the elicitation of *narrative* ma-terial, which called for a more "passive" interviewer.

The interview lasted between 1 1/2 and 2 hours. The interview manual was subdivided into the areas of work, family, peers/leisure, and personal ideology, though as noted above, room was left for the addition of other lifeworlds rele-vant to the interviewee. A fourth part centred on self-image, a subject spanning across individual lifeworlds. In this area, topics were discussed which could not clearly be classified as belonging to a single lifeworld (e.g. health, body). Inte-grated in our interview manual was Marcia's identity status questionnaire (Marcia, 1993). Although our theoretical approach differed in many ways from Marcia's work, the inclusion of his questions in our own manual allowed for the comparison of our findings with results stemming from the Marcia tradition.

The three waves of interviews called for differing positioning impulses in the interview manuals. In the first interview, the interviewee's biography and expectations for the time up to the next interview constituted the main topics. In the second and third interviews, on the other hand, reflection on the time since the last interview and previously formulated expectations played an important role.

While the interview manual outlined the structure and topics of the inter-view, further tools were introduced during its course. Of central importance was the *social network chart* (Straus, 2002). An I-centred version was employed, depicting the size and subjective relevance of the interviewee's social network. The chart was introduced at the beginning of the interview and gradually completed in accordance with the topic under discussion. It consisted of a sheet of paper on which seven concentric circles are marked around a central point, symbolising the self. The interviewee was asked to mark the relevant persons on the chart. Relevant dimensions of the subsequent network-analysis are (a) the structural dimension, e.g. density: are the persons in contact with each other; multiplexity: how many persons appear in more than one lifeworld; distance; conflictuality of relationships; (b) the functional dimension, e.g. relevance and use of one's network as a coping resource; individual effort to actively design or redesign one's network.

The *life-event questionnaire* was designed with the various lifeworlds in mind. It focuses on the previous twelve months and asks, whether a given event, for instance "I was sick", or an evaluation, like "I felt happy", is true or not. In the present study, interviewees completed the questionnaire during a short interview break. The questionnaire proved useful in touching on topics involving taboos or inducing shame and guilt which would not have deliberately been brought up during the interview (e.g. "I had problems with the police"). Furthermore, this instrument allowed for comparisons with (quantitative) life-event-studies.

Two *deictic tools* were used. The first consisted of the presentation of two *sets of photos* during the (first) interview. The photos depicted young women and young men and helped to initiate a discussion on self-image and on imagined partners. The issue of how to interpret the answers in the face of such a complex stimulus pattern was of minor importance, given that our interviewees were asked to explain their choices. The second deictic tool was the drawing of a "life-line" or *"story line"* (Gergen & Gergen, 1988) during the course of the third interview. The drawing of this line was expected, within a final step, to elicit the "mythopoetic construction" (McAdams, 1985) of the time span since the first interview and to record it in the form of a narrative. Construction takes place with the interviewee drawing a line (often resembling a temperature-chart), which is supposed to represent his or her feelings with respect to the years since the first interview. Having finished the drawing, he or she is invited to narrate his or her life "along" the line. This provided us with a retrospective self-narrative based on the years since the first interview.

3.3   Looking back/forward: Experiences/ideas

Lifeworld-focused change of I-positions shows the dynamic interplay of the various lifeworlds with regard to identity construction

Our decision to examine the various lifeworlds proved positive in many ways. First, we were able to confirm the heterogeneity of identity development in the various lifeworlds, as James Marcia had already shown. One pattern found, for instance, followed a model of "crop rotation", where investment in the specific lifeworlds changed over the course of time. Second, the preliminary offer of three lifeworlds to the interviewees facilitated a first orientation during the interview, which was then subject to individual refinement. Third, our offer of additionally introducing other lifeworlds helped to adapt the instrument to the individual's needs. Moreover, the individual lifeworlds were not discussed as separate parts but rather in their relationship to one another. This change of perspective resulted in a considerable increase in the differentiation of the self-narratives. Thus, a lifeworld-oriented strategy diminishes the danger of precluding one single context from other lifeworld-specific positions. Here we found parallels to the positioning theory of Harré & van Langenhove (1999).

The network-chart documents the dynamics of change in the individual networks and their quality as identity capital

Besides the positioning strategy, the network chart also proved an important tool, not only fulfilling its role in documenting the social relations in the various lifeworlds and their quality as social resources, but also visually displaying this information during the interview. The network chart, which was created anew in each interview, also enabled us to account for changes in the network, and to elicit explanations for them. Identity construction is not only carried out in relation to others, but also by leaving others behind, by cutting off ties. The chart allowed such changes to be documented, i.e. the exclusion of ex-friends, ex-lovers, ex-colleagues etc. from the new map, and interviewees to be questioned regarding these changes. Finally the network analysis enabled us to distinguish various types of social networks with respect to their functionality for identity construction (Keupp et al. 2006, p. 153 f.). Theoretically of most interest is the "individualised network" type, which is accompanied by a self-narrative showing one's agency.

A longitudinal design demonstrates the volatility of identity statuses

Identity achievement is not the endpoint of identity development. Instead it can be followed by various changes in identity status with regard to the various life-worlds. Here, external factors, i.e. the resources, indeed play a very important role. This is also the case with regard to identity diffusion. The theoretically discussed post-modern pattern of joyful diffusion does indeed appear to exist. It is, however, in need of personal and social resources before it can be experienced as such. If these are not sufficiently available, identity diffusion becomes a painful experience, even when prolonged on account of the adaptive potential of this status in the sense of Marcia's culturally adaptive identity diffusion.

Self-narratives are not the talking about identity. They are the doing.

The question of coherence as a basic concept in identity theory accompanied us for the duration of the project. We approached it from various angles, e.g. with regard to a narrative coherence (Kraus, 2000) or research on the sense of coherence (Höfer, 1997). Inspired by the dialogical and narrative turn in social science we came to understand that individuals do not first do identity work and then talk about it. The talking is the doing. It is not only a narrative focus which is being emphasised here, but also the performative side of interaction. If we take the proposition that the talking is the doing seriously, we will subsequently have to consider its consequences on the theoretical and methodological level. Theoretically, this entails scrutinising many more forms of discourse and self-expression than self-narratives alone.

The long view inspires the look into "small stories"

Methodologically we have come to realise that in studying the performative part of doing identity, more than one interactive situation is required. Indeed more than a few such situations are necessary, when these situations, because of the time in between, prove hard to relate. A plausible strategy may be to focus on identity development through the study of "small stories" (= stories-in-interaction). Identity is not only about big stories, stories of your past, self-stories, biographic stories, with you as the main agent but about all kinds of small stories during conversation, where the process of positioning and being positioned takes place and nourishes the identity process (Bamberg, 2006). Thus, in the end "the long view" adopted in our project ironically lead us to engage in our current research on identity construction as a situative process, the focus on individual agency further caused us to emphasise the discursive co-construction of identity, and an examination of comprehensive self-narratives revealed the importance of small stories.

Notes

1   I appreciate the comments of my colleagues: Heiner Keupp, Thomas Ahbe, Wolfgang Gmür, Renate Höfer, Beate Mitzscherlich, Florian Straus.
2   Many of the references above were published after our project had started. I have, however, selected them on account of their poignancy.
3   For a more elaborate presentation of our theoretical argument see Keupp et al. (2006).

References

Baethge, M. (1988). *Jugend: Arbeit und Identität* [Youth, work, and identity]. Opladen: Leske & Budrich.

Bamberg, M. (2006). Stories: Big or small? Why do we care? *Narrative Inquiry, 16,* 147–155.

Beck, U., Giddens, A., & Lash, S. (Eds.) (1994). *Reflexive modernization. Politics, tradition and aesthetics in the modern social order.* Cambridge, UK: Polity Press.

Bourne, E. (1978). The state of research on ego identity: A review and appraisal. Part II. *Journal of Youth and Adolescence, 7* (4), 371–392.

Bruner, J. (1990). *Acts of meaning.* Cambridge, MA: Harvard University Press.

Cavalli, A. & Galland, O. (Eds.) (1993). *L'allongement de la jeunesse* [The prolongation of youth]. Poitiers: Actes Sud.

Claes, M. (1986). *L'expérience adolescente* [The adolescent experience]. Brussels: Mardaga.

Coté, J.E., & Levine, C.G. (2002). *Identity formation, agency and culture. A social psychological synthesis.* London: Lawrence Erlbaum.

Erikson, E.H. (1968). *Identity, youth, and crisis.* New York: Norton.

Geertz, C.J. (1973). Thick description: toward an interpretive theory of culture. In C.J. Geertz (Ed.), *The interpretation of cultures: selected essays* (pp. 3–30). New-York: Basic Books.

Gergen, K.J., & Gergen, M.M. (1988). Narrative and the self as relationship. In L. Berkowitz (Ed.), *Advances in experimental social psychology* (pp. 17–56). New York: Academic Press.

Gergen, K.J. (1991). *The saturated self.* New York: Basic Books.

Giddens, A. (1991). *Modernity and self-identity. Self and society in the late modern age.* Cambridge, UK: Polity Press.

Harré, R. (1995). Discursive psychology. In J. A. Smith, R. Harré, & L. van Langenhove (Eds.), *Rethinking psychology* (pp. 143–159). London: Sage.

Harré, R., & Langenhove, L.v. (1999). Reflexive positioning: Autobiography. In R. Harré, & L. van Langenhove (Eds.), *Positioning theory* (pp. 60–73). London: Blackwell.

Haußer, K. (1983). *Identitätspsychologie* [Identity psychology]. Berlin: Springer.

Höfer, R. (2000). *Jugend, Gesundheit und Identität* [Youth, health, and identity]. Opladen: Leske & Budrich.

Keupp, H. & Höfer, R. (Eds.) (1997). *Identitätsarbeit heute. Klassische und aktuelle Perspektiven der Identitätsforschung* [Identity work today. Classical and current perspectives of identity research]. Frankfurt/M., Germany: Suhrkamp.

Keupp, H., Ahbe, T., Gmür. W., Höfer, R., Kraus, W., Mitzscherlich, B. & Straus, F. (2006). *Identitätskonstruktionen. Das Patchwork der Identitäten in der Spätmoderne* [Identity constructions. The patchwork of identity in late modernity]. Reinbek: Rowohlt Enzyklopädie.

Krappmann, L. (1997). Die Identitätsproblematik nach Erikson aus einer interaktionistischen Perspektive [The identity question after Erikson from an interactionist perspective]. In H. Keupp & R. Höfer (Eds.), *Identitätsarbeit heute* (pp. 66–92). Frankfurt/M.: Suhrkamp.

Kraus, W. (2000). *Das erzählte Selbst* [The narrated self]. Pfaffenweiler: Centaurus.

Krüger-Müller, H. (1990). Berufsfindungsprozesse – Forschungsergebnisse und Methodenfragen [Processes of job decisions – Research results and methodological questions]. In Deutsches Jugendinstitut (Ed.), *DJI-Information "Arbeitsweltbezogene Jugendsozialarbeit"* (pp. 16–23). München: dji.

Marcia, J.E. (1966). Development and validation of ego-identity status. *Journal of Personality and Social Psychology, 3* (5), 551–558.

Marcia, J.E. (1989). Identity diffusion differentiated. In M. A. Luszcz, & T. Nettelbeck (Eds.), *Psychological development across the life-span* (pp. 289–295). North-Holland: Elsevier.

Marcia, J.E. (1993). The status of the statuses: Resarch review. In J.E. Marcia, A.S. Waterman, D.R. Matteson, S.L. Archer, & J.L. Orlofsky (Eds.), *Ego identity. A handbook for psychosocial research* (pp. 22–41). New York: Springer.

McAdams, D. (1993). *The stories we live by: personal myths and the making of the self.* New York: William Morrow.

Melges, F.T. (1990). Identity and temporal perspective. In R.A. Block (Ed.), *Cognitive models of psychological time* (pp. 255–267). Hillsdale, NJ: Lawrence Erlbaum.

Miller, R. (2000). *Researching life stories and family histories.* London: Sage.

Münchmeier, R. (1998). Entstrukturierung der Jugendphase [The destructuring of adolescence]. *Aus Politik und Zeitgeschichte, 31,* 3-13.

Sampson, E.E. (1985). The decentralization of identity. Toward a revised concept of personal and social order. *American Psychologist, 40,* 1203–1211.

Straus, F. (2002). *Netzwerkanalysen* [Network analyses]. Wiesbaden: Deutscher Universitätsverlag.

Thomson, R., Plumridge, L., & Holland, J. (2003). Longitudinal qualitative research: a developing methodology. *International Journal of Social Research Methodology, 6* (3), 185–187.

Wagner, P. (1994). *A sociology of modernity. Liberty and discipline.* London: Routledge.

Ziehe, T. (1991). Vom vorläufigen Ende der Erregung – Die Normalität kultureller Modernisierungen hat die Jugend-Subkulturen entmächtigt [On the preliminary end of excitement – The normality of cultural modernisations has disabled youth subcultures]. In W. Helsper (Ed.), *Jugend zwischen Moderne und Postmoderne* (pp. 57–72). Opladen: Leske & Budrich.

Chapter 4

A Content Analysis of Narratives from a Categorical and Holistic Point of View to Study Changes after a Rite of Passage

Alejandro Iborra
University of Alcalá
Spain

In 2000 I began research in an attempt to study whether people changed after experiencing a special kind of transition: a rite of passage. I chose a rite of passage as an example of a ritualized transition where I expected it would be easier to observe processes of change. Among different kinds of changes, I was interested in studying changes in the identity of the participants. Would their identity before the ritual be different compared with their identity after the rite, as expected according to classical anthropological literature (Dunham, Kidwell, & Wilson, 1986; Rappaport, 1999; van Gennep, 1909)?

4.1   Introduction

In my opinion, rites of passage and their liminal transition phase were a good context in which to study the complexities of the processes related to changes in identity, understanding the rite as a moment of fragility that can threaten the coherence of the narrative or story that people have constructed about themselves (Devís and Sparkes, 1999).

One of the interesting aspects of a rite of passage is that the transformation expected to take place happens, formally speaking, at a specific point in time. This concrete moment has been termed a "performative act with an illocutionary force" (Rappaport, 1999, following Austin, 1962), those discourses and conventional acts that achieve their effects in their very utterance or enactment: *"I name this ship the Queen Elizabeth;" "I swear to tell the truth;" "We find the defendant guilty, etc"*. Conventional procedures are employed during a ritual for achieving conventional effects, and to be successful, performative acts should be performed by properly authorized persons under proper circumstances, being executed correctly and completely.

As Rappaport (1999) suggests, *"the informative capacity of ritual, its ability to form and transform, rests not only upon its special mode of transmission but also upon its reception by specially prepared receivers"* (p. 111). Participants must give meaning to the ritual that will probably influence the quality of those achieved changes. A method to study these phenomena should then consider those meanings provided by the participants in order to understand their own development. One of these methods would be the analysis of their narratives.

The use of qualitative methodologies has been common in the study of identity from an Eriksonian perspective, at least since interviews have been employed as a research tool to collect data from participants. And, in the last 10 years, there has been a growing tendency to make narrative analysis in a more explicit way (Grotevant, 1993; Whitty, 2002; Kroger, 1993, 2003; Kunnen & Wassink, 2003), although this kind of analysis is still a minority approach.

There is growing consideration to understand the narrative as one of the main processes we employ to construct a coherent and integrative sense of identity. According to McAdams and Janis (2004), *"the central idea animating narrative based approaches to theory and research in the behavioral and social sciences is that human beings make sense of their lives and their worlds through stories"* (p. 160). People make sense of the world by taking their experiences of life into narrative frames.

In my opinion, a narrative approach could complement and frame those processes involved in the formation of identity such as exploration and commitment (Marcia, 1966), communion and individualization (Adams and Marshall, 1996), attachment and individuation (Kaplan and O'Connor, 1993), differentiation and integration (van Hoof and Raaijmakers, 2003), and assimilation, accommodation), and evaluation (Breakwell, 1986; Bosma and Kunnen, 2001).

4.2   Methodology description

Sample

I based my research on the stories told by 16 subjects who had participated in a rite of passage: a wedding or a competitive examination[1]. They were between 26 and 50 years old (nine between 26 and 35 = young adulthood; seven between 36 and 50 = middle age). I used an intentional sampling procedure based mainly on the strategy of maximum variation (Miles and Huberman, 1994) once every participant fulfilled the mentioned criteria of having participated in a rite of passage. Every participant was interviewed at least once during one hour.

Interview

I designed an interview following the schema proposed by Maykut and Morehouse (1994). It was structured in the following sections: (1) a brief personal introduction about the interviewer, (2) a brief description of the purpose of the research, (3) asking for his permission to record the interview, (4) sociodemographic questions (age, job, hobbies, family status, religious beliefs, main personal relationships, main life events), (5) general approach to the experience of the rite (You got married, can you tell me about your experience? Where did it happen? When did it begin? Who took part? What did it mean for you? etc.), (7) specific approach: stages and changes (What did you think and feel from what you consider to be the beginning to the end of the experience? Which was the most meaningful moment for you? Why? If you could divide it in stages, how many stages would you need? Did you experience any change after the experience? Did the rite influence those changes? How? What remained the same? etc.), (8) evaluation of the experience: learnings, purposes, and reasons for taking part, (9) conclusions and insights after the interview.

These questions were suggested in order to get information about how the participant was creating a meaning from the experience of the rite. From a theoretical point of view it was important to explore if the rite was considered a turning point for the participant, if there were three stages as the anthropological literature about rites of passage suggests, if those mentioned changes had a relationship with changes in identity, etc. All the questions were led by their theoretical importance despite their exploring nature.

My purpose was to invite participants to tell their story instead of asking for a report about what happened. I tried to make sure that participants were responsible for the meaning of their story emphasizing their experience. The interview was semi-structured in the sense that I had enough flexibility to adapt my questions to the answers of participants, changing the order of the questions or avoiding some issues when deemed necessary by the situation.

Theoretical considerations concerning the analysis

Every interview was digitally recorded and transcribed in order to make a categorical content analysis (Lieblich, Tuval-Mashiach and Zilber, 1998) with the purpose of developing a general knowledge about the main themes covered by participants in their stories. According to Lieblich et al. (1998) the narrative materials may be processed analytically by breaking the text into relatively small units of content: *"the narrative story is dissected, and sections or single words belonging to a defined category are collected from the entire story or from several texts belonging to a number of narrators"* (p. 12). The purpose of this "dissection" is to examine the thematic similarities and differences between narratives provided by a number of people. The strength of this form of analysis lies in its capacity to develop general knowledge about the core themes that make up the content of the stories[2] generated.

There have been some critics (Conrad, 1990; Riesman, 1990) about the dissection implied by this kind of categorical analysis because it stresses a detached analysis of the whole experience of participants. Following this idea, Charmaz (2000) states that *"criticisms of fracturing the data [. . .] lead to separating the experience from the experiencing subject, the meaning from the story, and the viewer from the view"* (p. 521). Taking these critics into account I collected quotes from the narratives of the participants to develop core themes or categories, but without detaching them from the personal contexts they came from. One way of achieving this was writing theoretic memos concerning every participant. In doing this, I reflected on their particularities using the same categories and core themes that were emerging through the analysis process. Besides, these memos helped me reflect on the categories, their connections, and the new themes that could emerge during the cyclical process that took place during the analysis.

Analysis

The analysis process followed a three-step sequence with every interview. The first step involved an initial categorization of the transcribed interview, using categories already created when the selected sentences or paragraphs were related to these categories (previously created during the analysis from an inductive point of view) or creating new categories whenever there was a new theme in the discourse of the participants. The second step implied the elaboration of a visual model to the case I was analyzing, selecting the key categories in order to understand it. In this model the relationships between the different categories were stressed. As a third step I wrote a memo about the case, taking into account the model I had outlined. In this memo I was able to describe the core categories that had emerged, reflect on how they were related, and compound a whole, noting the similarities and differences with other cases, participants, or narratives. Finally, I asked new questions and made new predictions about what I expected would be found in the following cases to be analyzed.

The following extract of a memo is an example of the use of the categories (in capital letters) in order to explain one of the cases.

Religious Wedding Without Religious Beliefs: Jred Memo

This case is quite integrative. Though he had a religious (Catholic) wedding, he considers himself as an agnostic. Nevertheless, the ceremony was very meaningful for him because the rite was coherent with his beliefs about the marriage: a relationship based in a lifetime commitment.

It is interesting because it shows how, regardless of religious beliefs, he is giving his own meaning to the ceremony. The idea of commitment is crucial for him. Commitment is beyond the two individuals that form a couple (beyond their fears, doubts, and difficult moments). Therefore, it has a transcendent meaning related to NUMINOSITY emotions such as respect for something bigger than individuals.

For Jred the most meaningful important moment was when he asked his wife to marry him. He was aware of being mature enough to ask her to marry him and he was also aware that he was going to commit himself to that relationship, a lifelong commitment. That commitment is the key for him, once it is taken from freedom. He has laid great stress on this idea.

The wedding is a rite that symbolizes this PERSONAL COMMITMENT but furthermore the wedding implies a SOCIAL COMMITMENT. He is aware during the ceremony of the importance of what he is doing. That is why his FEELINGS are so INTENSE. Some MEANINGFUL MOMENTS are (1) when he swears love to his wife (the moment of the rings is a good example of a peformative act), (2) when he is awaiting the arrival of the bride, and (3) when his father-in-law delivers him his daughter. This moment is lived with a lot of respect towards her father (this emotion of respect highlights his awareness of the decision he is making). As a consequence he feels a great RESPONSIBILITY towards the commitment he has made.

The main change for Jred comes when he asks his wife to marry him. Nevertheless, as a consequence of the personal and social commitment consolidated during the ceremony, there is a CHANGE in his IDENTITY. This change was also expressed by J. and J.G. (other cases) when they referred to the couple as being only one person. The change they are taking part in strengthens the couple. This change in his identity and his connection with the personal commitment is very clear.

Another change is the self-perception of being more INDEPENDENT and ADULT. This is related to a feeling of being more MATURE thanks to living with his wife in their own house. The idea of MEANINGFUL DEVELOPMENT appears: he is aware of making a meaningful progress in his life that will go on. This maturity is different than the maturity he felt in order to ask his wife to marry him.

One of the most important lessons he learns is when and how to give in when quarreling with his wife. This is related to the identity change in which two people become one. One way of achieving this is through individual renunciations.

Once I had finished the analysis of all the interviews, I began to select the most relevant categories, based on their frequency of appearance and theoretical

contribution. Even when they had been mentioned only by one or two participants, they were selected when their application to other cases improved understanding of their experience[3].

Finally, not forgetting the individual experiences of the participants, I
selected the key categories in order to situate every participant in accordance
with these categories.[4] My purpose was to provide a context that made it easy to
perform the construction of patterns, through the comparison between the combinations of different categories present in every participant in a unique way.
Moreover, I tried to answer the question concerning why only some participants
had presented changes. Could the core themes I had extracted explain the different experiences and meanings expressed by the participants?

This whole analysis was conducted with N'VIVO software (Richards, 1999;
Bazeley and Richards, 2000), which was very useful in order to manage the ongoing process of categorization and the organization of that categorization in a
structured system. The software provided fast and flexible access to the previous
categorized material, which helped me reflect on the categories. In the end, I
was able to draw models where it was possible to synthesize the information obtained (see figure 4.1).

Goodness criteria

With regard to the issue of goodness criteria, as discussed by Sparkes (1998), a
number of features of the current study may be considered in order to prove its
trustworthiness and authenticity (Manning, 1997) from a parallel perspective.
For example, in both the process of conducting in-depth interviews, and in actively listening to the participants, stories were deemed important for building
rapport and trusting relationships, and for contextualizing events and meanings
over time. It was also important that the subjectivity of the researcher conducting the interviews was monitored in order to be aware of how this might shape
the study. In order to do this, regular discussions took place between researchers
of the research team I belonged to, who acted as critical friends, and myself
(Maykut and Morehouse, 1994). This monitoring allowed concepts and categories to emerge as the study developed. These were then integrated with relevant
theory to provide further explanations.

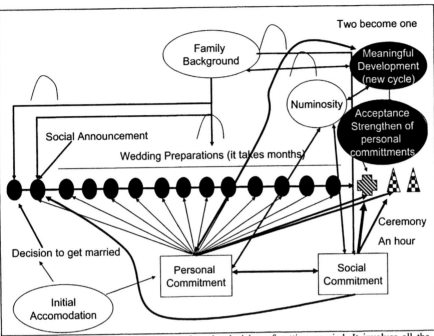

Note. Initial Accommodation: It is related to the decision of getting married. It involves all the changes undertaken by the participants in order to decide to get married. For example, a change in the personal values concerning the idea of taking part in a religious ceremony or to adapt oneself to the idea of getting married. It is quite related to a strengthening of previous personal commitments.

Personal Commitment: Adherence to a set of goals, values, and beliefs related, in this case, to the idea of getting married and becoming the husband of the former girlfriend. This personal commitment leads and gives meaning to all the small decisions that take place during the preparation of the wedding ceremony.

Social Commitment: External expression of one's personal commitment in front of a relevant audience (family and friends), who become witnesses of this personal commitment. It mainly happens during the day of the ceremony but also when the decision to get married is announced.

Family Background: Quality of support given by both partner families. It can be positive and supportive or negative and dissuasive. Depending on its intensity it can also be evaluated as positive or negative. It will be negative if the family pressure in order to influence the wedding decisions is too high or too low. It could influence a special meaning of the ceremony as a family ritual that highlights the importance of the continuation of a prior social situation.

Numinosity: Intense feelings lived during the ceremony characterized by emotions of respect, humility, and gratitude towards the guests, family members, and, in religious contexts, even towards spiritual beings.

Meaningful Development: Special meaning given to the rite, which expresses the beginning of a new cycle. There is one moment before and one moment after the experience of the rite that gives a sense of direction to one's life. One of the consequences of this meaningful development is a strengthening of one's own commitments, which are fully accepted.

Figure 4.1 *General Model for the wedding after comparing all participants narratives, memos and models*

Other techniques to achieve trustworthiness criteria (Lincoln and Guba, 1982) were, for example, the use of negative case analysis during the sampling process. Participants were selected according to those questions that emerged after the previous interview, depending on whether or not I wanted to confirm a hypothesis or simply enhance information about some issue. The criteria of transferability (external validity), which tries to warrant the transparency of the methods of analysis used by the researcher, was achieved through the registration of every step and decision made throughout the research. The use of a software such as N'VIVO makes it easy to achieve this process of registration, and to monitor the process, keeping all the information recorded in a concrete project that can be easily audited if required.

Report

I chose a realist tale in order to report my results. According to Sparkes (2002), realist tales are, firstly, characterized by the use of extensively edited quotations to express representative remarks transcribed from the mouths of the participants. A second characteristic is its interpretive omnipotence. An "experiential or narrative" description is tied to a theoretical problem of interest to the researcher's disciplinary community. And each element of the theory is illustrated by empirical data (the quotations of the participants). For the author (Sparkes, 2002) the most striking characteristic of a realist tale is the almost complete absence of the author from most segments of the text: only the words, actions, and thoughts of members of the studied culture are visible in the text. The author's voice is usually set apart to indicate that a dispassionate observer was there: *"these kinds of texts tend to be dominated by scientific narrators who are manifested only as dispassionate, camera-like observers and listeners"* (p. 44). These texts construct authority and objectivity through the use of a passive voice so as to obscure and apparently distance the disembodied author from the data.

The text of this chapter is not a realist tale but a narration similar to a confessional tale (Sparkes, 2002): tales of a representational genre that explicitly *"problematize and demystify fieldwork or participant observation by revealing what actually happened in the research from start to finish"* (p. 58). Therefore, the details that matter are those that constitute the experience of the author. These kinds of tales emphasize the researcher's point of view. Such writing is intended to show how each particular work came into being and to reveal the dilemmas and tensions contained in the process.

I paid close attention to how I reported my results because it is one of the topics that is usually taken for granted by scholars. Although in quantitative methodology it can be assumed that there is a single way of presenting information in order to provide objectivity (scientific tales), in qualitative methodologies, realist tales are assumed to be the standard way of reporting our research data, especially when there are more options that can be utilized. As Coffey and Atkinson (1996) have argued, researchers should be able to make disciplined, principled choices and strategic decisions when deciding how to represent and reconstruct social worlds and social actors, social scenes and social action. This is even more relevant if we take into consideration that each way of writing represents a different way of knowing. According to Richardson (1994), writing is a method of inquiry that helps us find out about ourselves and about our topic of inquiry: *"By writing in different ways, we discover new aspects of our topic and our relationship to it. Form and content are inseparable"* (p. 516).

4.3   Some reflections

After expressing these methodological tensions, I would like to go back to the beginning of my paper. Was the methodology I used appropriate in order to study those changes supposedly happening during a rite of passage? Was it appropriate in order to study the processes?

As I stated previously, I outlined a general model for every rite of passage where only the core categories appeared. This helped me understand how some changes in identity, autonomy, security, social relationships, etc. were reported only for some of the participants, and why other changes, or any change at all, were reported by others. Although I had termed some of their narratives as an example of some processes, such as assimilation, accommodation, personal commitment, social commitment, numinosity (humility, thankfulness, respect), etc., it is clear that, above all, they were examples of meaning making processes by way of a narrative. The participants were telling me their version of an experience, their effort to make sense of an experience they had gone through. And of course I was doing the same: making sense of their experiences from my theoretical point of view.

For example, in relation to the rite of passage of a wedding, I concluded that participants made sense of the ritual. They were responsible for its meaning. What four participants had in common in the research (Jose, J.G., Gin, and Jred) was that their wedding meant a change; it implied that their personal and social commitments would be made explicit and real. That's why the intensity of the emotions expressed during the ceremony had been so high for them. They were aware of the meaningful moment they had lived. They were aware that they had accommodated to that new situation when they decided to commit themselves to their partner. During the ceremony they expressed feelings of respect to the audience and to the father of the bride. They showed gratitude to the audience, and to their families, and they were aware of the personal evolution they were experiencing.

In contrast, the other three participants (J., Pi, and Jopelu) emphasized the social meaning of the wedding above the personal meaning. For them the function of the rite was just to formalize their personal commitments. The rite in itself was not very important. It was not transcending in its performance. It just signaled a continuity of a previous situation. They were valuing, above all, the social and family dimensions that surrounded the ritual. For them, the ritual was mainly a family ritual.

But even though there appeared to be accommodation processes in the case of Jopelu, and numinous feelings of gratitude and respect in J. and Pi, there were no personal changes. It is not the presence of an isolated category or variable that explains how the experience is going to be lived out, but rather the meaningful integration of all of them. For these people, the rite was an example of the continuation of the previous situation. There was no change because the personal dimension of the rite was not considered.

These kinds of conclusions are only possible if we emphasize personal experiences instead of variables through the content analysis of the narratives. A categorical or variable-oriented content analysis would have led to a description of the core themes mentioned or expressed in the narratives of the participants. But being isolated from their original contexts would prevent a complete understanding of the phenomena. That is why I think it is necessary to integrate this categorical analysis with another one that considers the whole experience of the person.

For example, it is interesting to note some identity changes[5] like these:

- I knew that whenever I got married I was going to stop being me, I was going to stop being J. and his world.
- J. is different, I mean, he is different five seconds before than five seconds after, that period of 10, 15 seconds –is there any variation?– with such an accuracy to say emphatically yes, I don't know, I don't know what to tell you. I mean, but however I told you before, I mean: now! Now it is! I did already! Maybe you are not aware about what you said or did, you are more aware, you rationalize it over time.

Or some non-changes to identity like these:

- I think that I really had few changes because I consider that what I was doing so far was what I had been doing and I've followed . . . and I've gone on doing. It is still complicated to call her my wife. We still call each other boyfriend and girlfriend.

These quotations are interesting as examples of a category of "changes in personal identity" but they are only meaningful when they are related to other categories. Only then can a reader or researcher try to understand not only that an identity change happened at least in these participants, but how it happened, what connections it had with other categories, etc. These quotations need to be framed in a wider perspective concerning the relationship between the categories. The categories should then be framed in the narrative of one participant, framed in the comparison of other participants, and finally framed with some relevant theories.

In relation to these ideas there emerge some theoretical issues. I wonder if this kind of narrative approach, based on a retrospective account of an experience, can really provide a description of actual processes taking place. I wonder if I could grasp these processes or whether I should limit myself to accessing a mere narrative or story told by the subjects (which is not the combination of processes that actually shapes the changes, probably actuating out of the awareness of the participant). I wonder if retrospective narratives are the only way we have of understanding our participants' experiences and their way of making sense, since it is very difficult to follow an ongoing experience, and easier to access multiple reports about past events.

According to these dilemmas, I wonder whether I achieved my purpose in studying processes concerning changes in identity. At least the last quotations give an example of how an interaction of meaning processes can lead somebody to become somebody else, or, conversely, to remain the same person.

Continuing this critique in my own work, I think that my analysis would need to pay attention to the form of the narratives and the interaction of this form with its content. It is interesting to note how scholars in other domains, such as sports and physical activity, are taking advantage of the use of qualitative research compared to our research field. For example, Smith and Sparkes (2005) provide an array of possibilities when carrying out an analysis of talk in a qualitative inquiry. As they state:

> life stories need to be subjected to multiple forms of analysis. If lives, stories, bodies, identities and selves [. . .] are multidimensional, constructed, complex and changing in time and with context, then researchers might seek forms of analysis that are sensitive to, and respectful of, this complexity and multiplicity (p. 214).

And taking into consideration, again, the way we report our data, I think that it would be interesting to explore different ways of writing our reports, going beyond realist tales, which are taken for granted. Different ways of expressing what we know about identity formation can add new insights and experiential keys to scholars and to readers. Alternative genres such as confessional tales, ethnographic fiction, and autoethnography provide different ways of reporting our research projects. As Sparkes (2003) reflects,

> writing autoethnographically has raised a number of issues for me. First, it has helped me recognize how, in my 'normal' academic writing I maintain tightly secured boundaries within me and beyond me, keeping various identities and selves separate, shored up, and protected from the swirling confusions I so often experience in my daily life. In this writing I tend to privilege rigor over imagination, intellect

over feeling, theories over stories, and abstract ideas over concrete events (p. 61).

He continues by quoting Bochner (1997, p. 421), who observes, *"the sad truth is that the academic self frequently is cut off from the ordinary experiential self. A life of theory can remove one from experience, make oneself feel unconnected"*.

I think that we, as scholars, should reflect more on different methods to report our data. For example, what are the advantages of using an autoethnography instead of a realist tale? What are the negative sides? Are the personal and private purposes of our research coherent with the method we choose to report our data, or is this method of reporting taken for granted as the only one? Are realist tales, or even scientific tales, taken for granted in our scientific reports? Does this have any influence on the growing knowledge of our disciplines?

I wonder if our academic field about identity would benefit if we began to practice different modalities of being more in touch with our experience and that of our participants. Producing personal stories can enhance a sense of connection with others. It could be a context to show identity processes in action, inviting the reader to engage in relation to their own experience as they read and participate with the text.

Notes

1   Competitive Examination: Special exam that must be passed in order to attain an occupation in public administration.

2   I agree with Smith and Sparkes (2005) when they note that *"the stories that people tell about their experiences should not be regarded as simple reflections of the teller's actual experiences or transparent windows to cognition and their inner private self that can be rendered visible through dialogue or a content analysis"* (p. 229). Narratives are social creations. Narrative is a form of social practice in which individuals draw from a cultural repertoire of stories that they then synthesize into personal stories.

3   For example, the category "Family Support" was not mentioned by all participants, but it was useful in order to have an idea of how the family context could influence the meaning of the wedding depending on the quality of their support.

4   The memo is an example of this. I was using the categories in the memos as an attempt to understand their experience. There were different categories in the stories of the participants, for example, the presence of numinosity feelings, related to positive support from the family and a strong personal commitment with changes in identity that had taken place.

5   I considered that there was a change in identity when this was pointed out by the participants (as in the examples mentioned) when talking about their changes after the rite. These changes usually were related to new self-references or self-perceptions, new behaviors or lifestyle, etc., due to the new social situation they had come into after the rite. It was important, again, that it was mentioned directly by the participant.

References

Adams, G.R., & Marshall, S.K. (1996). A developmental social psychology of identity: Understanding the person in context. *Journal of Adolescence, 19,* 429–442.

Austin, J.L. (1962). *How to do things with words.* Oxford: Oxford University Press.

Bazeley, P., & Richards, L. (2000). *The NVivo Qualitative Project Book.* London: Sage.

Bochner, A. (1997). It's about time. *Qualitative Inquiry, 3* (4), 418–438.

Bosma, H.A., &. Kunnen, E.S. (2001). Determinants and Mechanisms in Ego Identity Development: a review and synthesis. *Developmental Review, 21,* 39–66.

Breakwell, G. (1986). *Coping with threatened identities.* London & New York: Methuen.

Charmaz, K. (2000). Grounded Theory: Objectivist and Constructivist Methods. In N.D.Y. Lincoln (Ed.), *Handbook of Qualitative Research* (pp. 509–535). London: Sage.

Coffey, A., & Atkinson, P. (1996). *Making sense of qualitative data.* London: Sage.

Conrad, P. (1990). Qualitative research on chronic illness: a commentary on method and conceptual development. *Social Science and Medicine, 30,* 1257–1263.

Devis, J., & Sparkes, A.C. (1999). Burning the book: A biographical study of a pedagogically inspired identity crisis. *European Journal of Physical Education, 5* (2), 135–152.

Dunham, R.M., Kidwell, J.S., & Wilson, S.M. (1986). Rites of passage at adolescence: a ritual process paradigm. *Journal of Adolescent Research, 1,* 139–154.

Grotevant, H.D. (1993). The integrative nature of identity: Bringing the soloists to sing in the choir. In J. Kroger (Ed.), *Discussions on ego identity* (pp. 121–146). Hillsdale, NJ: Erlbaum.

Kaplan, K.J., & O'Connor, N.A. (1993). From mistrust to trust: Through a stage vertically. In G.H. Pollock, & S.I. Greenspan (Eds.), *The course of life: Volume II. Late adulthood* (pp. 153–198). Madison, CT: International University Press.

Kroger, J. (1993). Identity and context: how the identity statuses choose their match. In R. Josselson, & A. Lieblich (Eds.), *The narrative study of lives* (pp. 130–162). London: Sage.

Kroger, J. (2003). What transits in an identity status transition. *Identity, 3* (3), 197–220.

Kunnen, E.S., & Wassink, M.E.K. (2003). An Analysis of Identity Change in Adulthood. *Identity, 3* (4), 347–366.

Lieblich, A., Tuval-Mashiach, R., & Zilber, T. (1998). *Narrative research: reading, analysis, and interpretation.* London: Sage.

Lincoln, I., & Guba, E. (1985). *Naturalistic inquiry.* Thoushand Oaks, CA: Sage.

Marcia, J.E. (1966). Development and validation of ego identity status. *Journal of Personality and Social Psychology, 3*, 551–558.

Manning, K. (1997). Authenticity in constructivist inquiry. *Qualitative Inquiry, 3* (1), 93–115.

Maykut, P., & Morehouse, R. (1994). *Beginning Qualitative Research: a philosophical and practical guide.* London: The Falmer Press.

McAdams, D., & Janis, L. (2004). Narrative identity and narrative therapy. In L.E. Angus, & J. McLeod (2004). *The handbook of narrative and psychotherapy: practice, theory, and research* (pp. 159–174). London: Sage Publications.

Miles, M., &. Huberman, A.M. (1994). *Qualitative Data Analysis: An expanded sourcebook.* London: Sage.

Rappaport, R.A. (1999). *Ritual and religion in the making of humanity.* Cambridge: Cambridge University Press.

Richards, L. (1999). *Using NVivo in Qualitative Research.* London: Sage.

Richardson, L. (1994). *Writing.* In N. Denzin, & Y. Lincoln (Eds.), *Handbook of qualitative research* (pp. 516–529). London: Sage.

Riessman, C.K. (1990). *Divorce talk: women and men make sense of personal relationships.* New Brunswick, NJ: Rutgers University Press.

Smith, B., & Sparkes, A. (2005). Analyzing talk in qualitative inquiry: Exploring possibilities, problems, and tensions. *Quest, 57* (2), 213–242.

Sparkes, A.C. (1998). Validity in qualitative inquiry and the problem of criteria: Implications for sport psychology. *The Sport Psychologist, 12*, 363–386.

Sparkes, A.C. (2002). *Telling Tales in Sport & Physical Activity: A Qualitative Journey.* Champaign, IL: Human Kinetics Press.

Sparkes, A.C. (2003). Bodies, identities, selves: Autoethnographic fragments and reflections. In J. Denison, & P. Markula (Eds.), *Moving writing: Crafting Movement and Sport Research* (pp. 51–76). New York: Peter Lang.

van Gennep, A. (2004). *The rites of passage.* London: Routledge. (Original work published 1909)

van Hoof, A., & Raaijmakers, Q.A. (2003). The Search for the Structure of Identity Formation. *Identity, 3* (3), 271–289.

Whitty, M. (2002). Possible Selves: An Exploration of the Utility of a Narrative Approach. *Identity, 2* (3), 211–228.

Chapter 5

Qualitative Research on "Adolescence, Identity, Narration": Programmatic and Empirical Examples

Günter Mey
International Academy at the FU Berlin
Germany

To clarify the qualitative research approach to identity used in my study on "adolescence, identity, narration" I will present a case study. This case study will serve to explain the research methodology I employed and the specific interviewing, transcription and data analysis procedures utilized.

5.1   The study and research questions

In this study detailed problem-centered interviews with adolescents, 16 to 20 years of age, were conducted two times (with a time span between them of approximately one year). The interviews should help in analyzing how identity (Erikson, 1959) as a *feeling of the continuous sameness* and of *relative entireness* is constructed, and in which way such an experience of coherence is threatened or disturbed. This latter issue has become especially critical as a result of modernization in Western societies (Marcia, 1989; Darmstädter & Mey, 1998; Mey, 1999, chap. III; Kraus, 2000; Straub, Zielke, & Werbik, 2005).

Theoretically and methodologically I refer to the concept of "narrative identity," because it allows one to approach issues of development empirically. Such a "narrative" perspective, used since the middle of the 1990s, also for research on identity (see Habermas & Bluck, 2000; Brockmeier & Carbaugh, 2001; Bamberg, 2004), helps to reveal how individuals (re)construct experiences of continuity/coherence *and* discontinuity/incoherence during the process of autobiographical self-narration.

There were three guiding questions: 1) In what ways do individual conceptions of being a child, an adolescent, and anticipating being an adult change? 2) What subject (implicit) positions (for example, actively "producing" or being passively exposed to one's biography) do adolescents use in their narrative? 3) How do adolescents deal with discrepancies and contradictions: Is there a constant fundamental story adolescents use to present their life-stories over time?

5.2   Case study: Marion

The first interview

Marion was 19 years old when she was first interviewed. Since the divorce of her parents (when she was 15) Marion has lived with her mother, her mother's partner, and her 13 year old sister. After leaving high school, she began a retailer traineeship in a health food store; there were no alternatives at that time and her parents and her mother's partner forced this decision. Marion was interested in traveling and in learning foreign languages and made an earlier attempt at a traineeship in a travel agency, which failed. She also gave up on her original idea of being a biology teacher because of the vague job perspectives and the fact that her parents were not willing to pay.

In her leisure time Marion mainly stayed with scouts because she appreciated the values of tolerance and acceptance which, in her opinion, characterized the scout's life. The scouts were also important to Marion because she met her first two lovers there. One year prior to the first interview Marion was still single.

Biographic-dynamical approach

Marion's life as described during the first interview was characterized by a radical change. She lost the secure high school context and began to be confronted with the challenges of after-school life: "In earlier days one received pocket-money anyway [. . .] and during school one learned to be nice and (laughter) with equal rights and such things," she said. But now life –on the other side of freedom and the campfire romantic experience with the scouts– showed its harshness and the need to be tough –as Marion called it: "arseholeness." In a way it seemed as if Marion experienced herself as being exposed to an "enemy world" and her only choice was to accept the challenges and hardships without any chance to control them.

The situation became even more difficult as Marion had no concept of her own future. There was no partner and no idea of how such a person should be or act, no realistic personal project. Her decision to pursue the retailer traineeship only served as a shield against unemployment, but did not meet her interests and (personally anticipated) competences; it just had been the pragmatic ending point after frustrating attempts for a better job/traineeship.

Marion's story provided the image of an adolescent who gave up her aspirations without sufficient time to think about her own wishes and their possible realization. Consequently she suspended her wishes in a vague and far away future. Asked if she had "a future idea or image" of herself, she responded that she wished to become a person with "an own opinion and identity," accompanied by two further elaborations: "once to be married" and "to have some kind of job I am really interested in." Further definitions of adulthood according to Marion:

> You're adult with about 28 (she laughs). Yes, probably to have your own real existence, yeah, to work, to really earn money [. . .] and yes, maybe, to be grounded in your own life and tasks. Something like this, I think.

She also mentioned "to get clear" about herself, to gain "self-assurance" or "inner unity." Using such concepts Marion obviously tended to idealize adulthood as a state of "maturity." But she did not provide any details of *how* she expected to reach this state.

With the numerous facets revealed in the first interview with Marion, the picture of a young woman emerged, to her the own development –where she came from, the "how" of being an adolescent and of becoming an adult– was based on compromises. Marion passively accepted the "fate" of getting older and its affordances. During her narrative she seemed to be partly invisible against the overwhelming dominance of others (for example, forced by her parents and her mother's partner to accept a job she did not want), and she acted loyally against other's interests and orders, she tried to fulfill and justify them. So she stayed with her mother after her parents' divorce, although she disliked it, because "it was reasonable to keep the family together as far as possible." She then took a basement flat –and made it her "hut," while her younger sister lived in her mother's apartment.

The extent to which Marion's story can be reconstructed as an attempt to reach *her* idea of adulthood by loyalty and subordination I would like to analyze a sequence about a stay in the USA. Marion worked as an au-pair and felt very "lonesome" and thought about leaving the host family (and probably also the country) early:

M: But than my host mother fall ill
I2:   hmm
M: and stayed home for about two, three weeks, eh, did not work and so we started to come in contact with each other. Well, this was about Christmas time. After Christmas she again started to work, but eh, I were not sure at that time if I should stay or leave. [. . .]
I1:   Are you still in contact [. . .]?
M: After I returned [to Berlin] there had been no contact with my host family at all. (difficult to follow) this was really hard! Goodbye at the airport with tears and oh we will miss you and you are really important for us, and then . . . nothing.

This is the sequence as reported in the interview, now my interpretation. As her idea of leaving the host family coincided with the illness of the host mother, Marion decided to stay because she felt uncomfortable leaving the family in this situation. This again points to Marion's loyalty, her tendency to repress her own interests. But the main point, in my opinion, is another one: during this passage Marion stopped her rather controlled way of narrating and responded very excitedly and outraged; despite the "warm goodbye" and the tears at the airport afterwards there was no contact any more: *this* is what disappointed her. She obviously felt cheated as her efforts did not bear fruits, and the intensity of her emotional response is rather different from the calm and controlled way she described other difficult events (especially her parent's divorce and her partner leaving her). One possibility might be to think about a kind of emotional shift: the feelings and the involvement she was not able (and not allowed) to express at the "correct" place were linked (narratively and emotionally) to the seemingly more harmless scene with the host family. But if one takes into account that Marion's loyalty in a way served as the only anticipated and accepted strategy to fulfill her needs unobtrusively, the narrative takes on additional meaning: Marion's fear that loyalty would not sell, that making sacrifices would not necessarily lead to the reward she hoped for in the long run. And *this* would endanger her complete model of life, because hiding/giving up her wishes (for example her choice of profession), her obedience to her family (being the "cellar child"), all this is subordinated to one main aim: Marion's idea of a clearly defined life plan. Becoming an adult at the age of 28, gaining "self-assurance" and "inner unity," in some ways reminds of Erikson and his notion that the end of the moratorium adolescence is defined by integrity and by being socially accepted –and as the above story indicates, this aim might have been threatened.

The second interview

By the time of the second interview (one year after the first) Marion was living in a small apartment of her own. She had good prospects of receiving a regular contract (and of gaining financial independence), after finishing her final examination. Marion's social life also improved: she had a boyfriend and a significant female friend at her vocational college.

In a way the complete second interview follows one main motif: she *is* now the active planer and "producer" of her own development as she wished to be during the first interview. Interestingly, Marion now tells her story as if she had been this active person her entire life, and as if she never accepted others' rules. Even her choice of profession was, as she described it, *her* personal decision; that she once wished to study biology education is not even mentioned during the second interview. Also different from the first interview, she now says that she accepts and appreciates vagueness and unexpectedness as a necessary part of life instead of the "clear" life plan without any surprises. At the time of the first interview, Marion felt threatened by surprises. Finally, Marion's way of narration changed: While during the first interview she followed the communicative input from the interviewers (also in this respect she once acted "well-behaved"); in the second interview she is rather active, partly dominating the situation and sometimes responding "pertly" to the interviewer's questions.

5.3   Discussion

After offering some interpretation from the case study I now would like to discuss *possible generalizations*. In my opinion the story of Marion illustrates a partly complicated transition from adolescence to adulthood. In some ways in the case of Marion a more consistent concept of self would not have been possible (because of youth unemployment or of integrating family and profession as a still primarily female developmental task). Therefore, Marion's story –and also the stories of the other interviewees– is about (self) contradictions adolescents have to face. But the interviews also show that even if self and world concepts and experiences are crisis-prone, the adolescents find ways to establish a feeling of unity and uniqueness, even if temporary.

How do adolescents maintain such feelings of unity and uniqueness? Each interview followed its own (narrative) main logic –a kind of "great biographical story." This is what I tried to illustrate using Marion's case study. While during the first interview Marion continually tried to be "invisible," during the second interview she became an active and self-confident "advocate" of her own interests. And as each story deals with consistency in conflict with one another,

Marion in the second interview gives the impression as if the first interview never happened, or as if aspects seemingly discrepant between the first and second narration had always been "on the way" according to the main logic presented the second interview. This also includes recognizing and explaining differences: Marion emphasized that during the time of the first interview she preferred to fulfill her own wishes as inconspicuously as possible, while she imagined that in the next interview she probably would report on her "heroic deeds."

Although the self presentations seem to be different at first glance, there are shared dimensions which played a crucial role during both interviews: in Marion's case study autonomy vs. heteronomy, inclusion/acknowledgement vs. exclusion/isolation, and activity vs. passivity. These dimensions are stable, the differences in the narration occur while adolescents move between the poles of the respective dimension. And this move defines which part of a (his)story is considered at a time and in what way. This allows us to understand why Marion during the second interview did not mention her plan to leave the American host family; the negative connotation from the first interview was completely missing. Rather, during the second interview Marion exposes more detailed reasons for the decision to visit America and mentions people who told her after she returned to Germany that she had won self-confidence. It would have been possible to mention this also in the first interview (two years after the visit to America), but it did not fit the pole of the story Marion (re)constructed and experienced at that time.

5.4   Methodological background and methods used

I have attempted to demonstrate empirically how an individual (Marion) attempts to keep a "relative entireness" despite heterogeneity. I now will provide some methodological and methodical comments.

There were four main reasons why I chose a qualitative-empirical approach:

- The design would allow me to explore subjective meaning and to generate theory from the data.
- Qualitative research methods help to reconstruct personal life plans and interpretation patterns as well as their dependency on socio-cultural life worlds.
- Standardized questionnaires often used in traditional identity research do not allow for thorough analyses of identify construction processes because they define and measure self narration over time and for different dimensions with more stability than they occur in psychosocial realities.
- Analyzing the narrative construction of adolescent identity development requires an approach that allows the exploration of the

micro-narration, -presentation, and -construction logics of adolescents' stories.

Qualitative research

Doing qualitative research does not mean one is using so called "soft" methods. The qualitative approach is a way of doing research that leads one to a deep understanding of perceiving, describing, and interpreting reality. Among the central principles of qualitative research are a focus on single cases and a holistic stance. In accordance with Christa Hoffmann-Riem (1980), I would like to emphasize two especially important characteristics of qualitative research: the "principle of openness" and the "principle of communication."

According to the "principle of openness" research participants should have the opportunity to actively structure the research situation (interview) rather than be dominated by the (theoretical) pre-assumptions of the researchers. This should allow for the exploration of the various manifestations of identity: Overall ascriptions such as "identity diffusion," (Marcia, 1989) "patchwork identity" (Kraus, 2000) should be used very carefully as they may lead the researcher to ignore the biographical continuity from the participant's perspective. In contrast, generalizations about coherence and continuity as central ingredients of identity should be avoided, because they may lead the researcher to ignore incongruence and contradictions.

The "principle of communication" is probably a characteristic that most prominently differentiates qualitative and quantitative research. This principle acknowledges the interaction between researchers and research participants as the constitutive element of understanding: *any* ("aroused") responses and utterances that occur need to be analyzed as co-constructions of the persons involved in the interview situation.

In the case of Marion the principle of communication played a crucial role in the interview and its subsequent interpretation, as she was interviewed by two women, one 32 years old, the other 35 years old. This design unintentionally led to a kind of re-producing, as only very little information about Marion had been available, because in some regards Marion's behaviour towards the two interviewers had important similarities to her behaviour towards her mother and her mother's female partner. Therefore the analysis of the interview situation helps us understand the way Marion tended to "act loyal." She was well-behaved during the interview as she did with her complete obedience narration. It therefore is not only important to include in the analysis *what* an interviewee says but also *how* she acts toward the concrete other, how she does not use the potentials offered by an open interview design.

Data collection

The problem-centered interview. I decided to use the problem-centered interview (Witzel, 2000) because it relies on important commonalities with qualitative research (especially the principles of openness and communication) by using different question forms. Witzel differentiates "general exploration" and "specific explorations," from "mirroring," with "clarifying questions" and "confrontations" belonging to the latter.

In my opinion the problem-centered interview is better suited for research than are semi-structured interviews (like the identity status interview, see Marcia, 1966) because of its dialogic-discursive character. Interviewees have a chance to play an active role (if they choose it), while interviewers at the same time have the freedom to discuss possible contradictions and ambivalences with the interviewees. Interviewees are acknowledged as experts and theorists, and their history and interests are recognized. Consequently, communicative validation is made possible in the interview situation.

Interview schedule. Deciding to concentrate on a particular age group also means having to decide on the foci: currently no identity research per se is being done (see the different versions of the identity status interview for early/late adolescence and adulthood by Marcia et al., 1993, Appendices A, B and C). The particular age group being focused on needs to be kept in mind while selecting research instruments. In the case of the problem-centered interview the interview schedule needs to be defined according to the research focus. In the interview schedule for my research the following topics were included: family, peers, partners, school/work, leisure time, gender, ego-self-body, values, future (see figure 1, Mey, 1999, pp.152ff for the complete schedule with detailed comments):

Table 5.1

Interview schedule (Mey, 1999, p.152)	
Opening question	"You are now xx years old. Please try to look back on your life. And please tell us –as detailed as you like– how you experienced not being a child any longer and how the story continued from that point on."
Family	Familial constellation ([step-]brothers/sisters, [step-]parents, grandparents etc.); different relations to family members; education style; processes of exchange in the family and concrete ways to deal with personal problems and conflicts (also conflict causes); model function of the family members
Friendships	Definition of friendship; concrete descriptions of relations to friends; experiences with and expectation towards "real good" friends; controversies and conflicts with (female/male) friends

Table 5.1 continued

Love relations	(Sexual) relations in the past and present; activities shared with a partner; imagines o. "long-term" relations and partnership; expectation toward partnership (individual norms/concepts); reflection on starting and maintaining partnership (concepts of "being in time"/different stages)
School/job/work	General view on personal school/job situation; (self) construction of being a student/worker; relation to teachers/superiors and bosses/school fellows/colleagues; self evaluation of motifs for choice of/performance at school/vocational career
Leisure time	Activities; interests/hobbies; time budget (typical everyday); financial situation
Gender/sex (roles)	Concept of being a man/a woman; sex/gender stereotypes; sex and work; sex and partnership; ideas of sharing tasks (family, household and work) in a future life plan
Concept of youth and adulthood	Self concept and self image of being an adolescent; definition of and criteria for child/childhood, adolescence/adolescent, adult/adulthood
Ego-self-body	Self image and ideas of the way self is perceived by others; relevance of the body/body action (sport; drugs); wishes/ activities to body change; causes for and ways of self reflection
Values/moral development	Moral, religious and political attitudes; ideology; life principle(s)
Future	Near/distant vocational/private future (partnership; children; concept of an own family life; ideas of balancing family and job; career choice/aspiration); concepts of future; life goals (the future in 20 years)
Ending question (sum up refection)	"If your life would be the subject to a movie: what, in your opinion, would be necessary to receive an accurate portrayal?"
Interview closing questions	Aspects of the interviewee missed during the interview; experience of the interview (like/dislike etc.)

In identity research it is assumed that there are different dominant "logics" for different areas of life:

- Different areas of life may be differently important for the adolescents' identity development.
- There may be conflicts between such areas, which possibly make the processes of identity development more difficult.

- Adolescents may use different "subject positions" for different areas of
  life; this means that experiencing (and describing) oneself to be active
  vs. passive may change between these areas.

The importance of different areas and the interplay between them was also
obvious in the case of Marion: While she described becoming a girl scout (area
of leisure time) Marion mentioned that a girlfriend introduced her to the scouts
and she "just stayed" after the girlfriend left the group. This reminds us of the
passive self Marion chooses time and again. She draws a picture of herself as a
person who accepted (and in a way learned to love) what was left within the
well-defined frames others provided (e.g. the basement flat assigned to her became her "hut"). But: The scout story reads in some ways differently from
Marion's choice of profession story, because she resisted her mother's and her
mother's partner's pressure to leave the scouts because of her age while she accepted their influence on her professional development.

Beginning and ending an interview. Beginning and ending an interview requires special attention, as both serve as "frames" for the interview, which
–according to the principle of openness– are subject to the interviewee's structuring competences.

In the case of my research the *opening question* was: "You are now xx
years old. Please try to look back on your life. And please tell us –as detailed as
you like– how you experienced not being a child any longer and how the story
continued from that point on."

The question is intended to invite adolescents to provide their own view on
their lives, to act as auto-biographers. But the narrative opening in some cases
did not work. For example, Marion did not produce a detailed narration. Nevertheless the way she responded helped to understand *her* story; it gave interesting
insights in *her* way of being a biographer of *her* own history.

Marion considered the start of the high school and being assigned her own
room to be markers for the end of her childhood. Then she stopped, and after the
interviewers explicitly encouraged her again just to tell *her* story she delivered a
formal curriculum vitae, always mentioning the respective class she visited and
some "important events": her parents' divorce, becoming a girl scout, the two
love affairs, her travel to America.

Her response shows the extent to which Marion during the first interview
was delivered from a school (class) perspective and helped to understand the
importance of school as structuring life frame at that time. The formal chronology she provided ("and then [. . .] and then") indicated developmental processes,
but she obviously did not experience herself as an active producer of the own
development. So in a way she *was not* her own biographer or, more accurately,
it was not her *own* biography she talked about. Linking her response to the opening question to of her story provided above, one might say that her "and then"
culminated in her definition of adulthood: to achieve "an own opinion and iden-

tity" more or less automatically as a natural ending point of the chronology: "And then one is adult." So the internal dramaturgy of Marion's story was already present at the beginning of the interview.

As all interviews typically begin with a similar opening question, they also end with one final question, that should help to reflect on the main topics mentioned during the interview, and to provide a kind of final personal summary. The adolescents were asked to imagine the following: "If your life would be the subject to a movie: what, in your opinion, would be necessary to receive an accurate portrayal?"

Also, the responses to this question provided very precious insights, and this, similar to the opening question, even if the question did not work at a first glance. "I would not allow such a movie," Marion said at the end of the first interview, because she anticipated a curious and obtrusive public penetrating in the private life of sport stars and actors. Then she added, obviously trying to fulfil her interviewee task, she would like:

> to achieve something in my life, writing a book or so if nothing else works, but surely not, yeah, but surely trying to receive acknowledgment in a more invisible way, not by a movie or something splendid, but in a way [. . .] Yes, to win impact over other's life without being visible. This is why I would dislike such a movie, cause you suddenly would be in the center of the scene and, don't know you would become completely fragmented.

In this response Marion provides some central topics already mentioned above. She disliked the exploratory character of this question; Marion did not accept any surprises at this time. And she helped lend some understanding to the purposes of being loyal and obedient; it helps to avoid becoming visible, touchable, and open to attack.

Transcription

The interpretation mainly relies on the written interview transcripts (audio tapes are used when deemed necessary), so it is important to decide how detailed transcriptions need to be (see Kowal & O'Connell, 2004), how the verbal content and its expression (pitch, loudness) should be handled as well as non-verbal characteristics, accompanying the narration (e.g. clearing one's throat, laughter, but also mimicking and other non-verbal gestures). And it also must be decided if the entire interview should be transcribed or only extracts, and which ones.

In my study I decided to employ literary transcription as opposed to a more detailed "eye dialect" or phonetic transcription, which are especially useful in the case of linguistic/conversation analyses. In this study the complete interviews were transcribed. For sure in the case of Marion it would have been possible to use summaries for her partly very long explanations why generally, and in her own case, it would have been not reasonable to study biology education, her "dream job." But this would have meant neglecting Marion's way of using public arguments to hide her personal reasons and sentiments; namely, her disappointment that her parents were not willing to pay. Additionally, the contrast between such very detailed passages and other parts of the interview which also needed explication but did not receive it would have been lost. Summarizing instead of transcribing would have risked losing important insights because the decision to omit passages would follow the manifest content and ignore the communicative and latent structure of such passages.

Analysis

For examining the data I developed a frame for analysis combining grounded theory methodology (GTM): the original variants of Glaser & Strauss (1967), Strauss (1987) and Strauss & Corbin (1990) and an adaptation of GTM, "Global Analysis" (Legewie, 1994) and the "Method of Circular Deconstruction" (Jaeggi, Fass, & Mruck, 1998) as well as selected rules from objective hermeneutics (as modified with links to biographical research and analysing narratives by Rosenthal (1993). (For a detailed description of methods of analyses of developmental processes see Mey, 2003, 1999, chap. IV.2.2.):

- First, I began with a global *getting into contact* with the interview and with *reflecting first on emotional reactions* to the data;
- secondly, emerging interpretations were *unfolded and systematized*;
- finally, the core interpretations for each single case were *condensed and evaluated*.

It is necessary to stress again that qualitative research, according to the "principle of communication," requires the researcher to reflect on his or her subjectivity during the whole process of collecting and analyzing data. That researchers respond emotionally to a person or a text is a *condition sine qua non*, and so is the reflection on researchers' subjectivity for an adequate understanding of all data. One consequence is that the complete research process, from posing a research question to the formulation of a grounded theory, needs to be done by a research team. If this is not possible at least the data analysis should be conducted by a team (see Mruck & Mey, 1998, for theoretical considerations and suggestions for how to organize interpretation groups).

Step 1: Getting into global contact and reflecting on first emotional reactions to the data. This first step serves to focus on the first ideas of the research participant and his or her history and way of self presentation. This means:

- getting familiar with the data,
- receiving a first overview of the interview, and
- allowing a first emotional response and reflection.

During this first step more principled questions are asked concerning the complete text: "What is going on here?" It may be helpful during this first getting in contact to condense what seems to be central into a kind of "motto" which serves as a global summary for the first line of interpretation.

The first interview with Marion was given the following motto (after several mottos had been discussed by the research team): "I really would love to be a girl scout also in the future." The motto for the second interview was: "Really don't know what heroic stories I may tell in the future [. . .]." The process of deciding on a motto by the research group helps to simultaneously create a dense and colourful picture for each interview. As this creative act is useful to generate first interpretations, for the following analysis it should not be given up for a more detailed and systematic analysis of concrete passages too early. This is because the reflection of the first emotional responses (e.g. sympathy, antipathy, compassion) often is helpful for the second systematic approach by asking for example "Why do you suffer with Marion?" "What makes you think of Marion as a weak person?" "In which way does Marion remind you of your own adolescence?"

Step 2: Unfolding and systematizing emerging interpretations. This second step aims at analyzing single transcribed passages word-by-word or sequence-by-sequence. During this first interpretation, available from Step 1, are successively revised, unfolded, or given up completely if they do not fit the data during the ongoing analyses.

During this phase the overt structure of the content is explored analytically by using questions to the phenomenon being examined. This step is rather well known from different qualitative methods (e.g., "open coding" in the case of GTM, "sequential analysis" in the case of objective hermeneutics, or "detailed analysis" in the case of narration analytical approaches).

According to GTM (Strauss & Corbin, 1990) the so called "paradigmatic model" may be used while coding: it asks for causes, conditions, context, interaction, phenomenon, strategies, and consequences, using questions like:

- *what* –what is the phenomenon the sequence/text deals with;
- *who* –who participates, which roles are used/ascribed;
- *in which way* –which aspects are elaborated (and which are ignored);
- *at what time, how long, where* –which role the place and time play in the narration (biographically, for a single act/sequence);
- *why* –which causes/arguments are provided (in)directly;
- *how* –which strategies are used;
- *to which purpose* –which consequences were experienced/anticipated.

Some of the interpretations mentioned in the case study above only make sense with such questions in mind. To mention just the most important interpretations: The challenging situation after high school (condition), the parents' pressure (context), Marion's being passive and her tendency to suspend own wishes and interests (strategies), and her hope that adulthood will "occur" at the end of the development (anticipated consequence).

To respond to the theory generating questions the background knowledge of the researchers should be used. Most times these questions receive two answers: one refers to the overt meaning (as provided during the narration), the other relates to (latent) meaning/the researchers' interpretation (this difference was crucial for the various interpretations of the American sequence).

As not all interviews could be exposed to open coding completely (in my research there had been roughly 150-200 pages per interview) it is necessary to account theoretically for the decision which sequences had been selected:

- Often the opening sequence of an interview gains special attention. In my case this was because of the importance of the opening question for my research. More generally in the beginning of an interview the interaction between researcher and research participant is established, and many peculiarities important for the complete interview are already visible in this opening sequence.

- Sequences should be considered for open coding which deal in a central way with the phenomenon under research: In my study this had been the movie question, dealing with the adolescents' self perception and the way they believe they are to be experienced by others, and the question concerning their anticipation of the future.

- Those sequences should be interpreted more closely that cause special emotional responses or which at a first glance seem to be especially closed to interpretations. In the case of Marion her description of her visit to America was very emotional, which was very different from her narration during the rest of the interview.

Step 3: Condensation and evaluation of core interpretations. After systematizing the interpretations during detailed sequence analysis like those described above which are dedicated to generating a single case theory, all of the dimensions (categories) elaborated through the earlier steps are carefully evaluated, condensed, and revised, comparable to axial coding in GTM (via Strauss & Corbin, 1990). This is done by using sequences that directly indicate the phenomenon under research, in the case of Marion passages dealing with her obedience, etc. Additionally, sequences are included in the analysis which are linked to the phenomenon indirectly, for example the scout story which in a way contradicts all other sequences.

A single case analysis is finished after a "story" has been generated (comparable to selective coding in GTM; Strauss & Corbin, 1990), explaining consistently and systematically what is going on in this single case. It is important at this stage to ask if the complete data follow the major line of interpretation developed during the complete process of data analysis. This is what I tried to do with my case study. Furthermore, using this structure for my article I tried to give the reader an idea of the procedures I used to evaluate such major lines of interpretation.

5.5   Final remarks

The psychological developmental study of identity especially benefits from a qualitative approach and from employing and combining qualitative methods creatively.

In this study I attempted to demonstrate this with the single case presented in this article. My effort stands in a way as an example of the initial acceptance of qualitative methods within developmental psychology (see Mey, 2000, 2003; and more detailed, 2005); additionally, it illustrates some of the difficulties accompanying qualitative research and its presentation in publications. Related to the still difficult role of theory within qualitative research this especially concerns transparency of methods and interpretations on the one hand and the use of accepted qualitative "labels" on the other.

To report results from qualitative inquiry in research articles is difficult because of page restrictions that work against the need to provide detailed information about data and data analysis. In the case of Marion I did the analysis without extensive citations; I also omitted the description of more subtle interpretations. So in some regards readers are forced to trust instead of learning from a successive (and detailed) exposition of data and interpretation –that I tried to provide the case study to step by step give insight in my use of methods and in the interpretations I developed did probably only help partly. Interesting solutions to such a dilemma arise from online publications because there are less page restrictions and data (e.g., interviews) can be provided using a hyper text structure (I tried to realize this at least partly for a multi media text module for the FernUniversität Hagen in Germany, see Mey, 2004).

A second problem arises from the methods used for "making identities talk" (Kraus, 2000), and, more precisely, from the reputation methods acquire. Also, in qualitative research to mention special acknowledged methods is important as an act of authorization. Currently there is a growing number of German publications, using, for example, "problem-centered interviews" or "grounded theory" as a kind of label to prove that accepted routines had been used and in this way try to increase the dignity of the research. But just using labels is not sufficient for high quality qualitative research: *Application of* qualitative methods always means *developing* qualitative methods, and this requires presenting methods use and the interpretations done rather transparently. In this article I have attempted to show at least in a limited way that this may bring benefits.

Acknowledgements

Many thanks to Katja Mruck, my partner and colleague, for co-translating the text; and many thanks also to Robert Faux, my colleague from Pittsburgh, for the final look and copy editing.

References

Bamberg, M. (2004). Narrative discourse and identities. In J.C. Meister, T. Kindt, W. Schernus, & M. Stein (Eds.), *Narratology beyond literary criticism* (pp. 351–371). Berlin: de Gruyter.

Brockmeier, J., & Carbaugh, D. (Eds.) (2001). *Narrative and identity: Studies in autobiography, self and culture* (pp. 39–58). Amsterdam: John Benjamins.

Darmstädter, T. & Mey, G. (1998). Identität im Selbstwiderspruch oder "Die Schizophrenie des Lebens". Theoretische und empirische Einwände gegen "postmoderne" Konzeptualisierungsversuche von Identität [Identity contradicting itself or „The schizophrenia of life". Theoretical and empirical objections to postmodern conceptualisations of identity]. *Psychologie & Gesellschaftskritik, 22* (4), 65–94.

Erikson, E.H. (1959). *Identity and the life cycle. Psychological Issues 1* (Monograph 1). New York: International Universities Press.

Glaser, B.G., & Strauss, A.L. (1967). *The discovery of grounded theory. Strategies for qualitative research.* New York: Aldine de Gruyter.

Habermas, T., & Bluck, S. (2000). Getting a life: The emergence of the life story in adolescence. *Psychological Bulletin, 126,* 748–769.

Hoffmann-Riem, C. (1980). Die Sozialforschung einer interpretativen Soziologie. Der Datengewinn [Social research of an interpretative sociology. Data collection]. *Kölner Zeitschrift für Soziologie und Sozialpsychologie, 32,* 339–372.

Jaeggi, E., Faas, A. & Mruck, K. (1998). Denkverbote gibt es nicht! Vorschlag zur interpretativen Auswertung kommunikativ gewonnener Daten. *Forschungsbericht aus der Abteilung für Psychologie im Institut für Sozialwissenschaften der Technischen Universität Berlin, Nr. 98-2.* [also available online: http://www.tu-berlin.de/fb7/ifs/psychologie/reports/ber98_02.html or: http://psydok.sulb.uni-saarland.de/volltexte/2004/291/]

Kowal, S., & O'Connell, D.C. (2004). The transcription of conversations. In U. Flick, E. v. Kardorff, & I. Steinke (Eds.), *A companion to qualitative research* (pp. 248–252). London: Sage.

Kraus, W. (2000). Making identities talk. On qualitative methods in a longitudinal study [33 paragraphs]. *Forum Qualitative Sozialforschung / Forum: Qualitative Social Research [On-line Journal], 1* (2). Available at: http://www.qualitative-research.net/fqs-texte/2-00/2-00kraus-e.htm [Date of access: 15.04.2006].

Legewie, H. (1994). Globalauswertung [Global analysis]. In A. Böhm, T. Muhr & A. Mengel (Eds.), *Texte verstehen: Konzepte, Methoden, Werkzeuge* (pp. 100–114). Konstanz: Universitätsverlag.

Marcia, J.E. (1966). Development and validation of ego identity status. *Journal of Personality and Social Psychology, 3,* 551–558.

Marcia, J.E. (1989). Identity diffusion differentiated. In M.A. Luszcz, & T. Nettelbeck (Eds.), *Psychological development across the life-span* (pp. 289–295). North-Holland: Elsevier.

Marcia, J.E., Waterman, A.S., Matteson, D.R., Archer, S.L., & Orlofsky, J.L. (Eds.) (1993). *Ego identity. A handbook for psychosocial research.* New York: Springer.

Mey, G. (1999). *Adoleszenz, Identität, Erzählung. Theoretische, methodische und empirische Erkundungen* [Adolescence, identity, narration. Theoretical, methodical, and empirical investigations]. Berlin: Köster.

Mey, G. (2000). Qualitative research and the analysis of processes. Considerations towards a "Qualitative Developmental Psychology" [35 paragraphs]. *Forum Qualitative Sozialforschung / Forum: Qualitative Social Research [On-line Journal], 1* (1). Available at: http://www.qualitative-research.net/fqs-texte/1-00/1-00mey-e.htm [Date of access: 15.04.2006].

Mey, G. (2003). Qualitative Forschung: Überlegungen zur Forschungsprogrammatik und Vorschläge zur Forschungspraxis im Themenfeld der Frühen Kindheit [Qualitative research: Thoughts on research pragmatics and research suggestions for early childhood]. In H. Keller (Ed.), *Handbuch der Kleinkindforschung* (3rd revised ed., pp. 709–750). Bern: Huber.

Mey, G. (2004). Rekonstruktionen adoleszenter Identitätsbildungsprozesse: Eine qualitative Studie / Das problemzentrierte Interview [Reconstructions of adolescent identity development processes: A qualitative study / The problem-centered interview] (2 course packs). In H. Abels, W. Fuchs-Heinritz & S. Schönrath (Eds.), *Jugend: Theorie und Empirie. Mulitmedialer Dateikurs.* Hagen: FernUniversität Hagen [CD Rom].

Mey, G. (Ed.) (2005). *Handbuch Qualitative Entwicklungspsychologie* [Handbook Qualitative Developmental Psychology]. Köln: Kölner Studien Verlag.

Mruck, K. & Mey, G. (1998). Selbstreflexivität und Subjektivität im Auswertungsprozeß biographischer Materialien – Zum Konzept einer "Projektwerkstatt qualitativen Arbeitens" zwischen Colloquium, Supervision und Interpretationsgemeinschaft [The abilitiy of self reflection and subjectivity in the process of analyzing biographical data]. In G. Jüttemann & H. Thomae (Eds.), *Biographische Methoden in den Humanwissenschaften* (pp. 284–306). Weinheim: Beltz/PVU.

Rosenthal, G. (1993). Reconstruction of life stories. Principles of selection in generating stories for narrative biographical interviews. *The Narrative Study of Lives, 1* (1), 59–91.

Straub, J., Zielke, B., & Werbik, H. (2005). Autonomy, narrative identity and their critics. A reply to some provocations of postmodern accounts in psychology. In W. Greve, & D. Wentura (Eds.), *The adaptive self: Personal continuity and intentional self development* (pp. 323–350). Göttingen: Hogrefe .

Strauss, A.L. (1987). *Qualitative analysis for social scientists.* New York: Cambridge University Press.

Strauss, A.L., & Corbin, J. (1990). *Basics of qualitative research, grounded theory, procedures and techniques.* London: Sage.

Witzel, A. (2000). The problem-centered interview [27 paragraphs]. *Forum Qualitative Sozialforschung / Forum: Qualitative Social Research [On-line Journal], 1* (1). Available at: http://www.qualitative-research.net/fqs-texte/1-00/1-00witzel-e.htm [Date of access: 15.01.06].

Chapter 6

Analyzing Identity Using a Voice Approach

Mechthild Kiegelmann
University of Tübingen
Germany

My contribution in this paper is the introduction of a qualitatively oriented research methodology of psychology that can be applied to identity research. This methodology details the "Voice Approach" which was developed by Carol Gilligan and Lyn Brown together with their colleagues. The voice approach is a qualitative method, yet it is compatible with other modes of investigation and has been successfully combined with quantitative measures in mixed methods research.

6.1   Introduction

The conference "Identity Development – Toward and Integration of Quantitative and Qualitative Methods" in Braunschweig in November 2005 dealt with questions of identity research and empirical methodology. A special focus was on the identity status approach of James Marcia (see his contribution in this book), in which he describes how identity development can be traced in four statuses: achievement, foreclosure, diffusion, and moratorium. Statuses are marked by the absence or presence of commitment and exploration.

My contribution in this paper is the introduction of a qualitatively oriented research methodology of psychology that can be applied to identity research. This methodology details the "Voice Approach" which was developed by Carol Gilligan and Lyn Brown together with their colleagues (Brown & Gilligan, 1992; Gilligan, 1982; Gilligan, Spencer, Weinberg, & Bertsch, 2003). The voice approach is a qualitative method, yet it is compatible with other modes of investigation and has been successfully combined with quantitative measures in mixed methods research (e.g. Tolman, 2002). While this tool has been developed in the field of moral development and the development of girls and women, I argue that it can be used in investigations about other topics as well, such as identity development. Of interest for identity researchers is Gilligan's theory of girls' and women's development when being confronted with societal gender norms and expectations (Gilligan, 1990a & b; 1992).

Especially one feature of this research technique is its ability to provide insight on identity in the analysis of a "Voice of Self" via interview transcripts. In this paper I introduce the Voice Approach and illustrate with an empirical example how the concept of "Voice of Self" can provide insight on identity development. Here, I draw some connections of this type of research to Marcia's identity status theory.

While Marcia describes the process of identity development involving exploration and commitment, Gilligan and her colleagues emphasize authenticity in relationships and resistance to patriarchal norms. Yet, both approaches point to similar features of developmental processes when they address identity formation as active processes of human beings within their social surroundings. Identity formation involves exploration of various options in Marcia's terms or resistance to social pressures in Gilligan's terms. Both authors confront the lack of active deliberation by pointing out the pitfalls of foreclosure or capitulation.

In my own research I have used the Voice Approach to investigate how people can develop the ability to break silences in group settings (Kiegelmann, 1996, 2005). While I have not focused explicitly on questions of identity formation, I argue that an active sense of self worth and belief in one's own perception is a supportive measure in the ability to deviate from group norms. In order to "break the silence" one first must detect that silencing exists in a group, then use this knowledge to address the silenced topic, and subsequently acquire social support. Even though there does not seem to be a very large overlap between

Marcia's identity status testing and the Voice Approach, the Voice Approach has the potential to enrich the discussion on identity research and methods. In research on identity, information about how individuals bring themselves into relationships with others is essential. In this paper I introduce how a qualitative-psychological research strategy called "Voice Approach" can be a useful tool to assess information about identity. For my contribution I will use examples from my own empirical research in which I applied the Voice Approach (Kiegelmann, 2000, 2002, 2003, 2005) but focus on methods.

Below, I will first present the Voice Approach in the context of its theoretical background, i.e. relational psychology, and then move on to explain the specific steps in the method of analysis. Here, I proceed to an example to illustrate such an approach. Finally, I will come back to the relevance for identity theory and draw connections to Marcia's work.

6.2   Relational psychology

The Voice Approach was developed by Gilligan and her colleagues (Brown, 1991; Brown & Gilligan, 1991, 1992; Gilligan, Spencer, Weinberg, & Bertsch, 2003) at Harvard during the 1980's and 1990's in the context of their formulation of relational psychology, a feminist movement within psychology. They conducted a series of related studies on women's and girls' development, and refined the Voice Approach (Gilligan, 1982; Gilligan, Ward, & Taylor, 1988). Later, several researchers applied the approach to various other topics, such as the suicide of girls (Machoian, 1998), or the relationships of pre-school boys (Chu, 2000). Tamara Beauboeuf and myself were instrumental in applying more social context to the Voice Approach (Beaubeouf & Kiegelmann, 2000, 2006; Kiegelmann, 2005). This method is embedded in a theory of psychological development that Gilligan calls "relational psychology" (Gilligan, 2003). Gilligan and her colleagues emphasize the centrality of relationship by critiquing Kohlberg's notion that human development has the goal of achieving autonomy and independence from others. In relational psychology, development is viewed as a process in which human relationships change. An overemphasis on independence and autonomy is seen as a form of disconnection that could be detrimental to the individual. In addition, Gilligan proposes a multi-layered view on identity that describes a complex web of "voices," i.e. various experiences, emotions, cognitions, desires, and social relationships that mark people's identity. Relational psychologists point out that development occurs often in resistance to social pressures to conform to unhealthy norms and expectations, e.g. traditional views on femininity as subservient and selfless (Gilligan, 2003).

According to my reading of relational psychology there are several key aspects that can be relevant for the study of identity. These aspects are the following:

In order to understand psychological development, attention needs to be placed not only on a single individual, but also on how a person is connected with other people in immediate relationships. Furthermore, psychological insights about an identity can be gained by analyzing the word choices of a person talking about herself or himself. Also, development is framed as a relational process, not a process of striving towards disconnection and autonomy. Inherent in relational psychology is the assumption that authentic presentation of oneself in relationships is preferable over withholding aspects of self in order to avoid conflict or criticism. Here, the highly valued connectedness means involvement with other people, but also awareness and acceptance of multiple aspects of oneself (e.g. multiple voices).

Several later students of Gilligan and Brown have applied and modified this relational theory. For example, Taylor and Sullivan looked at the impact of racism on the development of girls (Taylor, Gilligan, & Sullivan, 1995), Tolman (2002) studied girls' ability to express sexual desire, and Balan investigated women's work place transitions (Balan, 2005). My own addition to this theory has been a special attention to social context (Kiegelmann, 2005). Here, I extend the notion of relationships as important aspects to psychology beyond immediate face to face relationships of a person. Drawing on concepts from social identity theory (Tajfel, & Turner, 1986; Abrams, & Hogg, 1999), I argue that information about salient group identifications can help understanding human development, especially when researching resistance to group practices such as silencing. This form of attention to social contexts informs both the general understanding of the main topics present in research data, and also adds to the notion of identity being structured with a layered set of multiple voices.

Before I discuss more of my own research, I will explain the procedure of data analysis that is derived from relational psychology. The Voice Approach consists of a set of strategies for analytical readings of transcribed research data.

6.3   Analyzing with the voice approach

There are several specific steps of analysis that constitute the Voice Approach. One step which is probably most relevant for identity research is the reading for a "Voice of Self" but for clarity, I will discuss all of the steps involved in the following paragraphs. For a more detailed description of the Voice Approach see Brown and Gilligan (1992), Brown (1998), Gilligan et al. (2003), and Brown et al. (1988).

The Voice Approach consists of a series of multiple readings of the research data. Most common data in this line of research are detailed transcripts from audiotapes of semi-structured interviews in which the researcher introduces her or his topics of interest and encourages the interviewee to explore her own thoughts, feelings, and experiences by avoiding interruptions (e.g. Brown & Gilligan, 1992). Each analytical reading focuses on a different aspect of analysis. Results of each step are summarized and later used to create an overall interpretation of the material. Findings from the earlier readings guide the subsequent steps. These steps in the analysis of the Voice Approach are (see Kiegelmann, 2005):

- Listening for plot
- Listening for readers response and social context
- Listening for self
- Listening for contrapuntal voices

An example of my own research can help illustrate this approach. I conducted a study with adolescent workers in the context of their learning about the Nazi history of their workplace (Kiegelmann, 2000). As part of their apprenticeship program, these young people visit a museum that was set up by political activists to educate the public about the history of a concentration camp located on the premises of the factory. I was able to conduct interviews with young workers right after they had visited this museum. In this paper I introduce an interview with a young man of Turkish decent in Germany who prior to this museum visit had not been aware that the company in which he had been employed had been founded during Nazi Germany as a weapon factory.

Plot

In the first step of analysis with the Voice Approach, the researcher outlines the content of a transcribed interview, i.e. the story line and the topics which the interviewee recalls in conversation with the interviewer. Similar to Kohlberg's mapping of logical arguments (for the purpose of identifying stages of cognitive moral development), the researcher with the Voice Approach codes the topics and argumentations of the interviewee. This first reading focuses on the explicit content of the material, as is common in other research approaches such as content analysis (Mayring, 1997). The young man in my study choose the following main topics when interviewed about his views on the local Nazi History: 1) The question about guilt and punishment of perpetrators of Nazi atrocities, 2) his status as a migrant in Germany and 3) the non-German nationality of the former concentration camp inmates who had participated in building the factory that now is his workplace. In my analysis, these choices of topics indicate that this man's experiences of being a member of a migrant community in Germany is a central aspect in how he relates to Nazi history in Germany. By focusing on the punishment of Germans (still alive) who had participated in the Nazi atrocities, he draws a link between the history and current times.

Along with this first step of documenting the content, the researcher also notes gaps in the story line or indicates places where information is missing in order to understand events or experiences of the interviewee. Attention to missing topics leads to the second step of analysis, i.e. the researcher's/reader's response, because it is the researcher who detects according to her or his own mindset what appears to be missing in order to understand the interviewee's topics more fully.

Readers' Response and Social Context

In the second step of analyzing, the interviewer goes back through the transcript and notes her or his reactions to the interview. Even if the researcher did not conduct the interview herself, in this step she places herself explicitly into relationship with the interviewee and pays attention to her own emotional and intellectual responses. Just as a psychoanalytic therapist reflects on instances of counter transference, the researcher pays attention to her own unresolved conflicts or important values that are being triggered by the words of the interviewee. If the researcher is identical with the interviewer, then the researcher responds to both the actual interview and the transcript as material. This second step helps to avoid traps where researchers remain preoccupied with their own favorite topics or their own problems, rather than listening to what the interviewee is expressing (see also Nadig, 1986). In addition, the researcher utilizes knowledge of the general socio-historic background of the interview, in order to assess social conditions that can be relevant to the experiences of the study participant. For instance, Gilligan interpreted a patriarchal history with specific gender role expectations and used this information as a background for understanding girls' and boys' psychological development (Gilligan, 2003).

In the example of my interview with the young worker, my initial reader's response to meeting him face to face during the interview and again when working with the transcript was my sense that his intellectual abilities were much higher than those of his colleagues. I wondered if his migrant status had prevented him from getting a more sophisticated education than his actual training as a blue color metal worker. My focus on access to education of this young man might be influenced by my own experiences of facing obstacles in access to education. Research shows that migrants of Turkish decent are over represented in the lower tracks of the school system in Germany (e.g. Ramm et al, 2003). This information about the social context supports my suspicion of disadvantage in schooling and subsequent job opportunities for this man.

Self

In the third step of analysis, the researcher pays attention to the way in which the interviewee talks about her- or himself and interprets these word choices within the context of the topics covered. How a person speaks about herself or himself provides information about confidence or unfinished processes of understanding, and shows how interviewees take a personal stance. Shifts in the forms of speaking about oneself are especially informative for understanding identity. For example, a person might speak in a distant manner using third person singular about typical daily routines, and then shift to first person singular when describing a recent personal conflict. This part of the Voice Approach is most relevant for identity research because it focuses on the way the interviewee views herself or himself. Illustrating the psychological processes which describe oneself in relation to others, Balan (2005) summarizes this third step in the Voice Approach by explaining how the word choices about the self are first coded in the transcript and then assembled in an "I poem:"

> According to Gilligan et al. (2003), two rules manage the construction of an "I poem." First, one is to extract every first person "I" within the given excerpt, along with the verb and any seemingly important accompanying information. Second, one is to maintain the precise sequence in which the phrases originally occurred in the person's story. As the researcher extracts the sequenced "I" phrases, she places them in separate lines, like the lines of a poem. Often, "I poems" capture concepts not directly stated by the informant, yet central to the meaning of what she has said. In any case, the "I poem" attends to an associative stream of consciousness carried by the first-person voice running through a narrative, rather than being contained by the full structure of sentences. Focusing just on the "I" pronoun, and at times, its relation to other pronouns, brings the informant's subjectivity to the foreground, providing the researcher with the opportunity to attend just to the rhythms and patterns in the informant's relationships to herself and to others as expressed in her narratives. (Balan, 2005, p 50)

In contrast to Balan, I suggest not limiting the search to the first person pronoun "I" but instrumenting a step of listening for self by including all pronouns which the study participant uses for herself or himself (Kiegelmann, 1996). This way, shifts in the Voice of Self can be traced more fully. Also, focusing on all namings of the self has the benefit that collectively oriented dialects and social cultures can be interpreted more adequately (Beaubeouf & Kiegelmann, 2006).

In order to illustrate the third step of the Voice Approach which is important when discussing identity, I will now introduce excerpt of an interview with the young study participant I mentioned above. In this excerpt he first recounts a discussion among his peers about whether or not a former Nazi should be sent to trial because of his human rights violations and murder of the concentration camp inmates. After summarizing the point of view from some colleagues who argue against prosecution of this particular man, the interviewee expresses his own contrasting view.

Original version

Also zum Beispiel die, ich weiß's nich genau, die eine Sache mit dem Doktor, glaub ich, das hat mich am meisten so intressiert gehabt. Ich kann mich kaum noch an die Sache erinnern. Ich glaub, dieser Arzt hatte, äh, die Aufsicht über die ganzen, äh, Arbeiter dort, über diese ganzen Juden, glaub ich, die dort gearbeitet haben und andere, und hat sich wahrscheinlich nich drum gekümmert. Und die sind dort irgendwie total verendet irgendwie so richtig in diesem Gefäng-, in diesem kerkerähnlichen Ge- Gebäude da zugrundegegangen so ne Art, obwohl er, (2) also, (2) ich glaube, die Macht hatte oder das Können hatte, zu s, zu sagen: „Hier, ich will, da, ich will, daß sich das von heut auf morgen so und so ändert." Ich glaub, das, dazu hat er eigentlich die Dings gehabt, glaub ich, [MHM] also, die Befugnis oder so. [MHM] Hat er ja, glaub ich, gehabt. Also, ich weiß es nich mehr genau, [MHM] soweit ich das weiß. Und, doch, er hat es nicht gemacht, und die Personen sind irgendwie dadurch zu Schaden gekommen, sind alle daran (2) irgendwie zugrundegegangen.

English translation

For example, I don't know exactly, the thing with the doctor, I think, that was something that I was interested in most. I can hardly remember this thing. I think, this physician was, em, the supervisor for all, em, workers there, for all these Jews, I think, who worked there, and for others; and probably he did not take any responsibility for anything. And then they somehow totally perished, somehow really in this priso-, in this dungeon-like build- building there, decayed in a way, even though he (2), well, (2), I think, he had the power or the ability to s-, to say: "Here, I want, there, I want that this will be changed right away in such and such a way." I think, that, for this he had had the whatcha ma call it, I think. [UHU] ahm, the permission or such. [UHU] He had had it, I think. Well, I do not know exactly, [UHU] as far as I know. But still, he did not do it, and the people somehow got damaged through this, because of this they all (2) perished somehow from this.

When isolating the wording this young man uses about himself in this quote, the following self poem results:

Original version	*English translation*
ich weiß's nich genau,	I don't know exactly,
glaub ich,	I think,
das hat mich	that I was
Ich kann mich kaum noch [. . .] er-	I can hardly remember
innern.	I think,
Ich glaub,	I think,
glaub ich,	I think,
ich glaube,	I think,
Ich glaub,	I think,
glaub ich,	I think,
glaub ich,	Well, I do not know exactly,
Also, ich weiß es nich mehr genau,	as far as I know.
soweit ich das weiß.	

In this list of words for self I notice a sense of vagueness in his voice. His summary of the information he had learned about one specific person he often interrupts with inserts in which he disclaims his knowledge. Thus, in a sense, he is providing information and at the same time claiming that he does not know this information. The Voice of Self shows hesitation in the way he relates to the history of a specific Nazi physician.

The initial uncertainty that I interpret as showing in this self poem could be a sign of an active process of exploration of his own position regarding the discussed question. As a German born young man of a Turkish migrant family, Nazi history is connected to Germany before his family migrated. Yet, a building located at his current work place is the site of a former concentration camp and thus close to his every day life. According to the information he gives at other places in this interview, he had learned about the concentration camp history of "his" factory only a day before. Without much time to form an opinion, he remains hesitant about prescribing actions resulting from this information. The disclaiming expressions (e.g. "I don't know [. . .]", etc.) in his utterance could be a sign of active exploration, as Marcia might say. In addition, his hesitance could be due to being intimidated by speaking about this history in the interview with me, a person from a university. Here, I do not see indications of commitment (as Marcia might find it), however, other cases also examined with a Voice Approach might, in contrast to this example, show a strong Voice of Self, presented without hesitation and with clear descriptions of the speakers' wishes, stands, or desires.

In sum, the analysis step called listening for self can shed light on latent expressions of how a speaker relates to the topic she or he is talking about. In research on identity, this technique could be used, for example, to gather information about the way study participants relate to controversial issues.

Multiple voices

Finally, the fourth and fifth and any subsequent readings that appear to be useful with any given data set for a research question, are listening for multiple voices. Here, researchers either investigate how theoretically derived categories of psychology can be identified in empirical data (such as "Voice of Care" and "Voice of Justice" in Gilligans early work), or researchers use the readings for multiple voices in order to detect new categories within the empirical material. For example, in the above quoted study with young workers in a German metal factory, I found an "educationally correct voice" in which the workers considered documentation of Nazi history as a preventative for further violence and genocide. Yet their answers to my questions in the interviews appeared to be conventional rather than expressing their own thinking and feeling about the topic (see also von Borries, 2001, 1995 about similar findings in large scale studies). Along side expressions that I coded as "educationally correct voices" were some signs of the young workers' ability conduct perspective taking and an ability to relate to the experiences of concentration camp inmates. The above quoted interviewee, for example, related his Turkish background and experiences as being labeled "foreigner" to the concentration camp inmates and focused on their nationality. In a voice that I coded as "migrant voice" he conceptualizes the concentration camp inmates as the founders of the factory and expresses his thankfulness towards them for providing him with the opportunity of employment. When discussing the question of prosecution of Nazi perpetrators who have not been taken to court at the time of the interview, he spells out arguments both for holding perpetrators accountable ("voice of punishment") and for an end of investigations ("voice of no punishment").

Thus, the reading for multiple voices is a tool that can help to construct a multi-faceted concept of the ways interviewees relate to the problem posed in a research question. Or, in more general terms, the Voice Approach, with its different steps of interpretation, is able to provide interpretations of human identities that are composed within a set of different voices.

In an analysis using the Voice Approach, the findings from all analytical steps provide the material for drawing conclusions on a particular transcript. The next step then is to move the analysis beyond single interviews or single cases and cross analyze a set of interviews from different study participants in order to answer the specific research question that guide the inquiry.

In conclusion to my brief introduction of the Voice Approach, I will address how this method could enrich the study of identity development in the following paragraphs.

6.4   Relevance of the voice approach for identity development

The Voice Approach could enrich identity research by providing a tool to trace latent information that is conveyed in speech through the patterns in which a person uses personal pronouns for addressing herself or himself. As I illustrate above, looking at a self-voice can help researchers to understand how a speaker relates to topics or persons she or he talks about. While Marcia stresses the importance of exploration and commitment when investigating identity statuses, the Voice Approach can trace issues such as self doubt, certainty, or capitulation to social pressures. Also, by relying on the choice of topics an interviewee presents as relevant to the issue as questions, there is the possibility that themes relevant to the speakers' identity will be addressed. For example, the identity of a German born member of a Turkish migrant community was relevant for the approach of a young worker to German Nazi history. He focused on the non-German nationality of the concentration camp inmates he learned about in an educational program.

Also, the Voice Approach offers a view to analyzing a multi-layered identity. This multi-layered identity is important, because depending on the specific social context, different aspects of identity become salient. Identities are complex as there are different facets of a person, depending on which relationships he or she finds herself in. These relationships are central and in turn because some aspects can be exaggerated or toned down depending on the situation. Whatever the situation, this approach promises to capture not just the loud and outspoken parts of a person's identity, but also capture the more subtle parts of identity that may be silenced. Often an interviewee struggles with conflicting voices in herself or himself and experiences difficulties in expressing all the nuances about her or his own experiences, views, and feelings. A researcher, using other methods, might inadvertently not be able to pick up the full complexity of this. Thus, relational psychology and the Voice Approach can complement identity research in their emphases on complexity of identity, and further, they can provide a tool to document subtle facets of meaning.

References

Abrams, D., & Hogg, M.A. (Eds.) (1999). *Social identity and social cognition.* Oxford: Blackwell.

Balan, N.B. (2005). Multiple voices and methods: Listening to women who are in workplace transition. *International Journal of Qualitative Methods, 4* (4), Article 5.

Beauboeuf, T., & Kiegelmann, M. (2000). *Toward a critical method of voice: Moving from first-person singular to first-person plural.* Paper presented at the 42. Kongress der Deutschen Gesellschaft für Psychologie, Jena.

Beauboeuf, T., & Kiegelmann, M. (2006). *Investigating the first-person plural in feminist research.* Second International Congress of Qualitative Inquiry, Chicago, USA.

Borries, B.v. (1995). *Das Geschichtsbewußtsein Jugendlicher. Eine repräsentative Untersuchung über Vergangenheitsdeutungen, Gegenwartswahrnehmungen und Zukunftserwartungen von Schülerinnen und Schülern in Ost- und Westdeutschland* [The consciousness about history of youth. A representative inquiry about interpretations of history, understanding of presence, and expectations of the future in high school students from East- and West Germany]. Weinheim: Juventa.

Borries, B.v. (2001). Lehr- und Lernforschung im Fach Geschichte [History classes: research on teaching and learning]. In C. Finkbeiner, G. Schnaitmann, J. Peterseon & G.-B. Reinert (Eds.), *Lehren und Lernen im Kontext empirischer Forschung und Fachdidaktik* (pp. 399–438). Donauwörth: Auer.

Brown, L. (1998). *Raising their voices: the politics of girls' anger.* Cambridge, MA: Harvard University Press.

Brown, L., Argyris, D., Attanucci, J., Bardige, B., Gilligan, C., Johnston, K., Miller, B., Osborne, D., Ward, J., Wiggins, G., & Wilcox, D. (1988). *A guide to reading narratives of conflict and choice for self and relational voice* (Monograph no.1). Cambridge, MA: Project on the Psychology of Women and the Development of Girls, Harvard Graduate School of Education.

Brown, L.M. (1991). Telling a girl's life: Self-authorizations as a form of resistance. *Women and Therapy, 11,* 71–86.

Brown, L., & Gilligan, C. (1992). *Meeting at the crossroads.* Cambridge, MA: Harvard University Press.

Brown, L., & Gilligan, C. (1991). Listening for voice in narratives of relationship. In M.B. Tappan, & J.M. Packer (Eds.), *Narrative and storytelling: Implications for understanding moral development* (pp. 43–62). San Francisco, CA: Jossey-Bass.

Chu, J. (2000). *Learning what boys know: an observational and interview study with six four year-old boys.* Unpublished doctoral dissertation, Harvard University Graduate School of Education.

Gilligan, C. (1992). Response to Melanie and the Melanie Case. In A. Garrod, L. Sullivan, S.I. Powers, & R. Kilkenny (Eds.), *Adolescent Portraits: Identity, Relationships, and Challenges* (pp. 19–47). Boston: Allyn & Bacon.

Gilligan, C. (1990a). Joining the resistance: Psychology, politics, girls, and women. *Michigan Quarterly Review, 29,* 501–536.

Gilligan, C. (1990b). Teaching Shakespeare's sister: Notes from the underground of female adolescence. In C. Gilligan, N. Lyons, & T. Hanmer (Eds.), *Making connections: The relational worlds of adolescent girls at Emma Willard School* (pp. 6–29). Cambridge, MA: Harvard University Press.

Gilligan, C. (2003). *The birth of pleasure: A new map of love*. New York: Random House.

Gilligan, C. (1982). *In a different voice: Psychological theory and women's development*. Cambridge, MA: Harvard University Press.

Gilligan, C., Spencer, R., Weinberg, M.K., & Bertsch, T. (2003). On the Listening Guide: A voice-centered relational model. In P.M. Camic, J.E. Rhodes, et al. (Eds.), *Qualitative research in psychology: Expanding perspectives in methodology and design* (pp. 157–172). Washington DC: American Pychological Association.

Gilligan, C., Ward, J., & Taylor, J. with Bardige, B. (1988). *Mapping the moral domain*. Cambridge, MA: Harvard University Press.

Kiegelmann, M. (1997). *Coming to terms: A Qualitative Study of Six Women's Experiences of Breaking the Silence about Brother-Sister Incest*. Ann Arbor, MI: UMI.

Kiegelmann, M. (2000). Handlungsrelevante und "pädagogisch korrekte" Stimmen von Auszubildenden zum Umgang mit Geschichte [Voices relevant to action and „educationally accurate" voices of trainees being exposed to history]. In C. Dalbert & E. Brunner (Eds.), *Handlungsrelevante Kognitionen in pädagogischer Praxis* (pp. 63–76). Hohengehren: Schneider Verlag.

Kiegelmann, M. (2002). Die soziale Dimension historischen Lernens in Gedenkstätten. In C. Lenz, J. Schmidt & O.v. Wrochem (Eds.), *Erinnerungskulturen im Dialog* [Memory cultures in dialogue] (pp. 133–141). Münster: Unrast-Verlag.

Kiegelmann, M. (2003). Umgangsformen mit der Geschichte des Nationalsozialismus [Different ways of dealing with national socialist history]. In M. Schweer (Ed.), *Die Neue Rechte. Eine Herausforderung für Forschung und Praxis* (pp. 125–131). Frankfurt a. M.: Peter Lang.

Kiegelmann, M. (2005). *Qualitative Methoden in der Psychologie. Eine Diskussion am Beispiel von Studien über Schweigenbrechen* [Qualitative methods in psychology. A discussion at the example of studies about silence breaking]. University of Tübingen: Habilitationsschrift.

Machoian, L. (1998). *The possibility of love: a psychological study of adolescent girls' suicidal acts and self-mutilation*. Unpublished doctoral dissertation, Harvard University Graduate School of Education.

Mayring, P. (1997). *Qualitative Inhaltsanalyse. Grundlagen und Techniken* [Qualitative content analysis. Basics and techniques] (6., durchgeseh. Aufl.). Weinheim: Deutscher Studien Verlag.

Nadig, M. (1986). *Die verborgene Kultur der Frau: ethnopsychoanalytische Gespräche mit Bäuerinnen in Mexiko; Subjektivität und Gesellschaft im Alltag von Otomi-Frauen* [The hidden culture of the woman]. Frankfurt am Main: Fischer-Taschenbuch-Verlag.

Ramm, G., Prenzel, M., Heidemeier, H. & Walter, O. (2003). Soziokulturelle Herkunft [Sociocultural background]. In PISA-Konsortium Deutschland (Eds.), *PISA 2003. Der Bildungsstand der Jugendlichen in Deutschland – Ergebnisse des zweiten internationalen Vergleichs*. Münster: Waxmann.

Tajfel, H., & Turner, J. (1986). The social identity theory of intergroup behaviour. In S. Worchel, & W. Wood (Eds.), *Psychology of intergroup relations*. Chicago: Nelson-Hall.

Taylor, J.M., Gilligan, C., & Sullivan, A.M. (1995). *Between voice and silence: Women and girls, race and relationship*. Cambridge, MA: Harvard University Press.

Tolman, D. (2002). *Dilemmas of desire: Teenage girls talk about sexuality.* Cambridge, MA: Harvard University Press.

Chapter 7
Draw your Life!
Investigations of Pictorial
Representations of Life Courses

Werner Deutsch & Christina Börges
University of Braunschweig
Germany

This paper is an explorative study of pictorial representations of life courses. In the history of art, staircases have been the most popular symbol for more than 450 years. Does this symbol still fit contemporary conceptions of life courses? Three case studies that illustrate other depictions of life courses are stars of life, a street of life, and a rock of life that deviate from the staircase tradition. Combined with a biographical interview, pictorial representations of personal life courses may offer a new approach to identity formation processes in different periods of life.

7.1   Staircases of life

At the "museum der kulturen" in the Swedish town of Lund one can find a painting that deserves a place in the history of developmental psychology. The only thing that is known about its painter are his initials, AK, which appear in the bottom of the picture between the number pairs 16 and 78 –the year of its completion. Stylistically, the painting can be classified as belonging to the Dutch School of Drawing. With a starting point in Amsterdam and Augsburg, the motif has been widely circulated in Europe since the middle of the 16th century. This circulation was boosted by the fact that the motif is seldom found in a painting –it was usually distributed by way of prints. Why would developmental psychologists bother to occupy themselves with a Dutch painting from Lund?

Developmental psychology as we know it today was developed in the 19th century and had its roots in child psychology. By means of youth psychology, the psychology of old age, and finally the psychology of adults, developmental psychology has conquered the entire life span of individual human development as its object of research. Developmental psychology as a science did not start from a complete concept but from one of its highly instructive chapters –the post-birth beginnings of development.

The painting from Lund shows a design of human age by means of a staircase of life that had surpassed another motif for depicting the human life course –the wheel of life. What kind of image of the human life course does the painting from Lund communicate? The life course is divided into decades that lead, step by step, up to an apex and from there, step by step, back down to the base level. Standing on the steps is a human couple that, depending on their gender and age, appear in different body postures and dress. Underneath the stairs there are three gates that clear the view on a landscape. The two small gates correspond to the first and the last three decades of life and show a hunting scene at the edge of a small wood as well as an idyllic homestead by the water. In between, the big gate underneath the three middle decades of life leads to a trading town by the sea. The mirroring symmetry of the composition covers the entire length of the painting. At the outer edges appear two motifs that characterize the ascending perspective of life as a tree in bloom and the descending perspective of life as dead tree stumps. The metamorphosis of the tree as a symbol for becoming and passing corresponds with two figures that are set in front of the middle gate between the sign with the date and the signature. To the right of the sign in front of the descending stairs is Father Death carrying arrow and sand. He has his eyes locked on a nude female beauty who is holding a crystal ball. The staircase of life from Lund is a composition that depicts the human life course as a geometrically structured arrangement. Becoming and passing are the corresponding faces of a coin. It is not just any human life course but its ideal. From the perspective of back then it encompasses the maximum life span that is organized in equal intervals –just like a flight of stairs.

Staircases of life like that from Lund are not copies but allegories of human life. Their message is to remind the beholder of the finiteness of human life. Even when the maximum life span can be savored without a break and changes in life occur in an orderly manner and at a consistent pace, the "Memento mori" does apply. Up into the 19th century such allegories were conceived as austere warnings to accept not only death but also the path that leads to it as an elemental part of human life. Associated with this warning was a hope that human life finds its fulfillment not in the earthly Here and Now but in the celestial afterlife. From this perspective it did not bother the beholder at all that the staircases of life idealized the human life course in such a way that the depicted order had no counterpart in real life whatsoever.

To modern empirical developmental psychology the design of the human life course as a mirroring symmetrical staircase of life is like a message from a different world. Back then the meaning of depictions was not aimed at how accurately they met the empirically captured reality but which transcendent meaning could be or was to be made and extracted for their own conduct of life. Are pictorial depictions of life courses relics from a time of pre-scientific developmental psychology that stand for a former human culture? What possibilities for occupation with life courses including one's own does modern developmental psychology offer? Has there ever been and is there now again an approach via the images that people perceive of their life courses? Or have pictures, as a way of giving light to the inner processes of the human person, his thoughts and feelings, long been outdated?

7.2   Responses

Students who have taken up their studies of psychology at the TU Braunschweig during the last two decades will have had a chance to get to know staircases of life as pictorial depictions of the human life course during their first or second semester. They were presented to visualize the change from a developmental psychology of human age and life courses determined by normative standards to an empirically directed identification of the courses of development of such functions as Perception, Memory, Thought, Language, and the like. Most students of psychology are only marginally interested in the historical roots of their field. They want to know the current state of knowledge and think of the historical path that has led to the present situation as superfluous knowledge. Strangely enough, the story is a very different one when it comes to the staircases of life. It happens again and again that the presentation of and the discussion about staircases of life that span from a period of time of more than 400 years motivates students to think about the structure of their own life course to date and what pattern it could take on in the future. Some students begin to reflect on the image of their life by producing drawings and collages –often after a long pause from creative engagement. It also frequently happens that former students discover staircases of life in books, museums, or while traveling that remind them of the staircases from their lecture, "Introduction to Developmental Psychology." These examples are then included in the current version of the staircase-lecture.

In this text, two examples will have to stand for the many more at hand. One good example is a postcard from a Jewish museum. To date, all of the known staircases of life started with the infant on the left side of the picture and closed with the old man on the right. The Jewish staircase of life runs in the opposite direction. It starts on the right side and closes on the left. The explanation for this change in direction is rather simple. Hebrew is written from the right to the left. In the Jewish staircase of life, events from the life course are depicted in the direction that corresponds to the direction of written language. The second example is also from a different culture group. In Bangkok, Thailand, on the wall of a Buddhist temple, a former student from Braunschweig came across a relief with a depiction of human age divided by decades in the form of a staircase of life as we know it. It shares similarities with the staircases of life known in Europe, but there are also a few differences. Origin and end of the individual human life are depicted as entrance to and egress from the globe, which is designed as a map. The two halves of life are associated with a red glowing sun in the ascent and a black and white moon in the descent. The beholder will easily notice that on the steps of life there is not consistently one individual, mostly –sorry– a man, ascending and descending, but a couple of mixed gender. On the second and third step of the staircase of life from Bangkok stands a man together with a woman, whereas on all the other steps there is only a man by himself. To understand this extraordinary staircase of life from a non-European culture group it is necessary to go into the texts on the relief in more detail and to get to know the history of the building of the temple. For now we will have to content ourselves with the fact that this staircase of life was adopted by another culture group and as a monumental relief has been integrated into a religious context of that culture area.

The students' interest in staircases of life as a symbolic depiction of life cycles is mainly personally motivated. On the one hand, the staircases of life inspire students to reflect on the classical questions of identity research: Who am I, who was I, and who am I going to be? On the other hand, the staircases of life symbolize a biographical identity that does not suit our everyday lives any more. Even from a normative perspective, its regularity of changes in the life course is barely acknowledged any more. We should, however, not refer to students in general but to those who –more or less voluntarily– have heard a lecture in "Introduction to Developmental Psychology." The confrontation with an abundance of staircases of life, where the rare examples from today tend towards caricature, and numerous examples from the past when many were convinced that after death in the Here and Now a new beginning in an afterlife would be possible, generates the question what iconographic structure matches the present-day life course, and especially one's own. It was this question that we posed to the students who heard the staircase-lecture during their "Introduction to Psychology" class at the TU Braunschweig in the winter semester of 2005/06. The response was a pile of drawings and collages that were handed on to us, mostly without reference to the artist. No grades or credit points were given for these works, so no pressure to perform interfered with the creative act of painting and drawing.

7.3 Productions

From the vast abundance of drawings, paintings, and collages we collected we have chosen three works that we would like to present here. For our selection, the following criteria were decisive: The examples display a different amount of proximity to the original staircases of life that initiated the task. They can be differentiated by the symbols that were used to depict the personal life course. The examples originate from students who could be allocated to the –originally anonymous– works and were glad to talk about their life-course drawings in an interview with one of us (C.B.). We will present each of the three examples in the following way: As a start, there will be a short pictorial analysis of the works that were carried out by W.D. independently of the knowledge of the content of the interviews. Those will be followed by excerpts from the –partly rather comprehensive– interviews that give additional information about the personal meaning of the life-course depiction on hand.

Stars of life

Case 1: The stars of life, U.M., female psychology student of U.S.-American origin, age 20 (see figure 7.1).

Pictorial analysis. The collage consists of two pieces of paper in DIN-A4 landscape format that have been joined together on the back with tape to make one single piece of paper. The color of the paper used is black. Spread across the whole two pages are little silver stars on a black background. In cursive with a silver pen the title "Stars of Life" was written on the upper left hand edge of the picture, as was the name of the artist on the lower right hand side. Aligned diagonally are six stars with five jags each. They were cut out from yellow paper and are in ascending order according to their size. The stars are glued onto the black background. Within the stars there are little drawings of the following motifs (from the bottom left-hand side to the upper right-hand side): a baby, a graduate student, clock, dollar sign and the word "profession", a family with father, mother, and two children, a car and a house framed by two trees, an old couple with a tree and a globe, and an angel in the clouds that is shone upon by the sun. In this depiction the life course has only one direction. Compared with the staircase of life there is only an ascent, but no descent. Nevertheless the stars of life encompass the whole life span from the beginning of life as a baby to the transformation of the deceased woman into an angel. Partners in life who are gained through the founding of a family (the star in the middle of the collage) are also part of the life-course. The stars of life depict a sequence of events that, in line with a quasi-law, will or ought to occur. At which star the author of the collage has presently arrived remains unknown. Past, present, and future are not clearly distinguished. The stars of life present an order of the life course that transcends time and the individual and that, in the collage, is set in space.

Figure 7.1 *Stars of life*

Excerpts from the interview.

C.B.:   *So, U., you have chosen stars for your life-course.*

U.M.:   Yes.

C.B.:   *Why? What do these stars mean to you?*

U.M.:   Um, well, you always, you always, well, well, here you always go up.
           Well, I think what we saw in the lecture comes, well, you start small
           and then somewhere, um, a climax and then you go back down. And
           in my opinion, really the older you become the happier, satisfied,
           and, yes, well I, I think you shouldn't regard old age as a negative
           thing, but that you have experienced many things and you've seen the
           world. That is something good, when you turn old, and also, well,
           there is also a meaning that, that um . . . yes . . . the sky's the limit,
           there is no, well there is no limit . . .

C.B.: *Mhm.*

U.M.: . . . somehow that you, you can never really end anywhere. There is no limit.

C.B.: *You reach for the stars.*

U.M.: Precisely.

C.B.: *And they become bigger because you . . .*

U.M.: Yes, well you start small, a little baby, and then you've graduated from university, then you're more grown-up and you have more, you have experienced even more and then profession, that really, the actual life begins here, and then it's also a big deal when you have a family and becoming old is, you have a big family, um, you've founded a family, many grandchildren, great-grandchildren, and then when you go to heaven that is the . . . that's the . . .the big star, what you have achieved . . .

C.B.: *Mhm.*

U.M.: . . . and the end of life.

C.B.: *And the globe here . . .*

U.M.: Ah yes.

C.B.: *. . . in the retirement . . .*

U.M.: Exactly.

C.B.: *. . . retirement star.*

U.M.: The world is, um, well, the tree here stands for, well, founding a family, and such a, um, family tree.

C.B.: *That you have roots.*

U.M.: Exactly. And then, well, here am I, well now I am twenty, but I know one day I will have children, then grandchildren and somehow, like my grandmother, I will have considerable influence on the children, and somehow I know: this is my family, and this family I have achieved and . . . yes, no one can take that away from me and . . .

C.B.: *And it grows larger, too.*

U.M.: Exactly.

C.B.: *So you start with your husband and your children, and then . . .*

U.M.: Precisely. And then the world stands for, that I, when I'm old I've been everywhere, I've seen lots of things, experienced many things and . . . then I'm a wise, wise old woman (laughs).

C.B.: *(laughs).*

U.M.: That is good (laughs).

C.B.: *And in the last star you have drawn an angel. What does this angel mean to you or for your life?*

U.M.: That is, um, well it, that here is no, uh, a little bit like a . . . my idea of a life, a life-course. Somehow I wanted to, I didn't think it was right how you, well the older you get, the lower you go on the life, the steps of life. And, um, I think then it is over, when you are that old and crippled, because, um, with the life-courses, that, well, steps of life that show, staircase, staircases of life, with the staircases of life that were shown it was over when you, um, old and crippled, when you couldn't move or feel anymore, and then it is over. But it was

C.B.:   *never shown that it is not over, and that somehow after life on earth*
          there is an afterlife, and, yes there is yet another life, somehow . . .
C.B.:   *Mhm.*
U.M.:   . . . something after you are old, and you can't, you can't take care of
          yourself anymore. That is why I think this should be the new stair-
          case of life (laughs).
C.B.:   *(laughs) So a, that corresponds to a life after death.*
U.M.:   Precisely.
C.B.:   *And that goes a little bit in the direction o f. . .*
U.M.:   Yes, well, um . . .
C.B.:   *infinite, no limits.*

Synopsis. Pictorial analysis and interview complete one another. U.M.'s
stars of life are her critical reaction to the classical ascending and descending
structure of the staircases of life. In her eyes, aging is not necessarily associated
with descent and demise. Quite the contrary: She views the second half of life as
an augmentation of the first. This view is probably rooted in her religious image
of the human person, according to which development does not halt in the Here
and Now but finds fulfillment in the afterlife. Will U.M still think about this ascending tendency in her life in the same way 20 years from now?

Street of life

Case 2: The street of life, G.V., male psychology student of German origin, age
22 (see figure 7.2).

Figure 7.2 *Street of life*

Pictorial analysis. G.V. used landscape format on a DIN-A4 piece of paper for this multi-colored pencil drawing. The title "My street of life" was written at the top middle of the paper and underlined. The work carries no signature. On the very outer left edge appears a sentence that is obviously irrelevant to the street of life. At first glance the drawing has a great resemblance to board games like ludo. A wide street leads from the lower left hand to the upper right hand side of the drawing where it ends at a map with two specified locations, BS (= Braunschweig) and Berlin, as well as five question marks. Underneath the map is a cycle that includes five symbols; arrows lead from (making) money to food, from food to sleep, from sleep to (making) money. Below that, at the lower right hand edge is a grave with a crucifix, a stone, and plants. The wide street has three junctions that lead to a house, a (school) building, and a forest. Left of the street are some big buildings, one of which carries a sign that says "kindergarten." The biggest building, which is green in color, could quite possibly symbolize the TU Braunschweig that G.V. studies at. The turnoff to the right leads to nature and technology. Near the institutions are stick figures of different sizes. Two bikes were drawn at the side of the (birth?) house and the kindergarten. The street ascends in a half-moon shape from the place of birth to kindergarten and school into the present and near future –graduation from university. Expectations for the future are vaguely implied but the street doesn't connect up to them.

This life-course depiction shows some significant differences from the staircase of life insofar as past and present life-stages are represented by formative institutions. These institutions are complemented by another two sources of influence concerning nature and technology. The street ends in the proximal future with the graduation from university. Its future course is yet undetermined apart from the fact that it will end at death someday. There are many details in G.V.'s street of life that are not self-explanatory and thus need to be addressed in the interview. The street of life offers an idea of development that places not the individual person but instead social systems at the center of attention. It is those systems that each of us depend on during the course of their development and that are left out of the picture in most depictions of staircases of life.

Excerpts from the interview.

C.B.:   *Just tell us a little bit about your street of life.*

G.V.:   Yes, I'd be happy to. I thought to myself that a staircase of life as the ones I saw in the lecture doesn't really match my life, I would have to make some changes. And then I gave some thought to it and I came to the conclusion that I will make a street with different stations. I started, um, here on the lower left hand side and drew my birth, symbolized by this little encircled star, um, that is where my life begins so to speak, and I grew up in a, um, in a small one-family house, or numerous one-family houses but I only drew one here, that's what this house is there to symbolize.

C.B.:   *Mhm.*

G.V.:   That is the, um, first path on my street that I am moving on, and the
        street starts down here at the very edge of the paper and then I join it,
        you could maybe say that life was already on its way before me and
        then I just join in, maybe, whatever (laughs). Well, um, the next sta-
        tion then, um, is my kindergarten where I then went, um, when I was
        a little bit older and where I experienced a lot and played with other
        children and so I then grew up a little bit. Then, um, came school.
        That was already the time of puberty, a little bit. The school is up
        higher a little bit, before that there's a branching that leads to a forest.
        That is really part of the time at school as well, um, I thought that be-
        cause then, um, I thought a lot about what kind of person I would
        want to become maybe, in hindsight and, um, I tried different, hm,
        things and that (laughs) maybe that was the best thing to do, maybe
        that's why I drew the forest. Um, yes, and in school once again I met
        many more people, I grew up a little more then, that's why I drew the
        small figure here, and then the bigger one. Hm, yes, but there was
        still a lot of play involved, we had this castle at school where we, um,
        studied a little and played a little, I always thought it was great when
        you were able to combine the two aspects, study and play. Then
        sometime after my 13th year, that's how long I went to school for,
        from the 1st to the 13th grade, that was a comprehensive school in
        Hannover . . .
C.B.:   *Mhm.*
G.V.:   . . . I, um, finished school and then I really went straight into my year
        of community service, that I didn't particularly mark in my drawing,
        but I have the university here as the next station. Uni, um, was a
        whole new chapter in my life, actually. Um (laughs), because the
        university happens to be in Braunschweig and because the A1 leads
        from Hannover to Braunschweig, I have built some kind of, um,
        highway on my street of life because so many things had suddenly
        changed then. All of a sudden you had to depend on yourself for eve-
        rything, you had go and hear all the lectures and remember all this
        knowledge and take notes in this short period of time, and that was,
        hm, yes that was a different feeling, which I found a bit stressful in
        the beginning, but in hindsight . . . I like it a lot now. Yes, and that's
        where I'm actually standing right now but my street of life will keep
        going of course. That's why I drew this little graduate student here
        who will hopefully emerge in the end, and then, um, will probably
        end up working somewhere in Germany, where exactly that will be I
        don't know yet. I would like to stay somewhere in the area maybe,
        but of course it is possible that I don't find work here and then I will
        have to go somewhere else, that's what this map of Germany with the
        question marks stands for.
C.B.:   *Is Berlin specially marked or is that just because it's our capital?*
G.V.:   I think that was for me, um, just the capital as a meaning. Um, that I
        want to go there in particular that is not the case, hm, no, I don't think
        so.
C.B.:   *Mhm.*

G.V.:   Braunschweig is simply where I am right now. Then sometime I want to, um, find my job somewhere or find a job and I don't really think about that too much. What comes to mind now, um, is I'm going to be working (laughs), eating, and sleeping, that's why I drew this cycle here. I hope that it'll be a little, um, more differentiated then. But I think at the moment that's how I imagine it and I don't give it too much thought, above all it'll simply be earning money, and that.

C.B.:   *Mhm.*

G.V.:   Yes and then sometime that'll all be done with, and then one day my life will be over and that's what this little cloud with the grave stands for. Now I forgot to explain this, um, Internet here, I should say a little bit about that. Well, um, when I was in school, around about the time of 10th grade, I think, my mother and I had an Internet connection for the first time. That was a real turnaround in my life because, um, on the Internet I was able to ask anything and look up practically everything I wanted. I'd always had all these ideas of what I wanted to do once I'd get the Internet and then when I sat in front of it for the first time I couldn't think of anything because suddenly the whole world was available to me.

C.B.:   *Mhm.*

G.V.:   But ever since then I have, um, worked with the Internet a lot, more and more often and that's really like a connection with the whole world. Where you have unrestricted access to an unbelievable amount of knowledge. That's why the Internet got a station of its own.

C.B.:   *Mhm. And, so, this cloud surrounding your grave, is that fenced off from the cycle? Does that have any particular meaning?*

G.V.:   Mh, well it is, um, maybe like a thought bubble. On the one hand it is there and it is present in my thoughts, but it is not so . . . this, death is not as present as work is, or later life as I imagine it . . .

C.B.:   *Mhm.*

C.B.:   *Yes, well I would say my questions are all answered so far, I don't know if, for the sake of completeness, you would like to somehow . . .*

G.V.:   Mhm.

C.B.:   *. . . add something else.*

G.V.:   Mh . . . let me think about that. Maybe I should once more draw your attention to these bikes I drew here.

C.B.:   *Mhm.*

G.V.:   That's really a very special part of my life. It's important that these bikes are there because I, um, I am a very avid bike rider, ever since kindergarten really, back then I already rode my bike to kindergarten and school all by myself and even when I, when we then moved house and lived a bit farther away I still rode my bike there quite often. Riding a bike is also part of my life, maybe that's what these bikes down there stand for.

C.B.:   *For you that also somewhat symbolizes independence and autonomy.*

G.V.:   Yes, certainly. Definitely.

C.B.:   *Mhm.*

G.V.:   Mhm. Yes but apart from that, um, I would say that was it for now.
         Mhm.
C.B.:   *I think it became quite clear, too.*
G.V.:   Okay.
C.B.:   *Well, then I thank you for the interview.*
G.V.:   Yes, you're welcome (laughs).

Synopsis. Without the interview, many of the drawings' details would have remained mysterious and may have induced wild speculations. With the interview at hand the meaning of such things as the bikes, for example, becomes quite clear and we understand how the ring of cloud around the grave is to be interpreted. Nevertheless, the interview leaves a few questions unanswered yet. Why, for instance, did G.V. choose to draw only one of the family houses that he grew up in and not the others?

Rock of life

Case 3: The rock of life, G.K., female psychology student of German origin, age 20 (see figure 7.3)

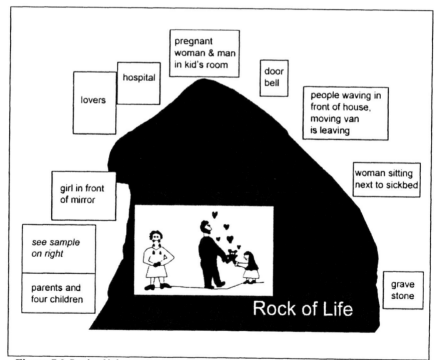

Figure 7.3 *Rock of life*

Pictorial analysis. G.K. decided to draw a rock that is framed from left to right by little sketches of important events from her life course. For her work, she used a white piece of paper in DIN-A3 landscape format. To the left of the rock, the sketches depict family situations. Behind a dark cliff at the side of the rock there are drawings of a couple who, behind the peak, become a whole new family. At the foot of the rock, on the bottom right edge of the paper, there is a tombstone that carries the couple's names. The composition of the drawing has symmetrical and asymmetrical aspects. Like the symmetrical staircases of life, the rock possesses an ascending and a descending side. However, it violates the mirror symmetry insofar as its ascent up to the cliff is rather steep. From there, we observe a continuous ascent up to the peak. The right side descends smoothly down to a few meters before the foot of the rock where the descent suddenly becomes more arduous again. Outline and texture of the rock correspond to the emotional significance of the life events that are depicted in pencil drawings surrounding the rock. On the right, the stony cliff is covered with a green pasture where flowers bloom. The life course seems to be overshadowed by events that happened within the family of origin. By leaving this family and founding one of her own, the artist has begun a whole new life, the fulfillment of which is the birth of her own child. From the depiction we cannot know where to draw the line between present and future. Is G.K. a mother already or is that one of her wishes for the future? This drawing deviates from the classical staircases of life not only in its structure but also in its content. The rock of life does not show which development task determines what age. Its objective is to demonstrate to the beholder which personally experienced situations have influenced the artist in a positive or a negative way. This format is applied to present, past, and future alike.

Excerpts from the interview.

C.B.:   *Yes, G., you drew a rock in the middle of your life-course and important life events are aligned around this rock.*

G.K.:   Um, I should start with, um, already at the beginning of my life things were somewhat tougher, well, my mother told me back then, um, when I was only seven years old, that, um, my father didn't love her anymore, and in the end that's what all these problems are based on. Even at the young age of seven I sensed and noticed that my mother was often sad, and now here, um, this picture, that he really, um, was more focused on me, that he regarded me as his daughter, his favorite daughter of three children in all, he is the biological father of only two of them though, and that, um, in the end he regarded me as his wife, and that, um, that it was about things like cuddling, about certain things especially during puberty with touching that had a tendency toward sexual abuse but then that's not really what it was, at least not as far as I know . . . maybe it's better that way . . . I don't know, and, um, because of that I only rarely perceived it, because there was also, um, of course I really only noticed sometime during puberty, I lost many friendships then, that's when I first, um, felt this

urge to get to work I would say and, um, also, hm, developed a tendency towards anorexia, so there was a bit of everything just to get
rid of these feelings of guilt towards my siblings and my mother
somehow and to somehow be able to survive, and, um, the rabbit I
drew because I, um, I was given a rabbit like that at about age twelve,
or really at age ten already, and, um, I treated this rabbit the same
way my father always treated me, so it was my little darling so to
speak and I took care of it and I lived for it because other than that I
wasn't particularly keen on living and this cliff here characterizes exactly that time when it became the most extreme, where it all kept ac-
cumulating. At some point my mother then took me to a psycho-
therapist, well, she just couldn't, um, watch me suffer anymore, she
noticed relatively late, well, my older sister with whom I get along
best and who also suffers from depression, she noticed earlier on and
protected me a little bit and, um, this cliff was really a scene where
you could say I was really close to the abyss, well that was . . . I always made an effort in school and did all these things and I really
never caused my parents any trouble but I just had these feelings of
guilt and everything else was also going wrong and I just tried to survive.

C.B.:   *So that's what this rough side of the rock symbolizes.*

G.K.:   Yes, that is . . . exactly, by and large. Well, but there are of course
many (laughs) more other factors, that contribute, but that is for now
. . . the most important points. And, um, yes during therapy I learned,
um, I realized for the first time what actually goes wrong in our family and then the situation improved (laughs), I'd like to say.

C.B.:   *Mhm. So this rough side at the beginning is more like, um, this . . .*

G.K.:   Fighting for survival, really. Well, emotional . . . well . . .

C.B.:   *The hardship of life in that case, eh?*

G.K.:   Mhm.

C.B.:   *But then on the other hand there is also a green surface to the rock,
an area where flowers grow.*

G.K.:   Mhm. Yes. That I would see, um, as a, um, that I really went through
this therapy and then, for that reason, noticed more and more that that
is how it is, but nevertheless with anorexia, well that still kept being a
problem for much longer, four years, and, um, at some point I really
finally made the decision to move out because I realized this is not
going to work out, and then my father told me, alright, he'll move
out, because he really didn't see a point in staying, after all he really
didn't want anything to do with that, and, um, then he moved out and
things did improve slowly, I should say. I have a very good relationship with my father, a friendly one but nothing more than that and,
um, yes, he then approached me again bit by bit because he realized
he's not just suddenly going to find another twenty-year-old woman
or something. And then in the end I really moved out and, um, that's
when I met my boyfriend and fiancé, that is Hans, well, back then I
had already got to know him at the archive because in school I was
always really involved and, um, yes and, um, that's when things

really started picking up, not just because of him, but because of the whole therapy, and that I'd moved out of course, that I noticed there is something else, you don't always have to be under this pressure and always suffer from watching what happens, um, to your own mother. And, um, yes and, that is really it so far, I estimate that it will keep going in that positive direction, certainly there'll be a couple of little pebbles along the way, as you can see, so that, that there'll still somehow be little quarrels, some problems where you run the risk of falling back into the old schemata of behaviour, for example that concerning eating, that in the end you always have to be careful, and that is what that characterizes really, but that, by and large, life now runs according to my rules and that I am able to say to my parents "Alright, it's enough, I'll go home now," well, that that is okay. And that other bigger rock again that is now, here you can see the hospital, I also wrote that down, um, because my boyfriend, um, he has a heavy scoliosis and, um, that was about, that's when we'd been going out for a year, well he's had that since puberty or birth, and then he had to have another big surgery and that's why at first I was like I need to somehow manage this, because at the same time I was finishing high school, I then went to the hospital on the weekends, and that was really tough for me once again, well, now, I mean, I knew that it is important for him, and I didn't notice it the same way at the time, but in hindsight, especially the fact that that was all in the intensive care unit and everything, it's really quite shocking.

C.B.:   *Mhm.*

G.K.:   You have, in that moment you just do that, and then only afterwards you notice how exhausted you really are.

C.B.:   *So then that's also such a, yes such a rock . . .*

G.K.:   Yes, also.

C.B.:   *Such an obstacle, tha t. . . where you then. . .*

G.K.:   Yes, well, that needed to be overcome . . .

C.B.:   *Exactly.*

G.K.:   . . . once again, but that was, well I have to say all went well (laughs), and of course things could have turned out much worse, so yes . . .

C.B.:   *Mhm.*

G.K.:   . . . and so, by and large, these are my further goals so that we, um, have a baby one day, um, or really we both plan that for the time of my studies already and, um, yes then my own practice, in the end, that I can accomplish that. Well my boyfriend has a house, and that I can really set up the practice there, that's what I always wanted to do ever since grade seven, then study psychology and then really, um, try to be self-employed after that. Maybe because of my past, because somehow I realized that you have greater insight when you've already been down that road yourself once. And yes, and that our child will move out someday, that it is a normal relationship, not like that with my parents, when they said "Please stay here, after all we need you to fix our marriage."

C.B.:   *Mhm.*

G.K.:   That it is something normal.
C.B.:   *Of course, and you're waving happily . . .*
G.K.:   Mhm.
C.B.:   *. . . and you're proud.*
G.K.:   Yes, and that I once again, um, took, now that my boyfriend is lying
         in bed, because after all he's twenty years older than me, I didn't
         really plan it that way, I didn't know that beforehand, it just happened
         and, um, of course he has these problems with his back, and, um, yes
         that's a bit difficult indeed, well that he needs to lie down so much,
         and that is only going to get worse with old age (laughs), they say,
         and that's why. And I guess, I took care of him after surgery, and so
         (laughs) . . .
C.B.:   *Mhm.*
G.K.:   . . . it's okay for me that way.
C.B.:   *Yes, there are some blooming flowers after all . . .*
G.K.:   Yes, it's okay. Certainly stands a little . . .
C.B.:   *. . . and only a few small pebbles.*
G.K.:   He once said, well, he wants to die at the same time as me, when he
         is a hundred and I am eighty years old. Well, so that really matched a
         little bit, that's why I then drew our joint grave (laughs).

Synopsis. The open questions from the pictorial analysis are addressed by
the information given in the interview. It is obvious how intensively G.K. has
coped with the painful experiences from her childhood and youth. This coping
has resulted in a scheme of life with clear-cut goals for the future. G.K. has expressed her life-course as a narrated sequence of events as well as a symbol (the
rock) whose features, outline, and texture correspond to these events.

7.4   Conclusions

"A picture says more than a thousand words" is a popular saying that is often
quoted. How do adults express themselves when experimenters in psychological
studies ask for their thoughts, feelings, memories, ideas, and desires? The preferred form of expression is mostly words, rarely pictures! That applies to quantitative and qualitative approaches alike. Why is it that empirical psychology
shies away from pictures and drawings unless they are artwork or research stim-
uli? The reasons are obvious. During childhood and sometimes into adolescence,
drawing and painting are popular activities. With some few exceptions, these
activities become less significant as children grow older. Spoken and written
language as forms of expression become so dominant that drawing and painting
are left to those who make a living from it, such as designers and architects, and
those who seek a creative outlet, such as hobby artists. The fact that drawing in
late childhood and early puberty is evaluated by the norm of realistic, foreshort-
ened depiction only contributes to this general trend. Without special training
though, most people never reach this stage of development in drawing (Schulz,
2006).

Even in the absence of special talent, it is important not to let drawing and painting subside (van Sommers, 1984). The study at hand proves that graphic expression can be revived if the research context provides the necessary motivation. The confrontation with artistically designed staircases of life can awaken a need to reflect the meaning of the topic for personal development and look for a symbol that may be more fitting to the personal life-course than the staircase. The four examples we presented show how critically the preset symbol is assessed and how strong the need for an individual personal form really is. Within a relatively homogenous subject group of only psychology students there is an abundance of life-course depictions that vary from the staircases of life to different extent. These results indicate a change in mentality for the development of a –biographical– identity. Life courses are no longer conceived as given models determined by social standing, gender, religion, and age but are interpreted as variable forms that –more or less accurately– match the personal life course. The appropriate form is chosen independently. For that process, the staircase of life often, but not always, acts as an outdated contrast.

None of the drawings we received in response to the task given in the lecture can be classified as artwork. At first glance most of the works look like children's drawings –this only goes to show that most of our students had likely taken long rests from creative engagement. Those who took on the task were able to dream themselves back to childhood and, like children, produce images from their subconscious, all in the absence of artistic ambition and/or pressure to perform. Many students were encouraged to tap their sleeping creative potential. The results are certainly no impressive artistic products. It is not their professionalism or virtuosity but their naïve authenticity that captures the beholder.

When we first started collecting data, we used the following approach: after the lecture about depictions of staircases of life we encouraged the participating students to create a picture of their own life-course without spoken comment. It was not until after evaluating the resulting works that we asked a select group of students for an interview to tell us about their picture and the corresponding life-course. Separating the pictures from the commentary turned out to be rather fruitful. No picture is self-explanatory, as Elfriede Billmann-Mahecha (2005) has demonstrated in a study researching the interpretation of children's drawings. Nevertheless, it makes sense to start with a pictorial analysis to be able to analyze the composition and the design of a picture independently of the personal meaning that is later derived from the commentary. In our study, this analysis proved to be quite uncomplicated because the pictures had a model in the staircases of life, be it evaluated positively or negatively. During this pictorial analysis many questions emerge, most of which can be answered in an interview with a second person, as our study shows. The separation and later consolidation of pictorial analysis and commentating biographical interview has the advantage that the process of interpretation is no act of arbitrariness but binds an outer objective *perspective* with an inner emotional perspective. Reservations towards the "random" interpretation of qualitative methods can thus be invalidated.

The interview situation is facilitated by the distribution of the pictorial representation of a life course and its biographical commentary. The picture offers the groundwork on the basis of which interviewer and interviewee can take up the interview with a clearly defined allocation of roles. The interviewee helps the interviewer understand the pictorial representation. He is the one that assigns the proper interpretation, not the interviewer. Thanks to the task of depicting a life course pictorially, an accepted regression is brought about, at least in adults who no longer draw and paint regularly. Pictorial representation can bring out ideas that are consciously much less controlled than those expressed verbally. The presented results motivate us to expand psychological research of biographies by methods that provide an outlet for pictorial expression even among adults.

How can our method be applied to identity research? As has been mentioned, the pictorial approach leads to life-course depictions that include the identity statuses from present, past, and future, despite the fact that no clear time distinctions can be identified. How do life-course depictions change when subjective and/or statistical life expectancy is taken into account? What constitutes the relationship between the identity statuses and the symbolism of life-course depictions? What is the symbolic correlative of diffusion, moratorium, foreclosure, and achieved identity that appear in life-course depictions? The pictorial approach offers a whole new set of possibilities –not only for biographical– but also for identity research.

References

Joerißen, P. & Will, C. (Eds.) (1983). *Die Lebenstreppe – Bilder der menschlichen Lebensalter* [Life's staircases – Pictures of human ages]. Köln: Rheinlandverlag.

Deutsch, W. & Krause, K. (1999). Was heißt Erwachsenwerden? [Growing up –What does it mean?]. In H. Schneider (Ed.), *Lieben und Arbeiten –Der junge Erwachsene und der Ernst des Lebens.* Heidelberg: Mattes Verlag.

Greve, W. (1999). Psychologie des Selbst [The psychology of self]. In W. Greve (Ed.), *Psychologie des Selbst.* Weinheim: Psychologie Verlags Union.

Further References

Billmann-Mahecha, E. (2005). Die Interpretation von Kinderzeichnungen [Interpreting children's drawings]. In G. Mey (Ed.), *Handbuch Qualitative Entwicklungspsychologie* (pp. 435–453). Köln: Kölner Studienverlag.

Deutsch, W. (1997). Wie in der Entwicklung des Zeichnens Kreativität wächst, vergeht und manchmal wieder neu entsteht [The development of drawing – How creativity comes, goes, and –sometimes– returns]. In H. Schneider (Ed.), *Mitte der Kindheit. Kreativitätsentwicklung – Kreativität in der Psychotherapie* (pp. 83–100). Heidelberg: Mattes Verlag.

Kaiser, H.J. (2005). Biographieforschung in der Entwicklungspsychologie [Biography research in developmental psychology]. In G. Mey (Ed.), *Handbuch Qualitative Entwicklungspsychologie* (pp. 233–263). Köln: Kölner Studienverlag.

Schulz, N. (2006). *Zeichnerisches Talent am Ende der Kindheit* [Drawing talent at the end of childhood]. Münster: Waxmann

Van Sommers, P. (1984). *Drawing and cognition. Descriptive and experimental studies of graphic production processes.* Cambridge: Cambridge University Press.

Chapter 8

Identity Development in College Students: Variable-Centered and Person-Centered Analyses

Luc Goossens and Koen Luyckx
Catholic University of Leuven
Belgium

According to Erikson (1968), adolescents have to develop a firm sense of identity. The essence of his theory can be summarized in two basic statements. First, some adolescents approach this developmental task in a very successful way and quickly forge themselves a well-defined identity, whereas others continue to struggle with this same task and find their identity slowly and with considerable difficulty. Second, adolescents who are quick to form their identity do so because they have the personal characteristics required and because they can muster the support from significant others in their environment. Erikson's theory, therefore, can be phrased in terms of two research questions or testable hypotheses. First, there is considerable variability in the development of identity among adolescents. Second, differences in the rate of identity development can be explained in terms of its main determinants, that is, adolescents' personality and their relationships with significant others. In this chapter, we will present the results of a research program that was specifically designed to address those two research questions in what was referred to as a model of identity formation.

8.1   Research options

Before we turn to our own study, we will detail the choices that were made regarding the methods used (quantitative as opposed to qualitative), the type of identity measure selected (continuous as opposed to categorical), the underlying view of identity development (a process view as opposed to an incremental view), and the statistical techniques of analysis (i.e., both variable-centered and person-centered analyses).

Quantitative versus qualitative methods

The two research questions to be addressed called for the use of quantitative methods. The first question (variability of identity development) calls for a strict approach to statistical inference. Specifically, we have to test whether the observed variability is significanly different from the "zero variance" baseline. The second question (determinants of identity development) calls for a statistical model of causal relationships between variables or a statistical description of associations among variables. Constructing such a model or providing such a description again calls for strict statistical inference. Specifically, we have to test whether the associations observed are significantly different from the "no association" baseline. Such statistical tests and models, and the underlying logic of strict statistical inference, represent the essence of quantitative methods. Adherents of these methods typically rely on more remote methods of data collection (e.g., pre-structured questionnaires) and on probabilities derived from the study of large numbers of randomly selected cases.

Qualitative methods, by contrast, tend to produce descriptive data with a strong emphasis on the person's own written or spoken words and observable behavior (Taylor, Bogdan, & Walker, 2000) and emphasize rich (or 'thick') descriptions of the individual's point of view (Denzin & Lincoln, 2000). Adherents of those methods typically rely on more detailed interviewing and observation and base their conclusions on a small number of individual cases. The issue of strict statistical inference (i.e., whether the observed results are non-trivial) does not present itself in qualitative methods, or put differently, statistical conclusion validity is implicitly assumed in those methods (Lund, 2005).

Dimensional versus categorical measures of identity

The two research questions, and the key issue of statistical inference, can be addressed somewhat more easily when using continuous (or dimensional) measures of identity. A greater variety of statistical techniques is available when using such measures. Inspired by Marcia (1966), we distinguished two dimensions of identity formation, that is, exploration and commitment. Exploration refers to the adolescent's active questioning and weighing up of various identity alternatives. Commitment refers to the presence of strong convictions or choices. Participants were asked to rate each of these two aspects of identity on a continuous scale. They rated those aspects as evidenced in two important life domains, that is, their current education/future occupation and their relationship with their best friend, and the scores obtained were averaged across the two domains.

Our use of continuous measures of identity represents a departure from standard practices in the domain of identity research that relies heavily on categorical (or configurational) measurement of identity. Following Marcia (1966), a distinction is typically made between four types (or categories or configurations) of identity that are referred to as identity statuses. These statuses are based upon the combination of the two dimensions of exploration and commitment. Adolescents who have arrived at clear commitments after exploring various alternatives are assigned to the Achievement status. Adolescents in the Foreclosure status also have made strong commitments but without going through a period of exploration. Adolescents in the Moratorium status are exploring various alternatives without arriving at firm commitments. Finally, adolescents in the Diffusion status have not yet made clear commitments. Moreover, they are not exploring thoroughly the different options at hand. (See Luyckx, Goossens, Soenens, Beyers, & Vansteenkiste, 2005, for an approach using categorical measures of identity).

Process versus incremental views of development

We relied on a process view on identity development because that view underlies a family of statistical techniques that has become available in recent years and allows researchers to address the two central research questions in this chapter in novel and informative ways. Our choice for this view on identity development again represents a departure from standard practices in the domain of identity research that has been inspired mainly by an incremental view on the development of identity and has relied on less satisfying statistical techniques that are based on such a view on development.

The incremental view of change emphasizes change as a series of starts and stops, rather than as a continuous process that takes place throughout the time span under investigation. When adopting such a view, researchers typically use a two-wave design (that represents a single start-stop sequence). The analysis of the available data concentrates on the comparison of the performance of a group of individuals at a given moment in time and at a later moment. If the group shows a higher level of a certain skill or characteristic at Time 2 as compared to Time 1, change is said to have occurred (Hartmann, 2005; Willett, 1988).

Such an approach, using categorical measures of identity (i.e., identity statuses) has long been the dominant approach to longitudinal research on identity. Using statistical tests specifically designed for that purpose (such as the McNemar test of change) researchers focused on transitions from one status to another. Specifically, they examined whether a net gain occurred for the more successful approaches to identity (i.e., the exploration-based statuses). So if the number of individuals who moved into the Achievement status clearly exceeded the number of individuals who moved out of that same status (from Time 1 to Time 2), change in the sense of an increment in a desired characteristic was said to have occurred. Similarly, if the number of individuals who moved out of the Diffusion status clearly exceeded the number of individuals who moved into that same status (from Time 1 to Time 2), change in the directon of a stronger sense of identity was also said to have occurred. When using continuous measures of identity, reseachers focus on the difference in scores obtained at the two measurement occasions. Specifically, they can test whether the gain from Time 1 to Time 2 (averaged across all individuals in the group) is significant.

These statistical approaches, based on an incremental view of change, do not provide an answer to the two research questions in this chapter. No statistical test is available to address the first research question (variability in identity development) for categorical or continuous measures of identity. The second research question (determinants of identity change) may be addressed through an examination of the correlates of individuals' difference scores for identity when using continuous measures of identity, but this type of statistical analysis is compromised by the notorious unreliability of difference scores. An additional problem is that the questions addressed in such a two-wave design cannot be generalized easily to multiwave designs that comprise three or more data waves (see Goossens, Marcoen, & Janssen, 1999, for an example of such a generalization to multiple waves using categorical measures of identity).

The process view of development, which has by now largely superseded the older incremental view of change and focuses on multiwave designs, views a person's scores as reflecting an underlying growth process and scores are linked to the time they are obtained. In this way, development is described in terms of a few aspects of change (labeled parameters of change; Hartmann, 2005; Willett, 1988). The first step is to represent each individual's pattern of growth (i.e., the intra-individual portion of the model). These individual scores can be averaged and a test can be used to address the first research question (variability in identity development). The second step is then to find independent variables that are associated with the parameters that are used to describe the growth process (i.e., the inter-individual part of the model). Put simply, corrrelational techniques can be used to address the second research question (associations with presumed determinants of identity development). The latter analysis is not plagued with problems of unreliability because the parameters of change are estimated using structural equation modeling (SEM).

The statistical techniques based on the process view of development are commonly referred to as Latent Growth Curve Modeling or LGCM. (See Wirtz, 2005, for a first introduction to this technique and McArdle & Nesselroade, 2003, for a more advanced introduction). These techniques describe individuals' development in a multiwave study in terms of two components (or parameters of change). The first one is the initial level at the first measurement wave (or intercept) and the other one is the rate of change (or slope). In this chapter we can forget about initial levels (or intercepts) and concentrate on the slope factor. This slope component represents the degree of change in a given identity dimension. And because every participant in any given study has a different degree of change, one can examine whether there is substantial variability among individuals in their degree of change (Research question 1) and correlate this change with change in other variables of interest, that is, the presumed determinants of identity change (Research question 2).

Variable-centered and person-centered analyses

Latent growth curve modeling, while fascinating in terms of the possibilities it provides, has one important drawback. The technique assumes that there is a single underlying trajectory and that young people's development can be described as variations on that common theme. In short, latent growth curve modeling is a particular type of variable-centered analysis.

To provide a complement to those techniques, one can proceed on the alternative assumption that there is heterogeneity in development and that different developmental trajectories can be distinguished for identity and its associated variables. In such a person-centered analysis (Magnusson, 1998), one again first determines the developmental trajectory of each individual and then groups them into different types or "clusters" of developmental trajectories. Each of these trajectory groups may then have its own set of determinants. In the study reported in this chapter, we will use both types of analysis (i.e., variable-centered and person-centered) to illustrate their complementarity when addressing the two research questions.

Testing a model of identity development

We tested a model in which personality characteristics and perceived parenting are considered to be antecedents of identity formation, whereas psychological adjustment is believed to be a consequence of identity formation. Two aspects of identity commitment were distinguished (i.e., Commitment making and Identification with commitment) and two aspects of identity exploration (i.e., Exploration in breadth and Exploration in depth; Luyckx, Goossens, Soenens, & Beyers, 2006). As regards personality, we used the Big Five and expected that Openness would be the most important determinant of inter-individual differences in changes in both types of identity exploration. High levels of Extraversion and Conscientiousness and low levels of Neuroticism were expected to be related to greater increases for both types of identity commitment. As regards perceived parenting, only the role of psychological control was examined. This intrusive parenting dimension is thought to inhibit and constrain adolescents' autonomy and was therefore expected to be related to smaller increases for both types of identity commitment.

8.2   The L-TIDES study

Design and participants

The data were taken from the Leuven Trajectories of Identity Development in Students study (or L-TIDES for short; Luyckx, 2006). L-TIDES is a seven-wave longitudinal study with a six-month interval between two adjacent waves. Data collection started in November 2002 and was completed in November 2005. All the participants in the study (initial $N = 565$) were college students in Psychology or Educational Sciences at a large university in the Dutch-speaking part of Belgium. This particular background of the sample explains why a large majority, about 83% of those students, were young women. For illustrative purposes, all analyses in the present chapter will focus on the first five waves of data collection.

Measures of identity and parenting were completed at each measurement wave (i.e., at six-month intervals), whereas measures of personality and adjustment were completed at the "odd" waves only (i.e., at yearly intervals: Wave 1, Wave 3, Wave 5, and so on). As a consequence of this intricate scheme of data collection, the data for the present chapter are taken, for the most part, from three of those waves (i.e., the first, the third, and the fifth wave, each one year apart) because all measures of interest were administered at these three waves. A total of 351 students (i.e., all the female students who completed all instruments at all three measurement waves) were included in the sample for those analyses. For some of the analyses, and for those regarding associations between identity and parenting in particular, the data were taken from all five waves. Sample size for those analyses was 364. (A total of 325 of those participants, or 89% of the sample, were young women).

Measures

Identity. The Ego Identity Process Questionnaire (EIPQ; Balistreri, Busch-Rossnagel, & Geisinger, 1995; Luyckx, Goossens, Beyers, & Soenens, 2006) was used to assess Commitment making and Exploration in breadth. All items were answered on a 5-point Likert-type rating scale, ranging from 1 (*"strongly disagree"*) to 5 (*"strongly agree"*). Sample items are "I have definitely decided on the occupation I want to pursue" and "I think what I look for in a friend could change in the future (reverse coded)" (Commitment making; 15 items), and "I have tried to learn about different occupational fields to find the best one for me" and "I have never questioned my views concerning what kind of friend is best for me (reverse coded)" (Exploration in breadth; 13 items).

The Utrecht-Groningen Identity Development Scale (Meeus & Dekovic, 1995) was used to assess Identification with commitment and Exploration in depth. Again, all items were answered on a 5-point Likert-type rating scale, ranging from 1 (*"strongly disagree"*) to 5 (*"strongly agree"*). Sample items are

"My education gives me certainty in life" and "My best friend gives me self-confidence" (Identification with commitment; 16 items), and "I think a lot about my education" and "I try to figure out regularly what other people think about my best friend" (Exploration in depth; 10 items).

Parenting. Psychological control was measured with the 8-item Psychological Control Scale –Youth Self-Report (PCS-YSR; Barber, 1996). Participants rated psychological control for both parents together. All items were answered on a 1 (*"does not apply at all"*) to 5 (*"applies strongly"*) Likert scale. A sample item is "My parents are less friendly to me if I don't see things like they do".

Personality. As a measure of Costa and McCrae's (1992) Five Factor Model of personality, participants completed the Dutch authorized version of the well-established 60-item NEO-FFI (Hoekstra, Ormel, & De Fruyt, 1996).

Adjustment. Self-esteem was measured using the Rosenberg Self-Esteem Scale (RSES; Rosenberg, 1965;Van der Linden, Dijkman, & Roeders, 1983). This scale contains 10 items scored on a 4-point Likert-type rating scale, ranging from 1 (*"does not apply to me at all"*) to 4 (*"applies to me very well"*). A sample item is "I feel that I have a number of good qualities". Depressive symptoms were measured using the Center for Epidemiologic Studies Depression Scale (CESD; Radloff, 1977) in a brief 12-item version (Hooge, Decaluwé, & Goossens, 2000; Roberts & Sobhan, 1992). Items are responded to on a 4-point Likert-type rating scale, ranging from 1 (*"seldom"*) to 4 (*"most of the time or always"*). Each item asks participants how often they had experienced symptoms of depression during the past week. A sample item is "During the last week, I felt depressed".

8.3   Empirical results

Variable-centered analyses

Research question 1 (Variability of identity development). Means and standard deviations for the two parameters of change (i.e., intercept and slope) are represented in table 8.1. The most important information in that table can be found in the last column, which indicates that the standard deviation for the degree or rate of change (i.e., the slope parameter) is significantly different from zero for all four aspects included in our identity model. These findings imply that the first research question in this chapter has been addressed conclusively or that the first hypothesis has been confirmed: There is substantial variability in the rate of change in identity among college students (Luyckx, Goossens, & Soenens, 2006).

Table 8.1

Change Parameters for the Multivariate Latent Growth Curve Model of Identity, Personality, and Parenting

Dimension	Intercept		Slope	
	Mean	SD	Mean	SD
Commitment making	3.15***	0.13***	0.03***	0.01***
Exploration in breadth	3.25***	0.19***	0.03***	0.01***
Identification with commitment	3.50***	0.10***	-0.01	0.01**
Exploration in depth	3.55***	0.10***	0.03***	0.01***
Neuroticism	2.95***	0.28***	-0.02	0.02
Extraversion	3.64***	0.19***	-0.01	0.03***
Openness	3.44***	0.13***	0.01	0.02**
Agreeableness	3.77***	0.10***	-0.01	0.02***
Conscientiousness	3.45***	0.16***	0.02	0.02*
Psychological control	1.91***	0.29***	0.01	0.01***

Note. $N = 351\text{-}364$; SD = Standard deviation. *$p < .05$. ** $p < .01$. *** $p < .001$.

The last column of table 8.1 also shows that most of the determinants of identity change show substantial inter-individual variability in the rate of change over time, with the exception of students' Neuroticism (Luyckx, Soenens, & Goossens, 2006; Luyckx, Soenens, Vansteenkiste, Goossens, & Berzonsky, in press).

Research question 2 (Associations with presumed determinants of identity development). Correlations between the rate of change (i.e., the slope component) for the determinants of identity and the rate of change (i.e., the slope component) for the four aspects of identity are represented in table 8.2. Changes in Commitment making were negatively related to changes in Neuroticism, and positively to changes in Extraversion, Agreeableness, and Conscientiousness. Increases in psychological control were associated with simultaneous decreases in Commitment making. Changes in Exploration in breadth were positively related to changes in Neuroticism and Openness and unrelated to changes in psychological control. The correlates of changes in Identification with commitment were identical to the correlates of changes in Commitment making, with the exception of Agreeableness. Finally, changes in Exploration in depth were positively related to changes in Extraversion, Openness, Agreeableness, and Conscientiousness and unrelated to changes in psychological control (Luyckx, Soenens, & Goossens, 2006; Luyckx et al., in press). These findings imply that the second research question in this chapter has been addressed conclusively or that the second hypothesis has been confirmed: Changes in identity formation are significantly related to simultaneous changes in personality and parenting along the lines predicted in our model.

Person-centered analyses

Research question 1 (Variability of identity development). To empirically identify the various types of developmental trajectories, we employed a statistical technique which is known as Latent Class Growth Analysis (LCGA; Nagin, 2005) and we used all four dimensions from our identity model as dependent variables in the analysis.

Table 8.2

Correlations Between Change in Identity and Changes in Personality and Parenting

Change in Person-ality	Change in identity			
	Commitment Making	Exploration in breadth	Identification with commitment	Exploration in depth
Neuroticism	-.56***	.61***	-.49**	-.16
Extraversion	.26**	-.13	.34**	.34***
Openness	-.09	.50***	.06	.37***
Agreeableness	.28**	-.21	.19	.23*
Conscientiousness	.29**	.12	.59***	.40***
Psychological control	-.47***	.14	-.28***	.12

Note. N = 351-364. * p < .05. ** p < .01. *** p < .001.

Using this technique, we have empirically identified four types of identity development and used labels initially used to denote different types of identity development in adult women (Josselson, 1996) to refer to them. Pathmakers (who may be compared to Achievers in Marcia's, 1966, original scheme) showed an increase over time in Commitment making and Exploration in breadth. Searchers (comparable to Moratoriums in Marcia's scheme) showed an increase in exploration in breadth and a decrease in Identification with commitment. Guardians (who may be compared to Foreclosures) showed an increase for Commitment making but no increase for Exploration in breadth. Finally, Consolidators (for whom there is no counterpart in Marcia's scheme) showed a marked increase for Identification with commitment, which seems to indicate that they consolidate the commitments they have made (Luyckx, Schwartz, Goossens, Soenens, & Beyers, 2006). The fact that we managed to distinguish different trajectories of identity formation is of course another indication that there is substantial variability in identity development (and again provides support for Hypothesis 1).

Research question 2 (Associations with presumed determinants of identity development). The four trajectory groups also evidenced a specific profile of scores on the parenting and personality measures as completed at the first measurement wave. The Searchers reported a significantly higher level of psychological control in their relationship with their parents than did both the Guardians and the Pathmakers, who scored higher than the Consolidators did. The four trajectory groups were rank ordered in the opposite direction for important personality dimensions such as Agreeableness and Conscientiousness (with the highest scores for the Consolidators and the lowest ones for the Searchers, and the other two groups scoring in between these two extremes; Luyckx, 2006). The fact that the four trajectory groups were each uniquely linked to the initial levels of perceived parenting and personality is of course another indication that these variables may be conceived of as determinants of identity development (and again provides some support for Hypothesis 2, even though the analysis did not concentrate on correlated changes in identity and its determinants).

It may be added here that the four trajectory groups were also linked, each in their unique way, to the type of development observed over time in psychological adjustment, as indexed through self-esteem and absence of depressive symptoms. The Consolidators showed the most positive profile of adjustment. Two thirds of them showed continuous high adjustment over time (labeled 'optimal adjustment'), one third showed increasing adjustment over time, and very few of them evidenced stable maladjustment over time. The Searchers presented the poorest profile of adjustment, with about a third of them showing stable maladjustment over time. The two other trajectory groups, the Pathmakers and the Guardians, also showed positive profiles of adjustment over time, though less clearly so than the Consolidators (Luyckx, Schwartz, Goossens, Soenens, & Beyers, 2006).

8.4   Discussion: Quantitative   and   qualitative methods

The present chapter has illustrated the use of quantitative methods in addressing two specific research questions regarding identity development that could be approached usefully with those methods. Other research questions regarding identity development may be approached more fruitfully using qualitative methods of inquiry. The two types of method can also be combined in what is referred to as a mixed methods approach (Mertens, 2005). In psychology, such an approach typically takes on a sequential format, such as a quantitative study followed by a qualitative study on the same topic (Waszak & Sines, 2003). An example of such an approach is provided by Kroger (2005) using categorical measures of identity. The author first conducted a larger-scale quantitative study on the incidence of the various pathways of identity and then conducted a small-scale qualitative study to better understand one particular type of pathway (i.e., from

Foreclosure to Moratorium to Achievement). Finally, a special type of qualitative methods, commonly referred to as the narrative study of identity, may provide information on identity formation that is only modestly related to the picture provided by quantitative methods such as the ones used in this chapter (McLean & Pratt, 2006).

References

Balistreri, E., Busch-Rossnagel, N.A., & Geisinger, K.F. (1995). Development and preliminary validation of the Ego Identity Process Questionnaire. *Journal of Adolescence, 18,* 179–192.

Barber, B.K. (1996). Parental psychological control: Revisiting a neglected construct. *Child Development, 67,* 3296–3319.

Costa, P.T. Jr., & McCrae, R.R. (1992). *Revised NEO Personality Inventory (NEO-PI-R) and the Five Factor Inventory (NEO–FFI): Professional manual.* Odessa, FL: Psychological Assessment Resources.

Denzin, N.K., & Lincoln, Y.S. (Eds.) (2000). *Handbook of qualitative research* (2nd ed.). Thousand Oaks, CA: Sage.

Erikson, E.H. (1968). *Identity: Youth and crisis.* New York: Norton.

Goossens, L., Marcoen, A., & Janssen, P.J. (1999). *Identity status development and students' perception of the university environment.* Unpublished manuscript, Catholic University of Leuven, Belgium.

Hartmann, D.P. (2005). Assessing growth in longitudinal investigations: Selected measurement and design issues. In D.M. Teti (Ed.), *Handbook of research methods in developmental science* (pp. 319–339). Malden, MA: Blackwell.

Hoekstra, H.A., Ormel, J., & De Fruyt, F. (1996). *NEO persoonlijkheidsvragenlijsten: NEO-PI-R, NEO-FFI. Handleiding* [NEO Personality Inventories: Manual]. Lisse: Swets & Zeitlinger.

Hooge, J., Decaluwé, L., & Goossens, L. (2000). Identiteit en psychisch welbevinden [Identity and well-being]. In H. De Witte, J. Hooge, & L. Walgrave (Eds.), *Jongeren gemeten en geteld. 12- tot 18-jarigen over hun leefwereld en toekomst* (pp. 35–58). Leuven: Universitaire Pers Leuven.

Josselson, R. (1996). *Revising herself: The story of women's identity from college to midlife.* Oxford: Oxford University Press.

Kroger, J. (2005, November). *Identity in formation: Qualitative and quantitative approaches.* Paper presented at the workshop Identity development: Toward an integration of quantitative and qualitative methods, Braunschweig, Germany.

Lund, T. (2005). The qualitative-quantitative distinction: Some comments. *Scandinavian Journal of Educational Research, 49,* 115–132.

Luyckx, K. (2006). *Identity formation in emerging adulthood: Developmental trajectories, antecedents, and consequences.* Unpublished doctoral dissertation, Catholic University of Leuven, Belgium.

Luyckx, K., Goossens, L., Beyers, W., & Soenens, B. (2006). The Ego Identity Process Questionnaire: Factor structure, reliability, and convergent validity in Dutch-speaking late adolescents. *Journal of Adolescence, 29,* 153–159.

Luyckx, K., Goossens, L., & Soenens, B. (2006). A developmental contextual perspective on identity construction in emerging adulthood: Change dynamics in commitment formation and commitment evaluation. *Developmental Psychology, 42,* 366–380.

Luyckx, K., Goossens, L., Soenens, B., & Beyers, W. (2006). Unpacking commitment and exploration: Preliminary validation of an integrative model of late adolescent identity formation. *Journal of Adolescence, 29,* 361–378.

Luyckx, K., Goossens, L., Soenens, B., Beyers, W., & Vansteenkiste, M. (2005). Identity statuses based upon four rather than two identity dimensions: Extending and refining Marcia's paradigm. *Journal of Youth and Adolescence, 34,* 605–619.

Luyckx, K., Schwartz, S.J., Goossens, L., Soenens, B., & Beyers, W. (submitted). *Developmental trajectories of identity formation and adjustment in female emerging adults: A multivariate latent class growth analysis approach.*

Luyckx, K., Soenens, B., & Goossens, L. (2006). The personality-identity interplay in emerging adult women: Convergent findings from complementary analyses. *European Journal of Personality, 20,* 195–215.

Luyckx, K., Soenens, B., Vansteenkiste, M., Goossens, L., & Berzonsky, M. (in press). Parental psychological control and dimensions of identity formation in emerging adulthood. *Journal of Family Psychology.*

Magnusson, D. (1998). The logic and implications of a person-centered approach. In R.B. Cairns, L.R. Bergman, & J. Kagan (Eds.), *Methods and models for studying the individual* (pp. 33–64). Thousand Oaks, CA: Sage.

Marcia, J.E. (1966). Development and validation of ego-identity status. *Journal of Personality and Social Psychology, 3,* 551–558.

McArdle, J., & Nesselroade, J.R. (2003). Growth curve analyses in contemporary psychological research. In I.B. Weiner (Series Ed.), J.A. Shinka, & W.F. Velincer (Vol. Eds.), *Handbook of psychology: Vol. 2. Research methods in psychology* (pp. 447–480). Hoboken, NJ: Wiley.

McLean, K.C., & Pratt, M.W. (2006). Life's little (and big) lessons: Identity statuses and meaning-making in the turning point narratives of emerging adults. *Developmental Psychology, 42,* 714–722.

Mertens, D.M. (2005). *Research and evaluation in education and psychology: Integrating diversity with quantitative, qualitative, and mixed methods* (2nd ed.). Thousand Oaks, CA: Sage.

Meeus, W., & Dekovic, M. (1995). Identity development, parental and peer support in adolescence: Results of a Dutch, national survey. *Adolescence, 30,* 931–944.

Nagin, D.S. (2005). *Group-based modeling of development.* Cambridge, MA: Harvard University Press.

Radloff, L.S. (1977). The Center for Epidemiological Studies-Depression Scale: A self-report depression scale for research in the general population. *Applied Psychological Measurement, 1,* 185–201.

Roberts, R.E., & Sobhan, M. (1992). Symptoms of depression in adolescence: A comparison of Anglo, African, and Hispanic Americans. *Journal of Youth and Adolescence, 21,* 639–651.

Rosenberg, M. (1965). *Society and the adolescent self-image.* Princeton, NJ: Princeton University Press.

Taylor, S.J., Bogdan, R.C., & Walker, P. (2000). Qualitative research. In A. E. Kazdin (Ed.), *Encyclopedia of psychology* (Vol. 6, pp. 489–491). New York: Oxford University Press.

Van der Linden, F. J., Dijkman, T. A., & Roeders, P.J.B. (1983). *Metingen van kenmerken van het persoonssysteem en sociale systeem* [Measurement of features of the person and the social system]. Nijmegen: Hoogveld Institute.

Waszak, N.K., & Sines, M.C. (2003). Mixed methods in psychological research. In A. Tashakkori, & C. Teddlie (Eds.), *Handbook of mixed methods in social and behavioral research* (pp. 557–576). Thousand Oaks, CA: Sage.

Willett, J.B. (1988). Questions and answers in the measurement of change. In E.Z. Rothkopf (Ed.), *Review of research in education 15: 1988-1989* (pp. 345–422). Washington, DC: American Educational Research Association.

Wirtz, P.W. (2005). Modeling developmental change over time: Latent growth analysis. In D.M. Teti (Ed.), *Handbook of research methods in developmental science* (pp. 367–378). Malden, MA: Blackwell.

Chapter 9

To Explore and to Commit: A German Version of the Utrecht-Groningen Identity Development Scale (U-GIDS)

Meike Watzlawik
University of Braunschweig
Germany

A German version of the modified Dutch Utrecht-Groningen Identity Development Scales II for adolescents aged 12 to 14 was evaluated with a younger sample (10 to 12 years of age). 214 children and adolescents (average age 11.2, SD=1.4) were interviewed to examine whether commitment and exploration in the life domains *siblings, best friend, intimate friend, school* and *hobby* differed between five groups of siblings (monozygotic, dizygotic same-sexed, and dizygotic opposite-sexed twins, as well as same-sexed and opposite-sexed siblings with a max. age difference of two years).

Hierarchical analyses showed that the type of sibling dyad (the five groups described above and different sex compositions) was not related to identity development. Only monozygotic twins –being of the same genotyp, same sex, and same age– derive more self-esteem from their sibling relationships.

The evaluation of the questionnaire leads to satisfactory results for the socially oriented scales (*siblings, best friend, intimate friend*), ambiguous results were found for the occupationally oriented scales (*hobby, school*); leading to the question if the dimensional approach (*examining exploration and commitment*) is appropriate for the examined age group.

9.1 Introduction

Identity and identity measures. Erikson's views on identity formation have had and still have an impact on empirical research in many ways. The most popular elaboration of his theory is Marcia's identity status model (1966), suggesting that identity development can best be described with the help of two core variables: the presence of *commitments* in specific life domains and their active *exploration*. The combination of these two variables leads to four identity states: identity diffusion, foreclosure, moratorium, and identity achievement.

Based on Marcia's model, Meeus developed questionnaires (Utrecht-Groningen Identity Development Scales I and II; U-GIDS I and II) to assess commitment and exploration in the life domains intimate relationships and school/occupation (Meeus & Dekovic, 1995). But instead of making identity status classifications, he analyzed developmental trends in the two core variables (slightly differently defined than in Marcia's model, see table 9.2).

Meeus and Dekovic tested 12 to 14 (U-GIDS II) and 21 to 24 year olds (U-GIDS) to examine identity development and parental and peer support in adolescence. They showed that relational identity becomes stronger as adolescents grow older. Less consistent or no developmental trends were found for school identity and occupational identity (Meeus & Dekovic, 1995). Peers mostly influenced identity development in these age groups, "with parents having only an additive positive influence" (Meeus & Dekovic, 1995, p. 931).

Siblings. In our ongoing study, the Brunswick Longitudinal Sibling Study, we examine a special group of "peers": siblings. Siblings have been examined in many ways. Adler (1926) and his followers concentrated on structural features of the sibling relationship –like birth order, age difference, or family size. The interaction of siblings and their mutual influence became more important with the establishment of modern family research in the 1970s. Independent of parental influence, the sibling relationship was then considered a subsystem within the family network (Cicirelli, 1995; Schmidt-Denter, 1996; Furman & Buhrmester, 1985). Looking at this subsystem (shared environment), it was surprising that siblings still turned out to be very different in many aspects, even though they shared 50 or 100% (monozygote twins) of their genes. Dunn and Plomin (1990) pointed out that not only the shared but –even more important– the non-shared environment accounted for many of these variations.

Siblings and identity development. Similarities between the siblings help to build up close relationships, whereas differences lead –at first– to more distant relationships between the children. By choosing different roles within the family, rivalry and the need to compete are diminished. This so called de-identification (Schachter, 1982) allows siblings to regain closeness in their relationships –although the harmonization does not have to take place (Bank & Kahn, 1990). Sibling relationships therefore differ in closeness, but they always demand to find one's own position within the sibling dyad or the family system by evaluating differences and similarities, by choosing to be different, or by sharing similarities.

Twins and identity development. Bank and Kahn (1990) claim that twins have a higher "access" to one another than other siblings, due to being of the same age, and –in some cases– the same gender or even the same genetic disposition. It is more likely for twins than for non-twins that the sibling becomes an attachment figure (Tancredy & Fraley, 2006), which is one reason why it is more difficult for twins to develop independence and a positive identity, as they have to emancipate themselves both from their parents and from their co-twins (Åkerman & Suurvee, 2003). It is important to note that we cannot talk about twins in general. The zygosity has to be taken into account when we examine (identity) development (Penninkilampi-Kerola, Moilanen, Kaprio, & Fine, 2005), since monozygotic twins seem to be a special case. Even in early childhood, they differ from other twins and siblings, e.g. in language acquisition (Deutsch et al., 2001) and self recognition (Deutsch, Schäfer, & Wagner, 1999). They also have higher dyadic identities in early adolescence and it can be assumed that they mirror one another. They have the unique possibility to watch "themselves" do things and then later decide whether or not they want to adapt a certain behavior. Both siblings use this possibility mutually (Watzlawik & Clodius, 2005).

Puberty as a crucial stage. Children reach a stage that is crucial for identity development with the onset of puberty (cp. Steinberg, 2002; Meeus, 1996; Marcia, 1993). During this period, important variations allow the child to become more independent of "others' expectations and directives" (Marcia, 1980, p. 160). Many relationships –including the sibling relationship– change within this period (Cicirelli, 1995). Due to the described differences between non-twins and twins, it can be assumed that identity development challenges non-twins and twins in different ways. We therefore interviewed children between 10 and 12 years of age, comparing how individual identity development differs between siblings (twins and non-twins) in the adolescents' important life domains *siblings, best friend, intimate friend, school,* and *hobby.* The U-GIDS II was chosen to measure the according variables (commitment and exploration), but it had only been validated for an older age group and for different domains. This leads to the following research questions:

1. Is the U-GIDS a reliable and structurally valid measurement for assessing commitment and exploration in 10-to-12-year-olds?
2. Do twins and other siblings differ in commitment and exploration in the life domains *siblings, best friend, intimate friend, school,* and *hobby?*

9.2   Method

Subjects

The 214 children were an average of 11.2 years old (SD = 1.4). The age difference between siblings was limited to 24 months. One-hundred six boys and one-
hundred eight girls participated in this study. We interviewed 24 sets of
monozygote twins (MT), 21 sets of dizygote twins of the same sex (DT-SS), 20
sets of dizygote twins of opposite sexes (DT-OS), 22 sets of siblings of the same
sex (S-SS), and 20 sets of siblings of opposite sexes (S-OS). Eighteen of the
twin pairs had already taken part in earlier projects of the Brunswick
Longitudinal Sibling Study. All additional families were contacted through the
media, schools, or already participating families. Trained students interviewed
the siblings separately, in their home environments, which was part of their research internships. The different groups of siblings do not differ significantly in
age, sex, schools attended (demonstrating their educational level), number of
other siblings, or family structure (parents married, single-parent households,
etc.).

Measures

Identity. The U-GIDS is based on Marcia's identity status model (1966). Its
scales measure exploration and commitment in different life domains. Differing
slightly from Marcia's definition of those two concepts[1], Meeus and Dekovic
define commitment as the extent to which adolescents feel committed to and derive self-confidence, a positive self-image, and confidence in the future from relationships, school, and work. Exploration is understood as the extent to which
adolescents actively engage in investigating relationships, school and work
(Meeus & Dekovic, 1995). In our study, we took on Meeus' definitions but still
modified and extended the U-GIDS II (12-to-14-year-olds) to measure commitment and exploration in the life domains *siblings, best friend, intimate friend,
school,* and *hobby.* The shortened scales for each life domain consisted of three
instead of five commitment items (scale sample presented in table 9.1) and three
instead of five exploration items (scale sample presented in table 9.2). In this
study, answers were given on a 4- instead of a 5-point Likert scale, with response categories ranging from 1 = "completely untrue" to 4 = "completely
true."

The children did not fill out the questionnaire by themselves. It was part of
a standardized interview conducted by trained interviewers (psychology students). This way, questions concerning the items were, if necessary, answered
right away using standardized explanations.

Table 9.1

Commitment items for the life domain "best friend": U-GIDS II and U-GIDS II modified for German sample

U-GIDS II (Meeus & Dekovic, 1995)	U-GIDS II modified Studies
1. My best friend gives me security in life.	1. I cannot imagine a life without my best friend.
2. My best friend gives me self-confidence.	2. I can better stand up for myself because of my best friend.
3. My best friend makes me feel sure of myself.	3. I can look ahead unworried because of my best friend.
4. My best friend gives me security for the future.	
5. My best friend allows me to face the future with optimism.	

Table 9.2

Exploration items for the life domain "best friend": U-GIDS II and U-GIDS II modified for German sample

U-GIDS II (Meeus & Dekovic, 1995)	U-GIDS II modified Studies
1. I try to find out a lot about my best friend.	1. I try to find out a lot about my best friend.
2. I often reflect on my best friend.	2. I often think about my best friend.
3. I make a lot of effort to keep finding out new things about my best friend.	3. I often talk with other people about my best friend.
4. I often try to find out what other people think about my best friend.	
5. I often talk with other people about my best friend.	

9.3   Results

Evaluation of the modified U-GIDS. Principal component analysis (varimax rotated) showed that all socially oriented scales (*best friends, siblings, intimate friends*) had the assumed factorial structure with two factors, representing commitment and exploration. The occupationally oriented scales (*school and hobby*) lead to different factorial structures with only one factor for the life domain *school* and two factors for *hobby*, which did not confirm the assumed underlying concepts. Due to these findings, low reliabilities, and insufficient discriminatory power ($r_{it} < .30$), *hobby* was excluded from further analysis. The total score of the life domain *school* stayed in the analysis: all items taken together were post hoc interpreted as "ongoing identity formation." The reliability coefficients of the new scales are shown in table 9.3.

Table 9.3

Reliability coefficients and item-total correlations of the different scales				
U-GIDS II (modified)	Number of items	Number of subjects	Cronbach's Alpha	r_{it}
siblings				
commitment	3	212	0.61	0.33 - 0.49
exploration	3	212	0.64	0.35 - 0.52
best friend				
commitment	3	208	0.71	0.46 - 0.59
exploration	3	208	0.65	0.34 - 0.54
intimate friend				
commitment	3	102	0.80	0.62 - 0.67
exploration	3	102	0.66	0.35 - 0.56
school				
total score	6	211	0.71	0.38 - 0.52

The number of subjects varies due to missing data (life domains siblings/school). A few children and adolescents said that they did not have a best friend, and more than 50% did not yet have an intimate friend.

Hierarchical Linear Modeling. Usual methods of analysis cannot be applied to the data set of this study because we interviewed children of the same dyad. Knowing that siblings influence each other, the data set now contains correlated answers. With the program Hierarchical Linear and Nonlinear Modeling (HLM) for Windows (Version 5.05; Raudenbush, Bryk, Cheong, & Congdon, 2000), the influence of the sibling relationship on exploration and commitment in the different life domains (individual parameters, level 1) was analyzed –accounting for the fact that sets of answers within the data set are not independent from each other. Hierarchical Linear Models use regressions to predict the mean scores for the different groups of siblings with the help of a group characteristic (level 2 predictor). In our case, this predictor is the kind of sibling relationship the children evaluate (for more details on the methodological approach see Raudenbush & Bryk, 2002, or Raudenbush, Bryk, Cheong, & Congdon, 2000).

The sibling relationship had a significant influence only on commitment and only in the life domain *sibling* (T[105] = -2.45; p < 0.05). Figure 9.1 shows that MT reach the highest scores; S-OS the lowest. For DT and S-SS, the mean raw scores for commitment in the life domain *siblings* are comparably high.

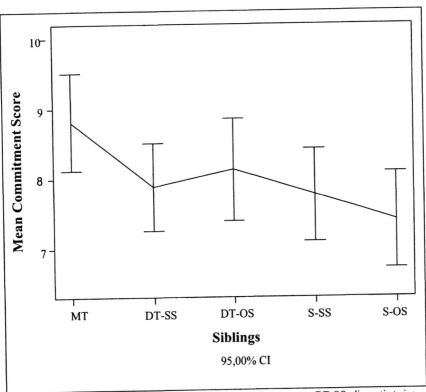

Note. MT=monozygotic twins, DT-SS=dizygotic twins of the same sex; DT-OS=dizygotic twins of opposite sexes, S-SS=siblings of the same sex, S-OS=siblings of opposite sexes.

Figure 9.1 *Mean commitment scores in the life domain siblings*

9.4   Discussion

Evaluation of the modified U-GIDS. A translated and shortened version of the U-GIDS II (Meeus & Dekovic, 1995) was tested with a younger German sample in different life domains. For the socially oriented life domains best friend, siblings, and intimate friend, satisfactory item-total correlations and reliabilities were reached. The factor analysis confirmed the assumed factorial structure (construct validity).

We did not succeed in separating commitment and exploration for the life domain *school,* and *hobby* had to be excluded from further analysis. The two possible explanations for these findings are that a) *hobby* and *school* differ from the socially oriented domains or b) the questionnaire did not use the appropriate items to measure commitment and exploration in these domains.

Assuming a), we can argue that the socially oriented domains all focus on relationships, whereas *school* and *hobby* also allow individual decisions that do not necessarily affect another person. In addition, it has to be considered that –at this age– *school* and *hobby* are still strongly influenced by parents (who want the child to succeed, who pay for hobby equipment and/or who drive and pick their kids up from the accordant classes), limiting the children's exploration and maybe even their commitment (e.g. Granic, Dishion, & Hollenstein, 2003; Wagner, Schober, & Spiel, 2005).

Assuming b), we need to have a closer look at the items themselves. In table 9.4 we compare the socially oriented life domain *siblings* with the domain *school*.

Table 9.4

Commitment and exploration items for the life domains school and sibling (German version of the U-GIDS)

Life domain siblings	Life domain school	
1. I cannot imagine a life without my brother/sister.	1. I like going to school every day.	commitment
2. My brother/sister makes me feel sure of myself.	2. School (my education) makes me feel sure of myself.	
3. My brother/sister gives me security in life.	3. School (my education) gives me security in life.	
4. I often think about my brother/sister.	4. I often think about school.	
5. I try to find out a lot about my brother/sister.	5. I try to take an active part in class.	exploration
6. I often talk with other people about my brother/sister.	6. I often talk with other people about school (my education).	

Item 1 differs in its emotional intensity. Liking something or even someone is less emotionally intense than not being able to imagine a life without another, so that –in the second case– maybe less commitment is described in the first place. Answering items 4 to 6 in the domain *siblings* may be motivated intrinsically, whereas evaluating the exploration items of the domain *school* may more easily trigger socially desired answers (extrinsically motivated, see explanation for a).

The one-factor structure of the domain *school* may therefore be caused by the fact that commitment is demanded from outside and exploration is limited in this domain. The less consistent picture found for the domain *hobby* may be due to this field being too inconsistent (kinds of hobbies, time investment, opportunities, etc.) to derive a consistent picture. Longitudinal studies will show if –as the children become older and the parental influence lessens— the scales *school* and *hobby* show the assumed two-factor structures and higher reliabilities.

Differences between twins and non-twins. Commitment and exploration of the life domains examined here do not differ between siblings. Only monozygotic twins are a clearly separate group with higher commitment rates in the life domain *siblings*, showing that their self-esteem is based more intensively on one another. In general, monozygote twins are not more self-confident than other siblings, as personality tests with the sample examined here showed (self-confidence scale of the PFK 9-14 from Seitz & Rausche, 2004; results: $F[4] = 0.28$; $p = 0.88$). Other siblings seem to use different resources than monozygotic twins to maintain or to build up self-confidence. The question of whether those resources are less important for monozygotic twins has yet to be examined.

Measuring identity development? Showing that the assumed factorial structure can only be found for scales with reference to social relationships, the presented findings suggest that identity development in early adolescence is strongly determined by social interaction. Adolescents discover new things and integrate them into their self-concepts through the acknowledgement of (significant) others. Identity development can then be considered to be a more inductive process, which leads to the question of whether measuring commitment and exploration (individual parameters) to determine identity development in adolescence —and maybe even earlier or later— is the appropriate approach. It is likely that a fuller picture of identity development can be reached if the individual's perception of the outside acknowledgement of his or her own discoveries and consequential decisions is integrated into questionnaires.

Especially for the here-examined population, we must also question whether difficulties in gaining independence from one's sibling would lead —as assumed— to higher or lower exploration and commitment rates in the chosen domains. It may be more useful to choose qualitative approaches (see corresponding chapters in this book), not to measure the effect of these difficulties, but to get an idea of what kind of difficulties occur and in what ways identity development can influence sibling relationships. For, e.g., counseling processes, this would probably be of greater value.

Acknowledgement

Thank you to all participating families and the following co-workers: Ina Popp and Sylvia Dzäbel.

Notes

1   Exploration "refers to a period of decision-making, of choosing among alternatives [. . .]; commitment deals with the individual's personal investment in the alternative chosen." (Marcia & Friedman, 1970, p. 250).

References

Åkerman, B.A., & Suurvee, E. (2003). The Cognitive and Identity Development of Twins at 16 Years of Age: A Follow-up Study of 32 Twin Pairs. *Twin Research, 6*, 328–333.

Adler, A. (1926). *Menschenkenntnis* [Knowledge of human nature]. Leipzig: Hirtzel.

Bank, S.P. & Kahn, M.D. (1990). *Geschwister-Bindung* [The sibling bond]. Paderborn: Junfermann.

Cicirelli, V. (1995). *Sibling Relationships across the Life Span*. New York: Plenum Press.

Deutsch, W., Schaefer, H. & Wagner, A. (1999). Mich gibt's nur im Plural. Ueber die Entwicklung der phaenotypischen Identitaet von mono- und dizygoten Zwillingspaaren [I only exist in plural! Phenotypic identity development of monozygote and dizygote twins]. In U. Fuhrer & I.E. Josephs (Eds.), *Persönliche Objekte, Identitaet und Entwicklung*. Göttingen: Vandenhoeck & Ruprecht.

Deutsch, W., Wagner, A., Burchardt, R., Schulz, N., & Nakath, J. (2001). Person in the language of singletons, siblings and twins. In S. Levinson, & M. Bowerman (Eds.), *Language acquisition and conceptual development*. New York: Cambridge University Press.

Dunn, J., & Plomin, R. (1990). *Separate Lives. Why Siblings Are So Different*. New York: Basic Books.

Furman, W., & Buhrmester, D. (1985). Children's perceptions of the qualities of the sibling relationship. *Child Development, 56*, 448–461.

Granic, I., Dishion, T.J., & Hollenstein, T. (2003). The Family Ecology of Adolescence: A Dynamic Systems Perspective on Normative Development. In G.R. Adams, & M.D. Berzonsky (Eds.), *Blackwell Handbook of Adolescence*. Oxford: Blackwell Publishing.

Marcia, J.E. (1966). Development and validation of ego-identity status. *Journal of Personality and Social Psychology, 3*, 551–558.

Marcia, J.E. (1980). Identity in Adolescence. In J. Adelson (Ed.), *Handbook of adolescent psychology*. New York: Wiley.

Marcia, J.E. (1993). The ego identity status approach to ego identity. In J.E. Marcia, A.S. Waterman, D.R. Matteson, S.L. Archer, & J.L. Orlowsky (Eds.), *Ego Identity*. New York: Springer.

Meeus, W. (1996). Studies on identity development in adolescence: An overview of research and some new data. *Journal of Youth and Adolescence, 25*, 569–598.

Meeus, W., & Dekovic, M. (1995). Identity Development, Parental and Peer Support in Adolescence: Results of a National Dutch Survey. *Adolescence, 30* (120), 931–944.

Penninkilampi-Kerola, V., Moilanen, I., Kaprio, J., & Fine, M. (2005). Co-twin dependence, social interactions, and academic achievement: A population-based study. *Journal of Social and Personal Relationships, 22,* 519–541.

Raudenbush, S.W., & Bryk, A.S. (2002). *Hierarchical Linear Models: Applications and Data Analysis Methods.* Newbury Park, CA: Sage.

Raudenbush, S.W., Bryk, A.S., Cheong, Y.F., & Congdon Jr., R.T. (2000). *HLM 5. Hierarchical Linear and Nonlinear Modeling.* Lincolnwood, IL: Scientific Software International.

Schachter, F.F. (1982). Siblings deidentification and split-parent identification: A family tetrad. In M.E. Lamb, & B. Sutton-Smith (Eds.), *Sibling relationships. Their nature and significance across the lifespan.* Hillsdale, NJ: Lawrence Erlbaum.

Schmidt-Denter, U. (1996). *Soziale Entwicklung: ein Lehrbuch über soziale Beziehungen* [Social development: a textbook on social relationships]. Weinheim: Psychologie Verlags Union.

Seitz, W. & Rausche, A. (2004). *Persönlichkeitsfragebogen für Kinder zwischen 9 und 14 (PFK 9-14)* [Personality questionnaire for children aged 9 to 14]. Bern: Hogrefe.

Steinberg, L. (2002). *Adolescence* (6th edition). Boston: McGraw-Hill.

Tancredy, C.M., & Fraley, R.C. (2006). The nature of adult twin relationships: An attachment-theoretical perspective. *Journal of Personalyity and Social Psychology, 90* (1), 78–93.

Wagner, P., Schober, B. & Spiel, C. (2005). Wer hilft beim Lernen für die Schule [Who helps with studying for school?]. *Zeitschrift für Entwicklungspsychologie und Pädagogische Psychologie, 37* (2), 101–109.

Watzlawik, M. & Clodius, S. (2005, September). *Paaridentität in verschiedenen Geschwisterkonstellationen* [Dyadic identity in different kinds of siblings]. Poster presented at the 17th Meeting of the German Society for Psychology/ Section Developmental Psychology, Bochum, Germany.

Chapter 10

Relationships with Parents and Identity in Adolescence: A Review of 25 Years of Research

Wim Meeus and Minet de Wied
University of Utrecht
Netherlands

We present an overview of 37 studies on parent–adolescent relations and identity. These studies were reported in 23 articles published in the period 1976-2000. Two approaches were used to study whether parent-adolescent relations are positively associated to identity development: by determining one score for every study and by counting the total number of associations. The main conclusion from our review is that parent-adolescent relationships are not linked to identity development in adolescence. Some associations between parent-adolescent relations and identity were found, but these are pertinent only to specific measures of parent-adolescent relations and identity: attachment and separation-individuation and general identity, and intergenerational boundaries and exploration of identity alternatives. Besides, these associations were not replicated in studies with multivariate designs. It is suggested that it may not be easy to find clear linkages between the nature of the parent-adolescent relationship and the development of identity because of the subtleties in the transformation process of the parent-child relation during adolescence.

10.1   Introduction

Adolescence is a period of intensive development. First, there is a change in the adolescents' relations with parents and peers. The parent-adolescent relation changes from a relation of authority into a more equal relation (Youniss & Smollar, 1985), and peer relations grow in intensity (Brown, 1990). Second, adolescence is the period in which identity is formed (Marcia, Waterman, Matteson, Archer & Orlofsky, 1993). An important question in present-day adolescent research is, therefore, whether parent-adolescent relations are associated with the development of identity. In this article we will give an overview of research conducted in this field over the past 25 years. With respect to the development of identity, we restrict ourselves to studies conducted on the basis of the Eriksonian concept of identity and its elaboration by Marcia (1966) into the identity status model.

A limited number of studies has been conducted to investigate the association between parent-adolescent relations and identity. Our search in the files of Psychlit, in review articles, and in the reference lists of articles, produced 23 articles published during the period 1976-2000. Only articles were included in the review when they had both an identity measure that fits Marcia's identity status paradigm and a measure of parent-adolescent relations. Our sample of articles includes most of the relevant publications, although we do not claim that our analysis covers all the articles ever published. Below we first give an overview of the theoretical perspectives to be found in these articles on parent-adolescent relations and identity. We then investigate in the same set of articles the extent to which these theoretical perspectives find empirical support.

10.2   Theoretical perspectives on parent-adolescent relations and identity

In the 23 articles, we found four perspectives on the association between parent-adolescent relations and identity: attachment theory, the separation-individuation hypothesis, the connectedness-individuality hypothesis, and the idea of intergenerational boundaries.

Parental attachment. Bowlby (1969) describes attachment and exploration as two complementary systems. Research into 'the strange situation' (Ainsworth, Blehar, Waters & Wall, 1978) confirms this idea. Securely attached children are more inclined to explore their surroundings than insecurely attached children. This idea is also found in identity research: a secure attachment to parents stimulates the development of identity (Quintana & Lapsley, 1987), especially because it promotes the exploration of identity alternatives (Marcia, 1983). Exploration of identity alternatives is, as we know, a necessary condition for attaining the status identity achievement.

Separation-individuation. The classic separation-individuation theory of Blos (1967) states that the adolescent has to let go of the child's internalized image of the parent as a precondition for individuation. In identity research this hypothesis has mainly been elaborated by Kroger (1985) and Kroger and Haslett (1988). They say that there is a parallel between the structure of the parent-child relation and the structure of the ego. In adolescence the young person no longer accepts the parents' omnipotence and their rules of conduct and defines him/herself and the parents as autonomous people in a relationship. This redefinition of the parent-adolescent relation makes it possible for the adolescent to give up his/her child's identity and to enter autonomously into new commitments.

Connectedness and individuality. This hypothesis was developed by Grotevant and Cooper (1985, 1986). It states that in adolescence the relation with the parents is changed, rather than abandoned, from a relation in which the authority of the parent is dominant into a relation of equality. The connectedness-individuality hypothesis complements the separation-individuation hypothesis, by stating that the adolescent has to give up his/her child's image of the parent, and qualifying the new parent-adolescent relationship. The connectedness-individuality hypothesis proposes that individuation depends on the degree of connectedness in the parent-adolescent relation: a high degree of connectedness offers the opportunity for individuality. Following the attachment theory, Grotevant and Cooper hypothesize that a high degree of connectedness leads to a high degree of exploration of identity alternatives, which promotes the development of identity.

Intergenerational boundaries. Some authors (Grotevant, 1983; Fullinwider-Bush & Jacobvitz, 1993; Perosa, Perosa & Tam, 1996) propose that strong boundaries between the generations, that is, parents and adolescents, promote the development of identity. If the boundaries are too rigid or too vague the development of identity does not proceed smoothly, for example because the parents do not give the adolescent enough support or space in which to develop. Inadequate boundaries between parent and adolescent are often seen in the literature as a cause of foreclosure. This is because the adolescents have not chosen their commitments themselves, but have been guided in their choice by parental authority (Bosma & Gerrits, 1985; Campbell, Adams & Dobson, 1984; Marcia, 1980; Waterman, 1982).

Summarizing, we may say that researchers working with both the attachment theory and the connectedness-individuality hypothesis, assume that a good bond with parents supports exploration and, therefore also, a successful development of identity. The connectedness-individuality hypothesis differs from attachment theory in that it is more specific about the characteristics of the parent-child relationship that promote the development of identity. The connectedness-individuality hypothesis also complements the separation-individuation hypothesis by recognizing that adolescents detach oneself from the parent-child relation of childhood, and by specifying the nature of the parent-child relation that is appropriate for adolescence. Finally, the idea of intergenerational boundaries focuses on the degree of connectedness in the parent-adolescent relation: it is not conductive to be too connected, neither to be unconnected.

10.3 An overview of empirical studies of parent-adolescent relations and identity

The main purpose of the present study is to examine to what extent the theoretical perspectives, mentioned above, find empirical support. In total, twenty-three articles were taken up in our analysis, and scored on the following criteria: (a) number and gender of the subjects, (b) type of sample high school (H-S), college or university (CU), (c) type and number of parent-adolescent relation measures, and (d) type and number of identity measures. For the identity measures, we noted the number (n), the name of the measuring instruments and also whether this measured overall (o) or domain-specific (d) identity.

The twenty three articles on parent-adolescent relations could be categorized into seven groups: 4 articles used measures of parental attachment, 4 articles used measures of separation-individuation, 5 articles used measures of connectedness and individuality, 2 articles used measures of intergenerational boundaries, 3 articles used measures of parenting, 2 articles used measures of parental support, and 3 articles used various measures of parent-adolescent relations. Table 10.1 gives an overview of these articles.

In these articles five types of identity measures were used: (a) general identity (is identity strongly or weakly developed?), (b) commitment (is commitment strong or weak?), (c) exploration (is exploration thorough or not?), (d) separate statuses (concerns studies in which for each individual a score was calculated for each of the four statuses), (e) between status contrasts (studies in which each individual was characterized with one status). As table 10.1 shows, most of the studies used self-report measures of global identity, that is identity across domains: Ego Identity Scale-Rasmussen (EIS Rasmussen), Ego Identity Scale-Tan (EIS Tan), Extended Objective Measure of Ego Identity Status (EOM-EIS), Objective Measure of Ego Identity Status (OM-EIS), Identity Exploration Scale of Grotevant (IE-G), Identity Achievement Scale (IAS), Ego Identity Scale (EIS) and Extended Objective Measure of Ego Identity Status 2 (EOM-EIS2). Only two studies used self-report measures of domain-specific identity: the Vocational Identity Scale (VIS), the Dellas Identity Status Inventory-Occupation (DISI-O), and the Identity Exploration Scale of Grotevant (IE-G). Also, only two studies used the identity status interview (ISI) to tap global or domain-specific identity. So, the majority of studies used quantitative self-report data, while only two studies made use of qualitative data to tap identity formation.

Table 10.1

Characteristics of the articles on parent-adolescent relations and identity

Authors	Sample				Type and number of measures			Identity (I)			
	Gender	n	High-school	College/University	Parent/peer-adolescent relation (P/P-A) Name	n		Name	Global	Domain-specific	n
					Studies of parental attachment						
Anderson & Fleming, 1996 (A. & F. 1996)	m/f	132		x	Emotional attachment	1		EIS-Rasmussen	x		1
Kendis & Tan, 1978 (K & T. 1978)	f	58		x	Evaluation of parents	4		EIS-Tan	x		1
Matos, Barbosa, De Almeida & Costa, 1999 (M, B, D-A & C, 1999)	m/f	361	x		Attachment	3		EOM-EIS2	x		4
Quintana & Lapsley, 1987 (Q & L. 1987), 1	m/f	101		x	Attachment	3		EIS-Rasmussen	x		1
2	m/f	101		x	Attachment	3		EIS-TAN	x		1
					Studies of separation-individuation						
Kroger, 1985 (K. 1985)	m/f	140		x	Harsburg's Separation-anxiety test	1		ISI	x		1
Kroger & Haslett, 1988, wave 1 (K & H. 1988, w1)	m/f	76		x	Harsburg's Separation-anxiety test	1		ISI	x		1
Kroger & Haslett, 1988, wave 2 (K & H. 1988, w2)	m/f	76		x	Harsburg's Separation-anxiety test	1		ISI	x		1
Lopez 1989, 1	m	114	x		Conflictual independence mother & father	2		VIS		x	1
2	m	114	x		Emotional independence mother & father	2		VIS		x	1
3	f	185	x		Conflictual independence mother & father	2		VIS		x	1
4	f	185	x		Emotional independence mother & father	2		VIS		x	1
Palladino-Schultheiss & Blustein, 1994, 1	f	82		x	Attitudinal independence father & mother	2		EOM-EIS	x		4
2	f	82		x	Conflictual independence father & mother	2		EOM-EIS	x		4
3	f	82		x	Connectedness: attachment	2		EOM-EIS	x		4
4	m	92		x	Attitudinal independence father & mother	2		EOM-EIS	x		4
5	m	92		x	Conflictual independence father & mother	2		EOM-EIS	x		4
6	m	92		x	Connectedness: attachment	2		EOM-EIS	x		4

Table 10.1 continued

Studies of connectedness and individuality in parent-adolescent relations

Study	Sex	N		Construct	k	Instrument				
Campbell, Adams & Dobson, 1984 (C, A & D, 1984), 1	m:f	286	x	Connectedness 1, father	1	OM-EIS	x			1
2	m:f	286	x	Connectedness 2, father	1	OM-EIS	x			1
3	m:f	286	x	Connectedness 1, mother	1	OM-EIS	x			1
4	m:f	286	x	Connectedness 2, mother	1	OM-EIS	x			1
5	m:f	286	x	Individuality 1 & 2, father & mother	4	OM-EIS	x			1
Cooper & Grotevant, 1987 (C & G, 1987), 1	f	44	x	Connectedness parents	10	ISI				2
2	m	38	x	Connectedness parents	10	ISI		x		2
3	f	44	x	Individuality	5	ISI		x		2
4	m	38	x	Individuality	5	ISI		x		2
Grotevant & Cooper, 1986 (G & C, 1986), 1	m:f	84	x	Connectedness	8	ISI	x			2
2	m:f	84	x	Individuality	4	ISI	x			1
3	m:f	73	x	Connectedness in 4 parent-adolescent types	32	ISI	x			1
4	m:f	73	x	Individuality in 4 parent-adolescent types	1o	ISI	x			1
Frank, Pinch & Wright, 1990 (F, P & W, 1990), 1	m:f	376	x	Connectedness	1	EOM-EIS-R	x			x
2	m:f	376	x	Individuality	1	EOM-EIS-I	x			x
3	m:f	376	x	Connectedness	1	EOM-EIS-R	x			x
4	m:f	376	x	Individuality	1	EOM-EIS-I	x			x
Kamptner, 1988 (K, 1988), 1	m	180	x	Connectedness	1	OM-EIS	x			1
2	m	180	x	Individuality	2	OM-EIS	x			1
3	f	230	x	Connectedness	1	OM-EIS	x			1
4	f	230	x	Individuality	2	OM-EIS	x			1

Studies of intergenerational boundaries

Study	Sex	N		Construct	k	Instrument			
Fullinwider-Bush & Jacobvitz, 1993 (F-B & J, 1993), 1	f	45	x	Connectedness & individuality	1	IE-G	x	x (3)	4
2	f	45	x	Overconnectedness father-daughter	1	IE-G	x	x (3)	4
3	f	45	x	Overconnectedness mother-daughter	1	IE-G	x	x (3)	4
Perosa, Perosa & Tam, 1996 (P, P & T, 1996), 1	f	164	x	No proximity differentiation	1	EOM-EIS	x		4
2	f	164	x	Generational hierarchy differentiation	1	EOM-EIS	x		4

Table 10.1 continued

Studies of parenting

Study	Sex	N		Variable	n	Measure			n
Adams & Jones, 1983 (A & J, 1983)	f	82	x	Perceived parenting styles father & mother	10	OM-EIS		x	1
Enright, Lapsley, Drivas & Fehr, 1980 (E, L, D & F, 1980), 1	m/f	202	x	Configuration of parenting father & mother	2	IAS		x	1
2	m/f	168	x	Configuration of parenting father & mother	2	IAS		x	1
LaVoie, 1976 (LaV, 1976), 1	m	60	x	Parenting father & mother	36	EIS		x	1
2	f	60	x	Parenting father & mother	36	EIS		x	1

Studies of parental support

Study	Sex	N		Variable	n	Measure			n
Meeus, 1993 (M, 1993)	m/f	261	x	Parental support school	1	DISI-O	x	x	1
O'Connor, 1995 (O'-C, 1995), 1	m	164	x	Emotional support father	1	EOM-EIS		x	4
2	m	164	x	Emotional support mother	1	EOM-EIS		x	4
3	f	254	x	Emotional support father	1	EOM-EIS		x	4
4	f	254	x	Emotional support mother	1	EOM-EIS		x	4

Studies of various parent-adolescent measures

Study	Sex	N		Variable	n	Measure			n
Adams, Ryan & Keating, 2000, 1, wave 1 (A, R & K, 2000, 1, w1	m/f	294	x	Family relations	1	EOM-EIS		x	2
2, wave 2	m/f	294	x	Family relations	1	EOM-EIS		x	2
3, wave 1 near wave 2, model 1	m/f	294	x	Family relations	1	EOM-EIS		x	2
4, wave 1 near wave 2, model 2	m	30	x	Identification with parents	1	ISI		x	1
Cella, De Wolfe & Fitzgibbon, 1987, 1 (C, DeW & F, 1987, 1)	f	258	x	Identification with parents	1	ISI		x	1
2	m/f	164	x	Family conflict	1	EOM-EIS2		x	1

Nelson, Hughes, Handal, Katz & Scanight, 1993 (N, H, H, K & S, 1993)

Note. EIS-Rasmussen = Ego Identity Scale-Rasmussen; EIS-Tan = Ego Identity Scale-Tan; ISI = Identity Status Interview; EOM-EIS 2 = Extended Objective Measure of Ego Identity Status 2; OM-EIS = Objective Measure of Ego Identity Status; EOM-EIS-R = Extended Objective Measure of Ego Identity Status-Relations; EOM-EIS-1 = Extended Objective Measure of Ego Identity Status-Ideology; IE-G = Identity Exploration-Grotevant.

We determined for each study how many associations between parent-adolescent measures and identity measures were investigated. This was done by multiplying the number of relation measures by the number of identity measures. In the study of Kendis and Tan (1978), for example, four parent-adolescent measures and one identity measure were used, so 4 associations in total were investigated. We then looked at whether the associations between the parent-adolescent measures were tested bivariately (B) or multivariately (M). The bivariate analyses concern the unitary associations between the parent-adolescent measures and identity. The multivariate analyses use not only the parent-adolescent measures but also other independent variables to predict the identity scores. Finally, for each investigated association, we scored whether a positive, negative or non-significant association was found between the parent-adolescent measures and identity. The authors upon request can provide detailed scoring. The findings for the different combinations of relationship and identity measures were summated and are presented in table 10.3.

A drawback of this approach is that studies testing many associations between parent-adolescent measures and identity have a stronger impact on the total score than studies testing fewer associations. An example: Anderson and Fleming (1996) studied one association between parent-adolescent relation and identity, while Kendis and Tan (1978) studied four. In this way the study of Kendis and Tan has four times as much influence on the total score than the study of Anderson and Fleming. To control for this effect, a systematic association between parent-adolescent measures and identity was determined for every analysis. This was performed by using criterion ≥ 50: if the number of positive relations is larger than, or equal to the number of summed up negative and non-significant relations, the analysis meets the criterion. In that case we assume that there is a systematical association between parent-adolescent measures and identity. In this way every study is assigned the same weight in the determination of the total score. An example again: Anderson and Fleming report one positive relation and Kendis and Tan two positive and two non-significant ones. Both studies meet the criterion ≥ 50 and receive the score 1. One has to keep in mind, though, that in studies with different sub-samples, separate analyses were carried out for each sub-sample. Accordingly, these studies have a larger influence on the total score. However, in our opinion to analyze them separately is more valid than to average the outcomes of the sub-samples.

Table 10.2 gives an overview of the data per study. In the columns under n the total number of studies are mentioned and under criterion ≥ 50 the number of studies with a systematic association between parent-adolescent measures and identity. The Table shows that our database of 23 articles on parent-adolescent relations and identity contains 26 bivariate and 11 multivariate studies.

Table 10.3 gives an overview of the unweighed number of associations and reports, in total, on 290 bivariate and 116 multivariate associations between parent-adolescent measures and identity (see cell 8F.B and 8F.M).

Table 10.2

Systematic associations, weighed per study, between parent-adolescent relations and identity

Parent-adolescent relations	A. General identity				B. Commitment		C. Exploration		D. Separate statuses				E. Between status contrasts		F. Total			
Identity — Bivariate (B) or Multivariate (M) test	B Studies		M Studies		B Studies		B Studies		B Studies		M Studies		B Studies		B Studies		M Studies	
	n	Criterion ≥ 50 (%)	n	C ≥ 50 (%)	n	≥ 50 (%)	n	C ≥ 50 (%)	n	C ≥ 50 (%)	n	C ≥ 50 (%)	n	C ≥ 50 (%)	n	C ≥ 50 (%)	n	C ≥ 50 (%)
1. Attachment	3	3 (100)	1	0 (0)							1	0 (0)			3	3 (100)	2	0 (0)
2. Separation-individuation	2	2 (100)	1	0 (0)							1	0 (0)	3	1 (33)	5	3 (60)	2	0 (0)
3. Connectedness & individuality			2	1 (50)	2	0 (0)	2	0 (0)	1	0 (0)	1	0 (0)	2	1 (50)	7	1 (14)	3	1 (33)
4. Intergenerational boundaries							1	1 (100)			1	0 (0)			1	1 (100)	1	0 (0)
5. Parenting	2	0 (0)	2	0 (0)									1	0 (0)	3	0 (0)	2	0 (0)
6. Support									2	0 (0)			1	0 (0)	3	0 (0)		
7. Various measures	1	1 (100)							1	0 (0)	1	0 (0)	2	2 (100)	4	3 (75)	1	0 (0)
8. Total	8	6 (75)	6	1 (17)	2	0 (0)	3	1 (33)	4	0 (0)	5	0 (0)	9	4 (44)	26	11 (42)	11	1 (9)

Note. In the columns n indicates the number of studies and criterion ≥ 50 (%) the number and percentage of the studies showing a systematic association respectively.

Table 10.3

Unweighted number of associations between parent-adolescent relations and identity.

Bivariate (B) or Multivariate (M) test

Parent-adolescent relations

Identity	A. General identity						B. Commitment			C. Exploration			D. Separate statuses						E. Between status contrasts			F. Total					
	B +	B −	B ns	M +	M −	M ns	B +	B −	B ns	B +	B −	B ns	B +	B −	B ns	M +	M −	M ns	B +	B −	B ns	B +	B −	B ns	M +	M −	M ns
1. Attachment	8	0	3	0	0	6										2	1	9				8	0	3	2	1	15
2. Separation-individuation	4	0	4	3	0	5										6	13	29	1	0	2	5	0	6	9	13	34
3. Connectedness & individuality				3	1	2	6	0	54	4	4	52	6	3	7	4	2	10	4	0	8	20	7	121	7	3	12
4. Intergenerational boundaries										9	0	3				2	2	4				9	0	3	2	2	4
5. Parenting	6	0	66	0	0	4							0	0	6				4	0	0	10	0	72	0	0	4
6. Support													7	1	8				0	0	1	7	1	9			
7. Various measures	1	0	0													0	0	8	2	0	6	3	0	6	0	0	8
8. Total	19	0	73	6	1	17	6	0	54	13	4	55	13	4	21	14	18	60	11	0	17	62	8	220	20	19	77

Note + indicates a positive, − a negative and ns a non-significant association.

We will discuss the results from tables 10.2 and 10.3 consecutively. In a few cases the results of table 10.2 and table 10.3 will be contradictory. In these cases we will let the findings of table 10.2 prevail in our interpretation, because in this table the same weight is assigned to different studies.

Findings

For parent-adolescent relationships the results are presented for each of the seven categories mentioned earlier. On the basis of the Tables, the following conclusions can be drawn.

Overall there is no association between the identity measures and the parent-adolescent relation measures (see cells 8F.B and 8F.M of table 10.2). Of the 26 bivariate studies 11 show a systematic association between parent-adolescent relations and identity and 15 do not. Of the 11 multivariate studies only 1 shows a systematic association between parent-adolescent relations and identity. The same pattern is found when we look at the number of associations (see cells 8F.B and 8F.M in table 10.3): with both bivariate and multivariate analyses, the number of non-significant associations is considerably greater than the number of positive and negative associations. In this connection it should be noted also that the number of negative associations is considerably lower than the number of positive associations. As a rule there is, also for the separate measures of parent-adolescent relations, no significant association with identity. In fact, there are no associations between:

- attachment and identity (multivariate, cell 1F.M in table 10.2 and 10.3);
- separation-individuation and identity (multivariate, cell 2F.M in both tables);
- connectedness and individuality and identity (cells 3F.B and 3F.M in both tables);
- intergenerational boundaries and identity (multivariate, cell 4F.M in both tables);
- parenting and identity (cells 5F.B and 5F.M in both tables);
- social support and identity (cell 6F.B in both tables);
- the various parent-adolescent measures and identity (cells 7F.B and 7F.M in both tables).

As to the number of studies, table 10.2 shows that bivariately there are three exceptions. Attachment, separation-individuation and intergenerational boundaries (see cells 1A.B, 2A.B and 4C.B respectively) are systematically positively associated to identity. As to the number of associations, table 10.3 shows that the same is true for attachment and intergenerational boundaries (see cells 1A.B and 4C.B), but not for separation-individuation (see cell 2A.B). Both tables show that these associations hold for specific identity measures only. Attachment and separation-individuation are associated with general identity, whereas intergenerational boundaries are associated with exploration. These positive associations between the quality of parent-adolescent relations and identity are absent in the multivariate analyses, however, where no associations emerged between attachment or separation-individuation and identity (see cells 1A.M and 2A.M in both tables). Our overview does not contain multivariate studies on intergenerational boundaries and identity.

Measured by the number of studies, no significant associations were found between the 5 distinguished identity measures and parent-adolescent relations across the various relation categories. Thus, general identity (multivariate, cell 8A.M in table 10.2), commitment (cell 8B.B), exploration (cell 8C.B), separate identity statuses (cells 8D.B and 8D.M) and between status contrasts (cell 8E.B) have no positive association with parent-adolescent relations. There is one exception, however: bivariately, general identity seems to be associated with parent-adolescent relations (cell 8A.B). When we take a closer look at the number of associations, this exception disappears and none of the 5 identity measures has an association with relation categories (see the corresponding cells in table 10.3).

Effects of sample type and type of measures

Of the 26 bivariate studies on parent-adolescent relations and identity, 9 were conducted on high schools and 17 on colleges/universities. Moreover, 13 studies used samples with a maximum of 110 respondents, 13 studies used larger samples. We checked by means of crossable analysis whether the nature and size of the sample had any influence on the association between parent-adolescent relations and identity. In these analyses we used dichotomized scores: positive associations versus the sum total of negative and non-significant associations. As to the multivariate associations, no differences due to type or size of sample were found for the number of studies, nor for the number of associations. In contrast, significant associations did appear in the bivariate associations. In the college/university studies significantly more associations were found then in the high school samples and in the large samples more than in the smaller samples, respectively $\chi^2(1, N = 290) = 45,56, p < 0,05$ en $\chi^2(1, N = 290) = 12,82, p < 0,05$. Finally, no differences in associations were found between studies that used quantitative self-report measures and studies using qualitative interview measures. This is of course mainly due to the very limited number of qualitative studies.

10.4 Discussion

The most important lesson to be learned from our review is that parent-adolescent relationships are not (strongly) related to identity development in adolescence. Relatively few positive links were found, but only between specific measures of parent-adolescent relations and specific measures of identity in bivariate designs, without replication in studies with a multivariate design.

In reviews (Marcia et al., 1993) and many empirical studies on parent-adolescent relations and identity, it is concluded that good relations with parents stimulate the development of identity. Our analyses challenge this conclusion. The number of studies in which negative or no associations were found between parent-adolescent relations and identity is superior to the number of studies in which a positive association was found. This is even more apparent in multivariate studies. With the exception of one single study, there are no associations between attachment, separation-individuation, connectedness-individuality, parenting, parental support and various measures of parent-adolescent relations and identity. This could mean that parent-adolescent relations, next to other environmental characteristics, exert no independent influence on the development of identity, or the various environmental characteristics exercise their influence at best through parent-adolescent relations. In the latter case parent-adolescent relations mediate environmental influences. On the basis of the existing research conclusions cannot be drawn, because very few studies checked mediation models.

The bivariate studies support the outcomes of the multivariate studies with regard to the association between identity and connectedness and individuality, parenting and parental support. Also bivariately there is no association between these measures of parent-adolescent relations and identity. This conclusion is an important addition to the conclusion of the multivariate studies. The absence of a bivariate association with identity makes it clear that the three measures mentioned, even cannot be considered as variables mediating environmental influences. A variable can only mediate the influence of another variable, when it has a significant association with the dependent variable. This means that of the four theoretical perspectives discussed in the introduction, the connectedness-individuality hypothesis has received the least support in the research so far. The idea of Grotevant and Cooper (1985, 1986), that a good relation between parents and children stimulates the exploration of identity alternatives, and therefore also, the development of identity, finds little empirical support. The notion that a safe and close attachment to parents incites the exploration of the environment, originates from attachment theory (Ainsworth et al., 1978). Remarkably enough this idea was not subject to study in all the five attachment studies which we included in our survey (Anderson & Fleming, 1996; Kendis & Tan, 1978; Matos et al., 1999; Quintana & Lapsley, 1987, studies 1 and 2).

This takes us to the three other theoretical perspectives from the introduction: parental attachment (Ainsworth et al., 1978), separation-individuation (Blos, 1967) and intergenerational boundaries (Fullinwider-Bush & Jacobvitz, 1993; Perosa et al., 1996). In contrast to the multivariate studies, the bivariate studies on the association between these measures of parent-adolescent relations and identity do show systematic associations. Parental attachment and separation-individuation are associated with a strongly developed sense of general identity, while intergenerational boundaries are associated with an intensive exploration of identity alternatives. This means that these measures of parent-adolescent relations can have the function of mediating variable in the prediction of general identity and exploration.

Although attachment, separation-individuation and intergenerational boundaries play a modest role in the development of identity, there is an important analogy between these perspectives. What emerges from these perspectives is the fact that both closeness to and detachment of parents can be significant for the development of identity. The idea of closeness can be found in the attachment theory and in the concept intergenerational boundaries. Attachment theory indicates that close relations with the parents can stimulate the development of identity, whereas the notion of intergenerational boundaries shows that too close relations can have negative effects. The idea of detachment is present in the separation-individuation hypothesis and also in the concept of intergenerational boundaries. The separation-individuation hypothesis states that the distancing from the image of the almighty parent is crucial for the development of identity, whereas the idea of intergenerational boundaries implies that the detachment should be within limits and that connectedness is necessary to a certain extent for the development of identity.

This is an important observation, because it characterizes the dilemma of the parent-child relationship during adolescence. Parents and children distance from each other more and more in the course of adolescence. Adolescents spend more and more time alone or with friends, without direct supervision of their parents (Larson, Richards, Moneta, Holmbeck & Duckett, 1996). At the same time they keep believing that the relation with their parents is important and they expect the contact to be more on the basis of equality (Youniss & Smollar, 1985). This points at the subtle transformation process of the parent-child relation during adolescence and this probably also explains why it is not easy to find a clear link between the nature of the parent-adolescent relationship and the development of identity. In this connection it is also relevant to note that good relations with parents hardly have a negative influence on the development of identity. The number of negative associations between parent-adolescent relations and identity is very limited.

Furthermore, it is important to note that twenty-five years of research have not made clear whether quantitative or qualitative methods should prevail in the study of parent-adolescent relations and identity. As yet, too few qualitative studies have been conducted too make a serious comparison between findings of quantitative and qualitative studies feasible. However, to our opinion this is really a matter of taste. We believe that the subtleties of parent-adolescent relations and identity formation can be captured with quantitative and qualitative methods.

To conclude this discussion, we present several somewhat more technical aspects. We showed that there are less associations between parent-adolescent relations and identity in the smaller samples than in the larger ones. Studies that use time consuming interviews, as in studies on Marcia's (1966) paradigm, usually involve small sample sizes. These studies have limited power, which makes it difficult to find significant associations. This could be one of the reasons for the absence of the association between parent-adolescent relations and identity. Aside from this, we would like to remark that an explanation is hard to give for the fact that there is a stronger association between parent-adolescent relations and identity at colleges/universities than at high schools. A second remark concerns publication culture in psychology. We showed that in the majority of the studies an association was not found between parent-adolescent relations and identity. After reading the abstracts of these studies we most certainly would not have drawn that conclusion. In the abstracts, but also in the discussion sections of the articles, there is a clear tendency to give positive associations more attention than negative or non-significant associations, which apparently can lead to the wrong conclusions.

References

Adams, G., & Jones, R. (1983). Female adolescents' identity development: Age comparisons and perceived child-rearing experience. *Developmental Psychology, 19,* 249–256.

Adams, G., Ryan, B., & Keating, L. (2000). Family relationships, academic environments and psychosocial development during the university experience: A longitudinal investigation. *Journal of Adolescent Research, 15,* 99–122.

Ainsworth, M., Blehar, M., Waters, E., & Wall, S. (1978). *Patterns of attachment: A psychological study of the strange situation.* Hillsdale, NJ: Lawrence Erlbaum.

Anderson, S., & Fleming, W. (1996). Late adolescents' home-leaving strategies: Predicting ego identity and college adjustment. *Adolescence, 21,* 453–459.

Blos, P. (1967). The second individuation process of adolescence. *Psychoanalytic Study of the Child, 22,* 162–186.

Bosma, H., & Gerrits, R. (1985). Family functioning and identity status in adolescence. *Journal of Early Adolescence, 5,* 69–80.

Bowlby, J. (1969). *Attachment and loss: Volume I. Attachment.* New York: Basic Books.

Brown, B. (1990). Peer groups. In S. Feldman, & G. Elliott (Eds.), *At the threshold: The developing adolescent* (pp. 171–196). Cambridge, MA: Harvard University Press.

Campbell, E., Adams, G., & Dobson, W. (1984). Familial correlates of identity formation in late adolescence: A study of the predictive utility of connectedness and individuality in family relations. *Journal of Youth and Adolescence, 13,* 509–525.

Cella, D., DeWolfe, A., & Fitzgibbon, M. (1987). Ego identity status, identification, and decision making style in late adolescents. *Adolescence, 22,* 849–861.

Cooper, C., & Grotevant, H. (1987). Gender issues in the interface of family experience and adolescents' friendship and dating experience. *Journal of Youth and Adolescence, 16,* 247–264.

Enright, R., Lapsley, D., Drivas, A., & Fehr, L. (1980). Parental influences on the development of adolescent autonomy and identity. *Journal of Youth and Adolescence, 9,* 529–545.

Frank, S., Pirsch, L., & Wright, V. (1990). Late adolescents' perceptions of their relationships with their parents: Relations among deidealization, autonomy, relatedness, and insecurity and implications for adolescent adjustment and ego identity status. *Journal of Youth and Adolescence, 19,* 571–588.

Fullinwider-Bush, N., & Jacobvitz, D. (1993). The transition to young adulthood: Generational boundary dissolution and female identity development. *Family Process, 32,* 87–103.

Grotevant, H. (1983). The contribution of the family to the facilitation of identity formation in early adolescence. *Journal of Early Adolescence, 3,* 225–237.

Grotevant, H., & Cooper, C. (1985). Patterns of interaction in family relationships and the development of identity exploration in adolescence. *Child Development, 56,* 415–428.

Grotevant, H., & Cooper, C. (1986). Individuation in family relationships. *Human Development, 29,* 82–100.

Kampter, N. (1988). Identity development in late adolescence: Causal modeling of social and familial influences. *Journal of Youth and Adolescence, 17,* 493–514.

Kendis, R., & Tan, A. (1978). Ego identity and perception of parents among female college students. *Perceptual and Motor Skills, 47*, 1201–1202.

Kroger, J. (1985). Separation-individuation and ego identity status in New Zealand University students. *Journal of Youth and Adolescence, 14*, 133–147.

Kroger, J., & Haslett, S.J. (1988). Separation-individuation and ego identity status in late adolescence: A two-year longitudinal study. *Journal of Youth and Adolescence, 17*, 59–79.

Larson, R., Richards, M., Moneta, G., Holmbeck, G., & Duckett, E. (1996). Changes in adolescents' daily interactions with their families from ages 10 to 18: Disengagement and transformation. *Developmental Psychology, 32*, 744–754.

LaVoie, J.C. (1976). Ego identity formation in middle adolescence. *Journal of Youth and Adolescence, 5*, 371–385.

Lopez, F. (1989). Current family dynamics, trait anxiety, and academic adjustment: Test of a family based model of vocational identity. *Journal of Vocational Behavior, 35*, 76–87.

Marcia, J.E. (1966). Development and validation of ego-identity status. *Journal of Personality and Social Psychology, 3*, 551–558.

Marcia, J.E. (1980). Identity in adolescence. In J. Adelson (Ed.), *Handbook of adolescent psychology* (pp. 159–187). New York: Wiley.

Marcia, J.E. (1983). Some directions for the investigation of ego development in early adolescence. *Journal of Early Adolescence, 3*, 215–223.

Marcia, J.E., Waterman, A.S., Matteson, D.R., Archer, S., & Orlofsky, J.L. (1993). *Ego identity*. New York: Springer Verlag.

Matos, P., Barbosa, S., De Almeida, H., & Costa, M. (1999). Parental attachment and identity in Portuguese late adolescents. *Journal of Adolescence, 22*, 805–818.

Nelson, W., Hughes, H., Handal, P., Katz, B., & Searight, H. (1993). The relationship of family structure and family conflict to adjustment in young adult college students. *Adolescence, 28*, 29–40.

O'Connor, B. (1995). Identity development and perceived parental behavior as sources of adolescent egocentrism. *Journal of Youth and Adolescence, 24*, 205–228.

Palladino-Schultheiss, D., & Blustein, D. (1994). Contributions of family relationship factors to the identity formation process. *Journal of Counseling and Development, 73*, 159–166.

Perosa, L., Perosa, S., & Tam, H. (1996). The contribution of family structure and differentiation to identity development in females. *Journal of Youth and Adolescence, 25*, 817–837.

Quintana, S., & Lapsley, D. (1987). Adolescent attachment and ego identity: A structural equations approach to the continuity of adaptation. *Journal of Adolescent Research, 2*, 393–409.

Waterman, A.S. (1982). Identity development from adolescence to adulthood: an extension of theory and a review of research. *Developmental Psychology, 18*, 342–358.

Youniss, J., & Smollar, J. (1985). *Adolescent relations with mothers, fathers, and friends*. Chicago: University of Chicago Press.

Chapter 11

Well-diffused? Identity Diffusion and Well-being in Emerging Adulthood

Aristi Born
University of Magdeburg
Germany

While Erikson (1959/1980) focuses on Identity Diffusion as the adverse pole of an achieved Identity, Diffusion can also be seen functioning with regard to the variable social and cultural conditions of emerging adulthood (Arnett, 2000). If commitments are loose and exploration engagement is low, one does not risk losing very much and stays flexible towards new opportunities (Krappmann, 1997). Marcia (1989) noticed a dramatic increase of Identity Diffusion among students already in the second half of the 1980s. He suggested splitting Identity Diffusion into four subgroups: *disturbed, carefree, developmental and culturally adaptive Diffusion.* In this study, a questionnaire was formulated to differentiate between the four subgroups and analyze their correlations with personal resources (self-efficacy, self-esteem) and subjective well-being. The results show evidence for differentiating between the different varieties of Identity Diffusion, but they do not prove the general functionality of a diffuse identity status in emerging adulthood.

11.1   Identity diffusion à la Erikson

In Erik H. Erikson's fundamental identity concept (1959/1980), he defines identity as a "direct perception of one's own consistency and continuity over time
[. . .] and the associated perception that others, as well, recognize this consistency and continuity" (p. 18). Based on this definition, identity is connected to a
striving for coherence and congruence throughout life. If the individual is not
able to integrate the contrasts and differences within the perceived and socially
mediated self in different situational contexts as well as over the course of time,
the incompatible elements stay separate and confused. This adverse pole of
Identity Achievement is called *Identity Diffusion*. Identity diffused people do not
interpret their experiences in a subjective and synthetic way. They are confused
concerning their ideas about such things as goals, occupations, sexual identity,
and gender roles. Erikson illustrates Identity Diffusion with a character in Arthur
Miller's "Death of a Salesman" (1949, cited in Erikson, 1959/1980): Biff, the
oldest son of the salesman, once a football star at high school for whom his father had great dreams, but for the last fourteen years unable to find himself, tells
his mother: "I just can't take hold of some kind of a life" (p. 91).

11.2   Identity diffusion à la James E. Marcia

According to the Ego Identity Status approach of James E. Marcia (Marcia
1966/1993a), people differ in their critical exploration and commitment in developing their own identity. Marcia describes identity development as changes
between four empirically confirmed identity statuses. It is possible to move from
one status to another all through one's life-span. Persons with conferred identities are called *Foreclosure* individuals. They often cling to parentally determined convictions, but do not engage in exploring different alternatives on their
own. Those with self-constructed and coherent commitments will be referred to
as *Identity Achievement* individuals. Persons who are in transition from conferred to self-explored commitments are called *Moratorium* individuals, and
those with low firm commitments towards personal beliefs and low critical exploration are categorized as Identity Diffusion individuals. *Identity Diffusion*
persons do not always care about their lack of commitment.

Different studies, summarized by Marcia (1993b), have shown that Diffusions, compared to the other three statuses, are high in anxiety, low in self-
esteem, low in autonomy and high in conformity. They have an external locus of
control, are more compliant to external pressure and are the most frequent drug
users. Diffuse people are low in moral development and cognitive performance
under stress, but they have an extremely complex, perhaps disorganized cognitive system. Their capacity for intimacy is low and they are more likely to use
bribes and deception to gain social influence. Diffusions report their families to
be more distant and rejecting. Kroger (1990, see Marcia, 1993b) found Diffuse

college students in New Zealand less secure and more anxiously attached to their parents. In adulthood, other studies presented Diffusion women as most masculine and less satisfied with marriage and parenting. In my own studies in Germany (Born, 2002), I found negative correlations between Diffusion and satisfaction with one's vocational, financial, interpersonal and health-related situation.

11.3   Different types of identity diffusion

Marcia (1989) noticed a dramatic increase of college students who were categorized as Diffusions from 20% in 1984 to 40% in 1989 in Western Canada as well as in the Eastern part of the United States. He perceived "a range of adaptability" (Marcia, 1989, p. 290) among his Identity Diffusions and pled for a reconceptualization and differentiation of this status. The Identity Diffusions in terms of Erikson, characterized by a discontinuous, inconsistent and not cohesive self-definition, are forming just one subgroup of Diffusion, called *disturbed Diffusion*. They are not pathologically affected like the self-fragmented borderline personality, but resemble a lonesome, possibly schizoid, maverick, "an isolated figure who might seek solace in fantasies of greatness or of having been greatly injured" (Marcia, 1989, p. 291). In contrast, the *carefree Diffused* is interpersonally skilled, especially in shortterm relationships. This type is an attractive partner for short projects, which do not call for strong commitment or reveal the person's inner emptiness. *Developmental Diffusions* are on their way to Identity Achievement, not vacant like the carefree or disturbed Diffused, but still indecisive about personal commitments. In contrast to Moratoriums they do not actively struggle with alternative points of view and do not invest much energy in exploring them. Marcia (1989) describes them as healthy and adaptive – "they are giving themselves a significant chance to think and to explore alternatives"– in a deliberate way. Another adaptive type is the *culturally adaptive Diffusion*. It is adaptive to a political-economic situation that calls for flexibility, such as that with which late adolescents and young adults especially are often confronted. Commitments are not functional when the situation requires quick adaptations to a variety of settings, and exploration is maladaptive if there are no viable alternatives. *Culturally adaptive Diffusions* have the potential to explore alternative ways and to make and commitments, but in their actual situation it is non-adaptive. As *culturally adaptive Diffusions* they are "able to jump at the first (or the next) opportunity" (Marcia, 1989, p. 292).

Kraus & Mitzscherlich (1995) observed similar identity types using a discursive analytical approach based on semi-structured interviews. In their project, 160 young adults between 18 and 22 years in East (Saxony) and West Germany (Bavaria) were interviewed about self-image, work and social network (see Kraus in this volume). In the terminology used by Kraus & Mitzscherlich (1995), the Carefree Diffusion type is a *Surfer* who changes positions easily out of aesthetic and hedonistic motives. Surfers were mainly young men in West German conurbations. The Disturbed Diffusion type is called the *Isolated*, not surfing but lost in the sea of possibilities, disoriented, lonesome and with low resources. Isolated were men and women without a continuous occupation who compensate their state of inner conflict with a special commitment to chosen hobbies. The third type of Kraus & Mizscherlich (1995) is a *Traditional* type, who is superficial and unreflected "normal". *Traditionals* stick to clichés, because they do not want to explore complex alternatives. The authors doubt if this "foggy" Diffusion type is a developmental stage or cultural adaptive.

11.4 The functionality of identity diffusion in emerging adulthood

The North American culture tends to have an ideology of individualism and a prolonged period of education (Arnett, 2000). Similar developments can be noticed in many European countries as well. In Germany, for example, we had 1,97 million students, including 356,000 freshmen, in the university winter term 2004/2005, of the latter, 37.3% were from the same age group (Federal Statistical Office Germany, 2004). That is 12% more than 1993. Because competition for jobs is fierce, more time is being invested in education. Many twentysomethings are in an extended adolescence and may not become full adults until they reach their mid-20s or even later, because they cannot follow clear guidelines to adulthood. More than 50% of emerging adults between 18 and 25 years answered the question, "Do you feel that you have reached adulthood?" with "Yes and no" (Arnett, 2000). In a German study (Born, 2003), 61.9% of the students and 50% of the non-students in this age period chose the ambivalent answer "yes and no" to this question.

Erik H. Erikson (Erikson, 1980) focuses on Diffusion as the opposite pole of a successful identity development, but under the variable social and cultural conditions in *emerging adulthood*, esp. the renunciation of clear societal norms and orientations, Diffusion can be seen functioning as well. New opportunities are easier to seize if commitments are loose and the exploration engagement is low (Krappmann, 1997).

Is it possible for emerging adults to be *"well-diffused"*? In this study, a questionnaire was formulated to differentiate between the four subgroups of Identity Diffusion ("Diffusion Questionnaire") and find out about their correlations with subjective well-being and the personal resources self-efficacy and self-esteem. Self-esteem relates to a person's sense of self-worth (Rodewalt & Tragakis, 2003), whereas self-efficacy relates to a person's perception of their ability to reach a goal (Bandura, 1977).

11.5 Hypothesis

The intention of this paper is to report on the construction and discuss the quality of the "Diffusion Questionnaire". Based on Marcia (1989) and Kraus & Mitzscherlich (1995) the following assumptions exist concerning the correlations of the four Diffusion subgroups with self-efficacy, self-esteem and subjective well-being:

1. The *disturbed Diffusions* are low on resources and suffer from their lack of social competence. There are negative correlations with self-efficacy, self-esteem and well-being.
2. The *carefree Diffusions* are reacting in a hedonistic way to external conditions. There are possibly negative correlations with self-efficacy, but positive correlations with self-esteem and well-being.
3. The *developmental Diffusions* are on their way to exploration and/or to becoming committed, but do not undergo a crisis like the Moratoriums. There is a tendency to positive correlations with well-being, self-esteem and self-efficacy.
4. The *culturally adaptive Diffusions* have the potential to adapt to actual conditions, but in a self-determined way and without inner conflict. There are positive correlations with self-efficacy, self-esteem and well-being.

11.6 Methods

Grounded in the theoretical work of Marcia (1989) as well as Kraus & Mitzscherlich (1995), 18 psychology students in four groups constructed twelve items for each Diffusion subgroup, concerning friendship and studies/work. Following Kroger (2000), these two domains are very relevant for self-related concerns in young adulthood. The final questionnaire contains the 48 items (six per subgroup and domain) which could be best classified as belonging to its special scale by the different student-groups (see figure 11.1 for an English translation of the German version).

Furthermore, sociodemographic data (sex, age, subject of studies, marital status, number of children, number of friends and acquaintances), the personal resources self-esteem (Rosenberg's scale in a German translation by Janich & Boll, 1982) and self-efficacy (Bandura's scale in a German translation by Schwarzer, 2000) as well as subjective well-being (Becker, 1989) were obtained. All items were collected using a five-point Likert-scale.

148 men (40%) and 224 women (60%) answered the questionnaire at the beginning of a lecture. Most of them studied economics (N=275), the others were students of different social sciences (N=97). The age mean was 21.9 years

for the female and 23.0 years for the male students. 95.4% were not yet married, but 28.9% lived with a partner. 96% had no children so far.

DISTURBED DIFFUSION

Friendship

1. I don't feel acknowledged by other people.
2. I spend most of my time alone.
3. I was hurt too often in the past to believe in real friendship anymore.
4. I feel less comfortable when I have to be with other people than when I'm by myself.
5. I don't dare speak to people.

6. What others say about my hobby is not important for me. (excluded)

Studies/Work

1. I prefer to work alone, because others don't like me.
2. No matter what I do, nobody pays attention to me.
3. I wonder why I actually study –I won't find a job anyway.
4. One day, everybody will wonder when I'll achieve something great. (excluded)
5. I prefer jobs I can organize by myself, because others don't appreciate my work.
6. I doubt very much that my subject was the right choice.

CAREFREE DIFFUSION

Friendship

1. I have a lot of short relationships.
2. People have fun with me.
3. I have a big and often changing circle of friends.
4. It is easy for me to make friends.
5. I am a party animal.
6. I have quite a number of loose relationships, but no close friends. (excluded)

Studies/Work

1. If I don't enjoy my job, I look for another one. (excluded)
2. Professional obligations terrify me. (excluded)
3. Some time or other, the right job will come up for me.
4. I don't know yet what to do vocationally, the main thing is it's fun.
5. It would be boring to do the same job all my life.
6. I don't care if I can't find a job right after I finish university. (excluded)

DEVELOPMENTAL DIFFUSION

Friendship

1. I am not sure if my friends suit me.
2. One day I will know who my close friends are.
3. At present I think a lot about what makes a good friendship.

Studies/Work

1. I have no concrete reason why I decided to opt for the subject I did.
2. Right now I can't say if my subject is the right one for me.
3. I don't know yet what do to after university, but I will find out.

4. I will find out if my friends are the right ones for me.
5. Lately I have been worried about my past and future relationships.
6. I'm increasingly noticing that a lot of my friendships are just superficial.

4. It will become clear what the right job for me is.
5. At the moment, I can't decide in which direction I want to go vocationally.
6. I still want to try many things at university, maybe I can find out what is suitable for me.

CULTURALLY ADAPTIVE DIFFUSION

Friendship

1. I am very busy, that's why I don't have time for intensive friendships. (excluded)
2. If I have enough time, friends can rely on me. (excluded)
3. After a relationship has split up, I don't mourn for it for long, but look for new opportunities.
4. Friends are important, but I don't get too attached. (excluded)
5. I look for friends wherever I happen to be. (excluded)
6. To my mind, friendship is connected with flexibility and adaptability. (excluded)

Studies/Work

1. I am very flexible with regard to my job.
2. For a good job, I don't mind moving around.
3. I leave my vocational situation open for any good opportunity.
4. I have no problem jumping into an ongoing project.
5. If there is a good chance for me in my job, I don't hesitate to take it.
6. I can imagine working in very different jobs in my life.

Note: (excluded) means this item was eliminated due to low and unspecific factor-loadings and a low corrected item-total-correlation.

Figure 11.1: *Operationalization of the four subgroups of Identity Diffusion*

11.7 Results

With regard to the results of *confirmatory factor analysis* (orthogonal rotation) and reliability analysis of our self-constructed Diffusion scales, we decided to eliminate items with low and unspecific factor-loadings and a corrected item-total-correlation lower than .30 (see figure 11.1). *Internal consistency* due to Cronbach-Alpha was finally .57 for carefree Diffusion (9 items), .79 for disturbed Diffusion (10 items), .64 for cultural adaptive Diffusion (7 items) and .78 for developmental Diffusion (12 items). It was .85 for the self-efficacy scale (10 items), .82 for the self-esteem scale (10 items) and .90 for the subjective well-being scale (19 items).

Figure 11.2 shows the *scale means* for the Diffusion subgroups according to the life domains friendship and studies/work.

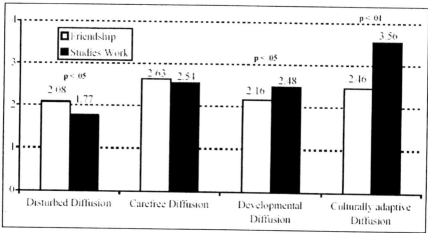

Figure 11.2: *Scale means for the Diffusion subgroups according to life domain*

On a five-point Likert scale, the scale means for disturbed Diffusion are relatively low, significantly lower for the life domain work/studies. The scale means for carefree Diffusion are slightly above the arithmetical scale median of 2.5 for both domains. The scale means for developmental Diffusion are slightly below 2.5, significantly lower for the life domain friendship. The scale mean for culturally adaptive Diffusion for the life domain friendship almost hits 2.5, whereas the scale mean for the life domain studies/work is significantly higher and the highest scale mean of all.

There are some *sociodemographic effects* on the Diffusion subgroups. With regard to the life domain friendship, men are more carefree Diffused (the mean for 146 men was 2.88, the mean for 224 women was 2.72, T = 2.50, p < .05) and more culturally adaptive Diffused (the mean for 145 men was 3.08, the mean for 223 women was 2.57, T = 4.17, p < .001) than women. Participants who are living with a partner have lower Diffusion values concerning all Diffusion subgroups than singles: developmental Diffusion (the mean for 260 single persons was 2.25, the mean for 106 persons with a partner was 1.93, T = -3.84, p < .001, domain friendship; the mean for 260 single persons was 2.57, the mean for 106 persons with a partner was 2.23, T = -3.76, p < .001, domain studies/work), culturally adaptive Diffusion (the mean for 261 single persons was 3.60, the mean for 106 persons with a partner was 3.45, T = -2.07, p < .05, domain studies/work), disturbed Diffusion (the mean for 260 single persons was 1.82, the mean for 106 persons with a partner was 1.67, T = -31.99, p < .05, domain friendship) and carefree Diffusion (the mean for 260 single persons was 3.09, the mean for 106 persons with a partner was 2.71, T = -4.10, p < .001, domain studies/work). The number of persons you visit at their home and invite to your home is positively correlated with culturally adaptive Diffusion (r = .12, p < .05, domain studies/work) and negatively correlated with disturbed Diffusion (r = -.25, p < .01, domain friendship; r = -.14, p < .01, domain studies/work) and developmental Diffusion (r = -.18, p < .01, domain friendship). The number of persons you arrange to meet at least once a month is positively correlated with culturally adaptive Diffusion (r = .20, p < .01, domain friendship; r = .13, p < .05, domain studies/work) and carefree Diffusion (r = .23, p < .01, domain friendship). It is negatively correlated with disturbed Diffusion (r = -.26, p < .01, domain friendship; r = -.21, p < .01, domain studies/work) and developmental Diffusion (r = -.17, p < .01, domain friendship). . Age is negatively correlated with developmental Diffusion (r = -.25, p < .01, domain studies/work) and carefree Diffusion (r = -.17, p < .01, domain studies/work).

Table 11.1

Pearson correlation coefficients (r) between the Diffusion subgroups by life domain, self-efficacy, self-esteem and subjective well-being.

Diffusion subgroup Life Domain	Self-efficacy	Self-esteem	Well-being
Disturbed Diffusion			
Friendship	-.33***	-.34***	-.52***
Studies/Work	-.26***	-.32***	-.46***
Carefree Diffusion			
Friendship	.23***	.14**	.16**
Studies/Work	n.s.	n.s.	-.17**
Developmental Diffusion			
Friendship	-.29***	-.30***	-.45***
Studies/Work	-.17**	n.s.	-.26***
Culturally adaptive Diffusion			
Friendship	.13*	n.s.	n.s.
Studies/Work	.17**	.14**	.16**

Notes. * = p < .05, ** = p < .01, *** = p < .001, n.s. = not significant.

Table 11.1 shows the *Pearson correlation coefficients (r)* between the Diffusion subgroups, self-efficacy, self-esteem and subjective well-being.

Disturbed Diffusion correlates significantly with self-esteem, self-efficacy and well-being in both life domains. Carefree Diffusion correlates positively with self-esteem, self-efficacy and well-being only with regard to the domain friendship. There is a negative correlation between carefree Diffusion in the domain studies/work and subjective well-being. Developmental Diffusion correlates in both life domains negatively with self-esteem, self-efficacy and well-being (only in the life domain friendship). The correlations between culturally adaptive Diffusion and self-esteem, self-efficacy and well-being are positive only with regard to the domain studies/work.

11.8 Conclusions

Despite different psychometric qualities of the four Diffusion scales, most correlations between the differentiated Diffusion scales, self-efficacy, self-esteem and well-being were theoretically coherent. They can be seen as an initial reference for the construct validity of the four Diffusion subgroup scales. The results show *evidence for differentiating between* the different varieties of Identity Diffusion, but they do not prove a general functionality of a diffuse identity status in young adulthood. There are positive and negative correlations between Diffusion, self-efficacy, self-esteem and well-being, depending on subgroup and life domain.

Without exception there were strong negative correlations between *disturbed Diffusion* self-efficacy, self-esteem and well-being for both life domains. They correspond with Marcia's description of this Diffusion subgroup which resembles the Identity Diffusion à la Erikson. It is characterized by low personal and social resources due to a discontinuous, inconsistent and not cohesive self-definition. The negative correlation between the number of friends and the disturbed Diffusion shows the loneliness of this type. Participants who are living without a partner have even higher Diffusion values than participants living with a partner. The disturbed Diffusion scale had the lowest scale mean compared with the other three subgroups, which can be seen as a sign that this dysfunctional Diffusion type is relatively low in emerging adults. This is probably an effect of social desirability which would be more avoidable in a qualitative interview. The Diffusion Questionnaire could not reflect the fantasies of greatness and the hobby engagement to compensate the inner emptiness. These two items were excluded because they reduced the internal consistency. In this case, content heterogeneity was limited for a more homogeneous and reliable scale.

The results concerning *carefree Diffusion* conform with the hypothesis only in the life domain friendship and only with regard to self-esteem and well-being. Here, the correlations between carefree Diffusion, self-efficacy, self-esteem and well-being were all positive. There was no expected negative correlation between carefree Diffuison and self-efficacy. It seems that carefree Diffusions change positions easily, but believe in their capabilities to execute the courses of social actions required to manage prospective situations in the domain friendship. They have quite a lot of friends they arrange to meet at least once a month. But with regard to the domain studies/work there were no significant correlations with personal resources and a negative correlation with subjective well-being. Carefree Diffusion is probably adaptive for the social life domain of emerging adults, who are still ambivalent. They explore their potential for emotional and physical intimacy but still avoid strong commitments like marriage or the responsibility of parenthood (Arnett, 2000), especially when they are not living with a partner. Carefree diffusion is not adaptive with regard to subjective well-being for the life domain studies/work, because competition for jobs is fierce and the carefree hedonism in this domain is limited. Emerging adults are open to new opportunities, but they care about education and a good job. That is what the items of the carefree Diffusion scale reflect. The results do not show that carefree Diffusions are personally competent with high self-esteem in the life domain studies/work. With regard to this domain, it may be difficult to build a belief of inner competence if you are a surfer in the sea of opportunities. Carefree Diffusion decreases when emerging adults are getting older or start living with a partner. It seems, that carefree Diffusion is more adaptive in early adulthood. Men have higher scale means in both life domains than women, which goes along with the findings of Kraus & Mitzscherlich (1995) that the surfer is rare but in most cases male. Emerging men probably have to care less about social and vocational commitments than emerging women.

Developmental Diffusions show significant negative correlations with self-efficacy, self-esteem (not for the domain studies/work) and well-being. This is not conform with the hypothesis, which was formulated in accordance to Marcia (1989), who described the developmental Diffusions as a healthy and adaptive subgroup. They are deliberately exploring their way to Identity Achievement, but do not struggle with alternatives like Moratoriums. They are probably on their way, which is not comfortable at the moment. They doubt their personal resources right now but their actual situation implies identity development, stronger personal resources and well-being in the future. It would be interesting to follow this subgroup longitudinally. Developmental Diffusion is correlated negatively with age and the number of friends (in the domain friendship). Participants who are living with a partner have lower values concerning developmental Diffusion than singles. In the Diffusion questionnaire this subgroup was measured by twelve items. Eliminations due to low and unspecific factor-loadings and a low corrected item-total-correlation were not necessary.

The *culturally adaptive Diffusion* seems to be more adaptive with regard to the life domain studies/work. In the life domain friendship, there is only one positive correlation with self-efficacy that indicates the belief in personal competences. Men have higher scale means than women. Young single adult women more frequently consult friends and their friendships are more intimate than men's interactions with friends (Kroger, 2000). Therefore culturally adaptive Diffusion seems less adaptive in women's social life. For the life domain friendship, the Diffusion questionnaire fails to measure the core of the construct in a reliable way. But in the life domain studies/work, culturally adaptive Diffusion was measured without item elimination in a consistent way and has the highest scale mean at all. It is adaptive to a vocational situation that calls for flexibility. Culturally adaptive Diffusions have the potential to make commitments, but actually they are not functional because the situation requires quick adaptations to a variety of settings. Culturally adaptive Diffusion (studies/work) is higher for single persons than for participants who are living with a partner and cannot jump independently at the first opportunity. Culturally adaptive Diffusion is positively correlated with the number of friends. Culturally adaptive Diffusions are probably socially competent and good at networking. This subgroup shows that Diffusion can be functional and adaptive in emerging adulthood, at least for the domain studies/work.

Exploration and commitment to self-elaborated beliefs, which are characteristic for an achieved identity, are probably more fruitful and constructive in young adulthood than "surfing around in the ocean of opportunities". Achieved identity goes along with a balanced relation of accommodative and assimilative processes (Whitbourne, 1996). These people know how to integrate new experiences in their self-theory and are able to use their self-conception to structure experiences. Achievement individuals know how they became who they are and have developed useful skills for the adaptive process of further identity regulation during adulthood.

This study will hopefully stimulate *further research* into the necessity of exploration and commitment in emerging adulthood for further identity regulation. The next step could be the optimization of the questionnaire. An ideal way to do this would be a longitudinal examination of a representative sample with the Diffusion questionnaire and a combination of quantitative and qualitative identity measures.

References

Arnett, J.J. (2000). Emerging adulthood: A theory of development from the late teens through the twenties. *American Psychologist, 55* (5), 481–487.

Bandura, A. (1977). Self-efficacy: Toward a unifying theory of behavioral change. *Psychological Review, 84*, 191–215.

Becker, P. (1989). *Trierer Persönlichkeitsfragebogen* [Trier personality questionnaire]. Göttingen: Hogrefe.

Born, A. (2002). *Regulation persönlicher Identität im Rahmen gesellschaftlicher Transformationsbewältigung* [Regulation of personal identity within the context of coping with social transformation]. Waxmann: Münster.

Born, A. (2003, November). *Developmental tasks and resources in transition to adulthood.* Poster presentation at the 1st conference on emerging adulthood, Harvard University, Cambridge, MA.

Erikson, E.H. (1980). *Identity and the life cycle* (2nd ed.). New York: Norton.

Janich, H. & Boll, T. (1982). *Übersetzung des Self-Esteem-Fragebogens von Rosenberg (1965)* [Translation of the self-esteem questionnaires from Rosenberg (1965)]. Trier: Universität Trier, Fachbereich I –Psychologie (unpublished manuscript).

Krappmann, L. (1997). Die Identitätsproblematik nach Erikson aus einer interaktionistischen Sicht [The identity discourse according to Erikson from an interactionistic point of view]. In H. Keupp & R. Höfer (Eds.), *Identitätsarbeit heute* (pp. 66–92). Frankfurt am Main: Suhrkamp.

Kraus, W. & Mitzscherlich, B. (1995). Identitätsdiffusion als kulturelle Anpassungsleistung [Identity diffusion as a cultural adaptation]. *Psychologie in Erziehung und Unterricht, 42*, 65–72.

Kroger, J. (2000). *Identity development: Adolescence through adulthood.* London: Sage.

Marcia, J.E. (1989). Identity diffusion differentiated. In M.A. Luszcz, & T. Nettelbeck (Eds.), *Psychological development: Perspectives across the life-span* (pp. 289–295). North-Holland: Elsevier.

Marcia, J.E. (1993a). The ego identity status approach to ego identity. In J.E. Marcia, A.S. Waterman, D.R. Matteson, S.L. Archer, & J.L. Orlofsky (Eds.), *Ego identity: a handbook for psychosocial research* (pp. 3–21). New York: Springer.

Marcia, J.E. (1993b). The status of the statuses: Research review. In J.E. Marcia, A.S. Waterman, D.R. Matteson, S.L. Archer, & J.L. Orlofsky (Eds.), *Ego identity: a handbook for psychosocial research* (pp. 22–41). New York: Springer.

Rodewalt, F., & Tragakis, M.W. (2003). Self-esteem and self-regulation: Toward optimal studies of self-esteem. *Psychological Inquiry, 14*, 66–70.

Schwarzer, R. (2000). *Stress, Angst und Handlungsregulation* [Stress, anxiety and the regulation of acting]. Stuttgart: Kohlhammer.

Whitbourne, S.K. (1996). Psychosocial perspectives on emotions: The role of identity in the aging process. In C. Magai, & S.H. McFadden (Eds.), *Handbook of emotion, adult development, and aging* (pp. 83–98). San Diego: Academic Press.

Chapter 12

Continuity, Change, and Mechanisms of Identity Development

Olaf Reis
University of Rostock
Germany

James Youniss and Hugh McIntosh
Catholic University of America
Washington D.C., USA

Jens Eisermann,
Free University of Berlin
Germany

This essay emphasizes the need to study developmental changes in identity and their underlying causes. Three studies are reviewed, each using a person-oriented analysis to find developmental trajectories in U.S. high school students as described by the identity scale of the Erikson Psychosocial Stage Inventory (Rosenthal, Gurney, & Moore, 1981). Both change and continuity were found during adolescence, but continuity prevailed during emerging adulthood. The data allow for the interpretation that different mechanisms are associated with continuous or changing identity trajectories. Self-fulfilling prophecies and self-chosen social companions seemed to explain continuity on a high level of identity clarity. Nonaccomplished developmental tasks, such as individuation from mother and friends, explained decreases in identity clarity.

12.1 Continuity, change, and mechanisms of identity development

The development of an ego identity is one of the most complex goals a person can achieve over the life course. This complexity is part of the construct itself. Since Erikson laid out a blueprint, this construct has been developed and operationalized in many different ways. According to Marcia (see chapter 1 this book), identity can be looked at from five different perspectives. From the beginning identity research sensu Erikson was approached via qualitative and quantitative methods. Questionnaire methods offered the advantage of administration to large samples in a short amount of time. Moreover, identity was conceptualized as a continuum, measurable by either Likert scales or Q-sort techniques (Wessman & Ricks, 1966).

One such questionnaire is the Erikson Psychosocial Stage Inventory (EPSI) by Rosenthal, Gurney, and Moore (1981). This questionnaire tries to operationalize the first six stages of Erikson's eight-stage model of psychosocial development, of which we used the identity scale (stage five). Each stage is assessed with 12 items, half of which reflect successful and half unsuccessful resolutions of the crisis associated with the stage (see table 12.1).

Table 12.1

Items of the EPSI identity scale (Rosenthal, Gurney, & Moore, 1981)

1. I've got a clear idea of what I want to be.
2. I've got it together.
3. I like myself and am proud of what I stand for.
4. I can't decide what I want to do with my life.*
5. I find I have to keep up a front when I'm with people.*
6. I know what kind of person I am.
7. I don't really feel involved.*
8. The important things in life are clear to me.
9. I feel mixed up.*
10. I don't really know what I'm on about.*
11. I change my opinion of myself a lot.*
12. I have a strong sense of what it means to be female/male.

Note. * = reversed items.

The items of the identity scale are oriented toward the crisis, which might be called "clarity about the self." For our analyses we omitted the item "I have a strong sense of what it means to be female/male" because it significantly reduced internal consistency (Reis & Youniss, 2004). For several items, we altered the wording slightly to make them more understandable to U.S. students. Respondents were asked to chose one of five possible answers from a Likert rating scale with the positions "strongly disagree" (1) to "strongly agree" (5).

We agree with Marcia and others that identity is more than just the visible coherence of items and, taking this reduction of our operationalization into account, we want to stress a second kind of complexity regarding identity development. Different mechanisms of the interaction between individuals and the environment may account for different trajectories in identity development.

Trajectories of identity development

Before we hypothesize about possible mechanisms, a few words should be said about identity development, ways of measurement, and data. First, development can be seen in different kinds of change. All kinds of change described by Craik (1993) for personality development may occur for identity, also. Identity may become "accentuated" by certain challenges, fundamentally change in structure and level, or change only in one facet. All these kinds of changes may be operationalized within qualitative or quantitative ways of measurement. As von Eye (2006) pointed out, both kinds of data, either qualitative or quantitative, might be used for exploration of the data or for confirming a set of a-priori hypotheses. In our view, it matters less whether a researcher uses categorical or continuous data. Of more importance is whether the data are used for exploratory or confirmatory purposes, or both (von Eye, 2006). For identity research, a mixture of both might be most appropriate (von Eye, 2006).

Exploratory as well as confirmatory studies of identity development have to deal with the problem that identity development is, at least in part, an unconscious, hidden process. Even if measurement of identity indicates continuity, identity might still "develop". First of all, quantitative comparisons of group means may indicate a kind of "*absolute* continuity" (Caspi & Roberts, 2001) which might mask intraindividual changes of various kinds. Absolute continuity might also be a problem within a more qualitative approach of identity measurement. For instance, a person who displays a continuous identity status in Marcia's sense, let us say a "moratorium", might be stable in absolute terms, but might fall behind if the sample of reference as a whole moves on to "achievement."

For that reason, identity development should also be investigated as *differential* continuity or change as suggested for personality development. Differential continuity means the consistency of individual differences within a sample of reference over time. Samples of reference may include persons of the same age, gender, or social class. In quantitative designs differential continuity is most often operationalized by correlation coefficients (Caspi & Roberts, 2001). This paper describes this method, but also introduces differential continuity modeled within a qualitative design, here as latent classes of patterns of change.

Structural continuity in the sense of Caspi and Roberts (2001) regards the composition of identity ingredients and will not be discussed in this paper. Examples for studies analyzing structural continuity are the papers of Goosens (chapter 8 this book) and Meeus (chapter 10 this book) studying the ratio of exploration versus commitment processes over time. The idea of structural continuity versus change was captured with the introduction of different identity styles (Berzonsky, 1992).

Research about absolute, differential, and structural continuity requires longitudinal data. Bosma and Kunnen (2001) have recommended that trajectories of identity might be developmentally more informative than statuses. Statuses may indicate the cumulative impact of experience at a given moment in time, and therefore they give a good description of individual needs and are very informative with regard to possible interventions. Statuses, however, do not tell us about the developmental course an individual may have traversed to reach the present state. To overcome this shortcoming, several researchers (Waterman, 1993) charted identity trajectories as sequences of statuses, thus, highlighting how individuals arrived at different statuses.

Development and context

According to Erikson (1968), transitions in context (for example, major life span changes) are occasions for intraindividual transitions from one identity status to another. This view calls for attention to continuity and change instead of a focus on momentary status. Bosma and Kunnen (2001) point out that trajectories of identity are informative from a transactional perspective. Identity development as a product of person-environment-person-transactions was highlighted by different approaches of identity research. Concepts that contain processes of comparison, such as Tajfel's concept (1982), or see identity as "capital" (Coté, 2002), emphasize the transaction between society and the inner self. Pals (2001) describes identity as an opportunity to contextualize personality development because identity is an even more "social" construct than personality is. For a full transactional model, certain requirements have to be fulfilled (Asendorpf & Wilpers, 1998): Continuity and change in both the individual and its context need to be monitored. There should be opportunities to connect change or stability in one domain with change or stability in another. Thus, cross-lagged-panel analyses become important in order to determine whether changes in context pace changes in statuses (Asendorpf & Wilpers, 1998).

12.2 Method

The identity scale of the EPSI (Rosenthal et al., 1981) was used in the three studies that are reported here. Each study operationalized continuity and change in a different way. In study A (Reis & Youniss, 2004; Youniss & Reis, 2001), identity trajectories were modeled as clusters of trajectories over a 3-year period from the sophomore to the senior year of high school. In study B (McIntosh,

Metz, & Youniss, 2005), students were assigned to identity trajectories using the sophomore year as the starting level, after which differences scores were computed with focus again on changes from Grade 10 to Grade 12. In study C (Reis, Eisermann, Azmitia, & Tonyan, 2006), latent classes of identity were measured in quartile distributions for fall, winter, and spring terms during the first year of college.

Samples and measures

Studies A and B were conducted to investigate effects of social service among high school students. Both studies also included measures of social support from family and friends and of identity clarity. Study A was conducted in two private Catholic high schools in the Washington, DC, suburbs. Students (N = 294) mostly came from middle- to upper-income families and were predominantly of European American descent. Measures of social support used in the first study are described in Ruth (2001). Participants also answered questions regarding developmental opportunities and challenges they experienced in doing service. These were measured by students' ratings of statements about their service such as "It helped me see the world in a new way," "It showed me I could do things I never thought I could do," and "I changed some of my beliefs and attitudes."

Participants of study B (N = 173) came from a suburban middle-class public high school near Boston. About 75% of the sample was of European American descent. Along with measures of community service, data were collected regarding peer relationships, crowd membership, family relations, personality, and extracurricular activities. A more detailed description of the measures is reported in Metz, McLellan, and Youniss (2003).

Study C was conducted to explore risks and protective factors of integration into college life during the first year at a major California university. About 35% of the sample (N = 150) was of European American descent, while other participants were of different ethnicities (24% Latino/Chicano, 28% Asian American or Filipino, 8% African American, 3% Native American, and others. Participants were on average 18.2 years old and predominantly female (61%).

12.3 Major findings

Continuity and change in identity development

Studies A and C dealt with empirically derived trajectories of identity. Therefore, the trajectories can be regarded as results themselves. In study A (Reis & Youniss, 2004; Youniss & Reis, 2001), four clusters of trajectories were found. One group consisted of persons who started and remained on a high level of identity clarity (42%). Another group started high but declined in clarity (24%). A third group started low but gained in clarity (34%). And the fourth group

(20%) started and remained low on clarity throughout high school. As many adolescents showed change (either as gain or loss) as continuity (either on a high or a low level). These results were obtained despite the fact that sample as a whole showed no gain in identity from the sophomore to the senior year (see table 12.2).

Table 12.2

Change in mean EPSI identity-scale scores in three studies

Study	M (SD)		r_{t1-t2}	t	df	p
	first measure-	last measure-				
A	3.64 (.64)	3.70 (.66)	.37	-1.58	293	n.s.
B	3.65 (.66)	3.69 (.67)	.52	-0.77	172	n.s.
C	3.45 (.69)	3.56 (.70)	.75	-2.97	166	0.01

In study C, however, Reis et al. (2006) identified four *patterns* of trajectories all signifying continuity in identity, either on a high (21%), moderately high (39%), moderately low (15%), or low level (25%). These trajectories of continuity were found despite the fact that the sample as a whole moved upward in identity during the first year of college (see table 12.2). Compared to study A and B, this study represents a categorical (qualitative) approach to the data. To demonstrate the usefulness of this approach we split the distribution of identity measures into quartiles and combined exploratory data analyses with confirmatory analyses. In the exploratory part we tested models with increasing numbers of factors until we reached a satisfactory solution, which is model 4 in table 12.3.

Table 12.3

Hierarchical modeling with latent classes of identity development

Model and number of classes	χ^2	L^2	df	$p(L^2)$	BIC	AIC	E	λ
2	126.63	123.52	44	.000	1159.43	1102.62	0.029	0.932
3	64.54	55.04	34	.013	1140.86	1054.14	0.038	0.923
4	29.99	28.59	24	.236	1164.31	1047.68	0.065	0.892
4 with large identity losses	58.43	52.52	29	.005	1163.29	1061.62	0.042	0.914
4 with small identity losses	43.32	41.82	29	.050	1152.59	1050.92	0.063	0.883
4 restricted	32.64	30.63	34	.634	1116.44	1029.72	0.048	0.913
5	14.72	16.06	14	.278	1202.22	1055.69	0.065	0.905
6	5.36	6.67	4	.154	1242.20	1065.76	0.088	0.885

To this exploratory analysis we added a confirmatory part testing the hypothesis that the transition to college is –at least for some– a time of loss in identity (or "clarity", in our terms). We used the starting partition of the best fitting model (with four patterns/classes/trajectories of development) and defined one of the patterns to be loss. By doing that, we added a hypothetical trajectory to the best fitting model. We calculated two different models containing losses, one containing a large (from a very high to very low level of clarity), one containing a smaller identity loss (from both higher levels to some lower level). Both models containing losses (see table 12.3) did not improve the fit compared to the original model 4. In other words: The hypothesis based on the results of study A was falsified for study C.

Factors associated with continuously high levels of identity

Continuously high levels of identity were found in studies A and C and were modeled as an independent variable in study B. Compared to other groups found or defined in all three studies, this group differed from the group with constant low levels of identity, but not from either change groups (studies A and B) or groups with moderately stable trajectories of identity (study C). In study A students with continuously high levels of identity did social service of a more challenging kind (Youniss & Reis, 2001). Community service of this kind meant direct exposure to poverty and hopelessness, for example, working in a soup kitchen or a shelter for the homeless. Interestingly, this difference appeared at the beginning of the high school experience only. Students constantly high on identity also scored higher on the scale for developmental opportunities.

In study B, students high on identity were separated into "gain" and "loss" groups (McIntosh et al., 2005, p. 347-348). Here, "gainers" participated more frequently in required community service. Again, this difference appeared only at the beginning of the program.

In study C, students constantly high on identity did not differ from groups with moderate levels, but from students constantly low on identity. To predict the identity trajectories, prediction analyses (von Eye, 1987) with median-split measures for self-esteem (Rosenberg, 1979) and social support from family and friends (Procidano & Heller, 1983) were conducted. Prediction analysis can be used to describe the association between categorical variables and is therefore suited to all sorts of confirmatory qualitative investigations. It compares values of expected variables obtained via rules of prediction with values obtained by chance. These rules of prediction may reveal interesting constellations of variables that are predictive. The important parameter is the increase of predictability, compared to chance, the del measure. Table 12.4 contains different models of prediction which can be compared by their fit (del measure). The del measures in table 12.4 describe the entire models and can be taken apart into partial del measures, which describe the proportion of different prediction-patterns (e.g., high self-esteem predicting the highest level of identity).

Table 12.4

Results of different prediction analyses in predicting identity trajectories during the first year of college

Predictors	L^2	df	p	Del
Family	8.99	3	.029	.14
Friends	8.85	3	.031	.19
Self-esteem	46.10	3	< .001	.46
Family & friends	17.51	9	.041	.30
Friends & self-esteem	55.30	9	< .001	.41
Family & self-esteem	47.98	9	< .001	.38

The best fitting model is the one in which self-esteem predicts identity development. However, other models with combinations of self-esteem and social support from either friends or family fit the data as well. High self-esteem enhances the prediction of trajectories with continuously high and moderate levels of identity by 61% (partial del = .61). When the prediction for continuously high levels of identity also contains high levels of social support from the family, it becomes even more pronounced (partial del of high self-esteem and high social support from family = .73). The inclusion of the friends system into the prediction did not increase the partial del for persons with continuously high levels of identity (.42), compared to the partial hypothesis including self-esteem alone.

Factors associated with continuously low levels of identity

All three studies also contained a group of students who were continuously low on identity. In study A these students chose rather unchallenging types of social service and reported less developmental opportunity from service than the others. In study B, few clues were found to explain trajectories that started on a low level of identity, either for "gainers" or for "losers."

In study C continuously low levels of identity development were predicted by low self-esteem. Knowing that a person had low self-esteem enhanced the prediction of trajectories with continuously low identity clarity. Interestingly, two constellations of the independent variables enhanced prediction of continuously low identity clarity trajectories if one also takes social support from the family into account. Not only did having low self-esteem and no support from the family increase prediction (31%) here, but so did the constellation of having good support from the family but low self-esteem (32%).

Factors associated with gains and losses in identity development

In all three studies, almost no associations of variables with gains in clarity were found. In study A "gainers" could not be further specified according to any of the potential correlative factors. In study B, gainers did more required service, but this was true only of students who started from a high identity level. In study C, an absolute gain in identity over the first year of college was observed for the whole sample. However, no identity trajectory group interacted with time in a repeated measures design. In other words, no differential change was found, despite the fact of absolute identity gains for the whole sample.

Only in study A were associations found for differential losses in clarity during high school. Students who lost clarity during this time showed a unique pattern of not improving in communicative relationships with their mothers, whereas all other students showed communicative gains (Reis & Youniss, 2004). Identity "losers" also did not resolve conflicts with their friends between the sophomore and the senior years. These patterns of differential continuity were covered by absolute continuity explained in mean comparisons over time for the whole sample. This absolute continuity depends also on the time of measurement, here sophomore and senior year. Studies A and B contained more than two points of measurements. In both studies, there was a highly significant dip in identity development around the 11th grade in high school. For study B this dip occurred with all participants, for study A only for participants from one school.

Second, study B used a regression design (McIntosh et al., 2005) wherein the same set of predictors was regressed to the level of identity at the beginning and at the end of high school. This procedure yielded two findings. First, gender was a major variable moderating the relationship between identity and other variables. Second, at the beginning of high school variables like personality, ethnicity, and positive peer attitude towards school were predictive while at the end variables like doing service, having friends who enjoyed school, and participating in a wide range of leisure activities were predictive.

12.4 Discussion

In the studies reported here, we found less evidence for identity change than we expected. The first conclusion we can draw from this fact is that identity development needs time to unfold. Even in the face of events that should have an effect on identity, such as being confronted with new gender, professional, ethnic, or intimacy roles during the first year of college, changes might not occur immediately. Perhaps the time of decision, such as the 11th grade in high school, might be more salient for identity discontinuities. After youth decide whether to attend college or not, the late teens and early twenties may occur as years of experimenting, wherein identity in the sense of clarity might not play a huge role. As shown by other studies, the period of "emerging adulthood" (Arnett, 2001) can be years of intense exploration, which might not lead automatically to answer the question "Who am I?" Following Erikson's traditional view, a young adult should have answered this question more or less, and should now be occupied with questions of intimacy. The studies reported here focused only on one of Erikson's stages, which might fall short of an adequate description (Rosenthal et al., 1981) of identity processes. However, describing the full process of identity development was not the purpose of this study. Rather we wanted to discuss variables that might be associated with changes in identity sensu Rosenthal et al., which we called identity clarity. In all three studies we found mechanisms which might account for differential continuity and change.

In our view, continuity is established via early onset of identity and subsequent mechanisms of self-selection. Students who know who they are tend to choose activities and friends supporting their view of themselves. As in self-fulfilling prophecies they reap developmental advantages out of challenging kinds of service, supported by friends who do the same. Another result pointing in this direction is that personality traits explained much of the variance in identity clarity at the beginning of high school, whereas the type of chosen friends and social service highly influenced clarity in the later school years (McIntosh et al., 2005). As indicated by the results of McIntosh et al., these students at the start of high school already had friends similar to themselves. Their friends were more positive about school and did more positive leisure activities. The timing of peer influence here was moderated by the gender of the student.

From our data we cannot determine whether these students with clear ideas about themselves are foreclosed or early achievers in the sense of Marcia (1966). Both mechanisms seem to be involved. As shown in several studies (Fletcher, Elder, & Mekos, 2000; Yates & Youniss, 1997) youth who engaged in service often had parents who belonged to service-promoting organizations, such as churches. Females and youth of highly educated parents tended to participate more in service activities than others (Youniss, Yates, & Su, 1997), which can also be interpreted as an adherence to traditional roles. On the other hand, Youniss et al. (1999) also found that community service might evoke rather unconventional constructions of identity and might lead to activities that challenge the existing order in multiple ways. It seems unlikely that students of this kind are foreclosed. The question of how factors of foreclosure and active exploration work together in identity development remains to be answered. Early commitment to community service seems to be a valuable paradigm to investigate these subtle mechanisms.

It might be that continuity in identity is produced by self-chosen continuities in the environment. The idea to explain personal continuities by continuities within the person's context is nothing but new. Two mechanisms are assumed for personality development. As Caspi and Robert (2001) wrote, individuals might actively seek out trait-matched environments and experiences, or their experiences may reflect social reactions to their personal characteristics. As McKinney (2002) assumed, it might be the first mechanism when adolescents decide to do community service voluntarily. For her, the intention to do something good with community service stems from a general attachment-attitude, which itself is a result of successful bonding to friends and parents. In other words, people who were cared for also care for the world.

From our data we can say that these students, foreclosed, achieved or attached, tend to organize their world according to their views. They are able to use different sources, such as parents, institutions, and peers, to do so. They tend more to assimilate their environment rather than accommodate to contextual changes. This kind of self-organized continuity resonates with results from personality psychology. Neyer and Asendorpf (2001) showed that individual differences in personality predicted individual differences in social relationships much better than vice versa. This process of self-organization seems to come to a preliminary stop when high school comes to an end. At this time, contextual factors, such as doing service and being integrated into wide networks of friends doing all kinds of activities, are more predictive for identity as it is measured here.

For study C we assumed that these "community-based identity constructions" (McIntosh et al., 2005, p. 345) might turn back into "home-based" constructions when students start college. Within the limits of the model used in study C, this hypothesis was supported. A major part of identity as measured by Rosenthal et al.'s (1981) scale turned out to be self-esteem. This self-esteem was closely related to social support from friends at home. For this reason, the special constellation of low self-esteem and high support from friends did not enhance the prediction of trajectories of continuously clear identity. At the transition to college, friends from home offer something like a "home-base" for identity construction. The transition to college study also asked for new relationships with friends at college, and the researchers plan to analyze whether these relationships are more closely related to identity than relations with home-based friends.

Mechanisms of identity continuity on a low level

Study A hinted that self-organizing mechanisms of continuity which account for high levels of identity might also work for continuities of low identity. Study A showed that students with low identity tend to choose for themselves the less challenging kinds of social service, when compared to others. Perhaps these students did not want to challenge their own identity by exposing themselves to strong environmental clues. This result was not replicated by study B, which used a different strategy to identify identity trajectories.

Study C revealed an interesting detail. Knowing the quality of support from the family increased the predictability of identity trajectories for trajectories low on identity. Here a lack of self-esteem could not be compensated by high support from the family during the transition to college. Obviously, "home-based" identities may come to their limit when the adolescent leaves home. In this sense, the hypothesis about the return to home-bases at the beginning of college must be seen differently: If students do not have solid self-esteem at the beginning of the college experience it will be hard for them to make gains in identity with the help of family only. They will probably need new outside sources to draw from.

Trajectories of continuously low identity levels, as found in studies A and C, might signal a constant low on identity capital (Coté, 2002). A strong association between continuously low identity and a lack of academic self-efficacy in study C (data not shown) points in this direction. However, it remains interesting and a challenge to identity research to determine how individuals make themselves comfortable within states that might be described as "constant diffusion."

Mechanisms of identity decrease

The major mechanism for a decease in identity found by study A was a lagging behind in individuation. Individuation theory describes the adolescent's active construction of relationships with parents and friends (Youniss & Smollar, 1985). It elaborated on Erikson's notion of the increasing influence of peers compared with the family. According to Youniss and others (Youniss & Smollar), youth learn to negotiate their way into adulthood while actively gaining critical looks at ideologies and different models of leadership. As long as an adolescent stays on conflictual terms with friends, she or he has fewer chances to explore values, goals, and commitments that serve a clearer sense of the self. In turn, the individual who does not fully individuate might have problems in communicating with parents (only mothers were investigated in study A). These mechanisms could not be verified for an older population in study C. Neither in the exploratory nor in the confirmatory part of study C identity decreases were observed. Again, "identity" was named by Erikson (1968) as a developmental task of adolescence, pre-staging intimacy in early adulthood. We can speculate that the measure we used was not sensitive enough to detect changes during emerging adulthood. A division into the components of exploration and commitment might be more helpful here (see Goossens, in this book).

Mechanisms of identity increase

As mentioned, we did not find mechanisms for differential increase, but only for absolute increase. In study C all students gained in identity (or clarity) over the first year of college. As claimed already by Erikson (1968) and later by sociologists such as Coté (2006) identity development is not only the unfolding of the self, but also "prescribed" by the society. In other words, increases in identity development can be observed because our society requires or allows for it

(Coté). As Coté describes the changing industrial society it might be a risk for personal development to know too early what to do with life. Openness, experiments, and postponed decisions are markers of "emerging adulthood" (Arnett, 2001), an institutionalized period of extended adolescence in industrial societies. On the other hand, increases of identity can become "identity capital" (Coté, 2002) that becomes even more salient within a world wherein commitments are necessary to reach certain goals, such as academic degrees. We can assume that freshmen at college develop this sense of capital as they transit through their first year.

Exploring the subtle balance between necessary commitments and openness to individual changes, as it might be required by our changing society (Crockett & Silbereisen, 2000), requires studies about structural aspects of identity development. Studies of this kind are even more predestined to mix categorical (qualitative) and quantitative data.

References

Arnett, J.J. (2001). *Adolescence and emerging adulthood. A cultural approach.* Upper Saddle River, NJ: Prentice-Hall.

Asendorpf, J.B., & Wilpers, S. (1998). Personality effects on social relationships. *Journal of Personality and Social Psychology, 57,* 481–492.

Berzonsky, M.D. (1992). Identity style and coping strategies. *Journal of Personality, 60,* 771–788.

Bosma, H.A., & Kunnen, E.S. (2001). Determinants and mechanisms in ego identity development: A review and synthesis. *Developmental Review, 21,* 39–66.

Caspi, A., & Roberts, B.W. (2001). Personality development across the life course: The argument for change and continuity. *Psychological Inquiry, 12,* 50–65.

Coté, J.E. (2002). The role of identity capital in the transition to adulthood: The individualization thesis examined. *Journal of Youth Studies, 5,* 117–134.

Coté, J.E. (2006). Emerging adulthood as an institutionalized moratorium: Risks and benefits to identity formation. In J.J. Arnett, & J.L. Tanner (Eds.), *Emerging adults in America: Coming of age in the 21st century* (pp. 85–116). Washington, D.C.: American Psychological Association.

Craik, K.H. (1993). Accentuated, revealed, and quotidian personalities. *Psychological Inquiry, 4,* 278–281.

Crockett, L.J., & Silbereisen, R.K. (2000). Social change and adolescent development: Issues and challenges. In L.J. Crockett, & R.K. Silbereisen (Eds.), *Negotiating adolescence in times of social change* (pp. 1–14). New York: Cambridge University Press.

Erikson, E.H. (1968). *Identity: Youth and crisis.* New York: Norton.

Fletcher, A., Elder, G.H. Jr., & Mekos, D. (2000). Parental influence on adolescent involvement in community activities. *Journal of Research on Adolescence, 10,* 29–48.

Marcia, J.E. (1966). Development and validation of ego-identity status. *Journal of Personality and Social Psychology, 3,* 551–558.

McIntosh, H., Metz, E., & Youniss, J. (2005). Community service and identity formation in adolescents. In J.L. Mahoney, R.W. Larson, & J.S. Eccles (Eds.), *Organized activities as contexts of development: Extracurricular activities, after-school and community programs* (pp. 331–351). Mahwah, NJ: Erlbaum.

Metz, E., McLellan, J., & Youniss, J. (2003). Types of voluntary service and adolescents' civic development. *Journal of Adolescent Research, 18,* 1–16.

Neyer, F., & Asendorpf, J.B. (2001). Personality-relationship transaction in young adulthood. *Journal of Personality and Social Psychology, 81,* 1190–1204.

Pals, J. (2001). Identity: A contextualized mechanism of personality continuity and change. *Psychological Inquiry, 12,* 68–72.

Procidano, M.E., & Heller, K. (1983). Measures of perceived social support from friends and from family: Three validation studies. *American Journal of Community Psychology, 11,* 1–24.

Reis, O., Eisermann, J., Azmitia, M., & Tonyan, H. (2006, March). *Latent classes of identity development during the first year of college: Correlates in self-esteem and relationships with friends and mothers.* Paper presented at the meeting of the Society for Research on Adolescence, San Francisco.

Reis, O., & Youniss, J. (2004). Patterns in identity change and development in relationships with mothers and friends. *Journal of Adolescent Research, 19*, 31–44.

Rosenberg, M. (1979). *Society and the adolescent self image*. Middleton, CT: Wesleyan University Press.

Rosenthal, D.A., Gurney, R.M., & Moore, S.M. (1981). From trust to intimacy: A new inventory for examining Erikson's stages of psychosocial development. *Journal of Youth and Adolescence, 10*, 525–537.

Ruth, A.J. (2001). *Relationships and crowds over time in adolescence*. Unpublished doctoral dissertation, Catholic University of America, Washington, DC.

Tajfel, H. (1982). Social psychology of intergroup relations. *Annual Review of Psychology, 33*, 1–39.

Von Eye, A. (2006, March). *Mightily mixing many multivariate methods*. Paper presented at the meeting of the Society for Research on Adolescence, San Francisco.

Von Eye, A., & Krampen, G. (1987). BASIC programs for prediction analysis of cross classification. *Educational and Psychological Measurement, 47*, 141–143.

Waterman, A.S. (1993). Developmental perspectives on identity formation: From adolescence to adulthood. In J.E. Marcia, A.S. Waterman, D.R. Matteson, S.L. Archer, & J.L. Orlowsky (Eds.), *Ego identity: A handbook for psychosocial research* (pp. 42–68). New York: Springer.

Wessman, A.E., & Ricks, D.F. (1966). *Mood and personality*. New York: Holt, Rinehart, and Winston.

Yates, M., & Youniss, J. (1997). Community service and political identity development in adolescence. *Journal of Social Issues, 54*, 495–512.

Youniss, J., McLellan, J., Su, Y., & Yates, M. (1999). The role of community service in identity development: Normative, unconventional, and deviant orientations. *Journal of Adolescent Research, 14*, 249–262.

Youniss, J. & Reis, O. (2001). Identitätsentwicklung und soziales Engagement bei amerikanischen Jugendlichen [Identity development and social engagement in American youth]. In H. Uhlendorff & H. Oswald (Eds.), *Wege zum Selbst* (pp. 249–260). Stuttgart: Lucius & Lucius.

Youniss, J., & Smollar, J. (1985). *Adolescent relations with mothers, fathers, and friends*. Chicago: University of Chicago Press.

Youniss, J., Yates, M., & Su, Y. (1997). Community service and marijuana use in high school seniors. *Journal of Adolescent Research, 12*, 245–262.

Chapter 13

Identity Formation:
Qualitative and Quantitative
Methods of Inquiry

Jane Kroger
University of Tromsø
Norway

"All theories and methods of research, however, pre-suppose a particular worldview [. . .]"

(Honeychurch, 1996, p. 339).

Out of the multitude of possibilities, how does one come to find (or not) a place within the surrounding social terrain? Once initial identity-defining decisions have been made, what circumstances precipitate ongoing identity revisions throughout adulthood? For many years now, these questions have intrigued me. I have attempted, over the past 25 years to investigate the development of identity by undertaking both quantitative and qualitative research studies, interviewing both adolescents and mid-life adults, and undertaking this work in a variety of social and cultural contexts. My investigations have all been grounded in the theoretical writings on identity that Erik Erikson (1963, 1968) has provided. In this chapter, I begin with a brief overview of Erikson's definitions of identity and the identity formation process, and I continue by noting some of the methodologies that have been used to examine various dimensions of the identity formation experience. I turn, then, to make explicit some of the assumptions underlying both quantitative and qualitative research methods and illustrate how both approaches can offer complimentary insights into related processes using an example from one of my own large databases. I conclude with some reflections on quantitative and qualitative methodologies and the potential that their combined forces have for elaborating various dimensions of identity formation and revision processes in greater details.

As a student in the University of California system in the late 1960's and early 1970's, when student demonstrations and protests over the Viet Nam War permeated many dimensions of campus life both inside and outside the classroom, I first became aware of the writings of Erik Erikson. Perhaps it was his work, *Ghandi's Truth: On the Origins of Militant Nonviolence* (Erikson, 1969), which had just won the Pulitzer Prize, or perhaps it was Erikson's (1968) *Identity: Youth and Crisis*, which made the concept of identity a term commonly in use among fellow students on campus, that first sparked my curiosity about Erikson and his work. Certainly, some of Erikson's writings galvanized student opinions in my courses on personality psychology, particularly his controversial ideas on womanhood and the inner space. Nevertheless, this European immigrant's insights into North American culture and the identity issues he described, have had a lasting influence on my own career and have provided a rich source of thought for identity theorists and researchers over the past half-century.

13.1 Identity and the identity formation process: Erikson's views

Identity, to Erikson, is an entity most clearly elucidated by its absence, or when it is called into question. Erikson (1963) developed his definitions of identity on the basis of his clinical work with veterans returning from World War II. He first described identity in the following way:

> What impressed me most was the loss in these men of a sense of identity. They knew who they were; they had a personal identity: But it was as if subjectively, their lives no longer hung together –and never would again. There was a central disturbance in what I then stated to call ego identity   (Erikson, 1963, p. 42).

Thus, through its absence, Erikson was able to pinpoint some of identity's key dimensions. Perhaps most critically, identity provides one with a sense of sameness and continuity across time and place. Identity (if functioning well) enables one to feel a sense of inner coherence despite the inevitable changes in social roles and historical circumstances that occur over time. Identity is tripartite in nature. It is based on *biological* capacities, individual *psychological* needs, wishes, interests, conscious and unconscious motivations, in interaction with the roles and values of a *social context* that compliment and confirm one in his or her sense of being. Simply stated, identity provides one with a sense of "fit"–a feeling of being at home in one's body, a psychological sense of well-being, and a sense of mattering to those who count (Erikson, 1968). With these elements in place, identity is what enables one to move with direction and purpose in life.

Erikson (1963, 1968) has also defined the identity formation process in a variety of ways. While identity and identification have the same linguistic root, identity formation involves the synthesis of important childhood identifications into a new whole, greater than the sum of its parts (Erikson, 1968). "Identity formation, finally, begins where the usefulness of identification ends [. . .]" (Erikson, 1968, p. 159). The identity formation process involves the ability to construct or choose one's own psychosocial commitments, to choose those values and roles to which one wishes to adhere in life.

This process often occurs during late adolescence, when decisions regarding vocational, ideological, and sexual/relational roles and values begin to press for some form of resolution. This identity formation process lies at the heart of Erikson's fifth psychosocial stage, Identity vs. Role Confusion. And while identity issues often come to the forefront of concern during adolescence, ongoing identity development may occur across the remaining adult years as earlier identity-defining decisions are re-evaluated and revised.

13.2 Assessing identity formation: Quantitative studies

In the years since Erikson's theoretical writings on identity first appeared in the 1950's and early 1960's, various measures have been used to operationalize some of identity's dimensions and chart its developmental course. Quantitative efforts to measure identity and the identity formation process have generally taken one of three general tacks. One body of work has focused on the relationship between resolutions to the "Identity versus Role Confusion" task of adolescence and other psychosocial stages in Erikson's eight-stage scheme of life-span personality development. Perhaps the most widely adopted measures using this approach are those by Constantinople (1967, 1969) and Rosenthal, Gurney and Moore (1981). These authors argue that in order to understand the role of identity in life-span personality development, research must examine how resolutions to earlier psychosocial stages impact upon "Identity versus Role Confusion" and how resolutions to "Identity versus Role Confusion," in turn, impact subsequent psychosocial stages of adult development.

A second general approach to assess Erikson's identity construct has come via measures that consider identity in bipolar terms, with one's resolution falling somewhere on a continuum between the high and low ends of an identity scale. Thus, identity has been assessed according "how much" or "how little" of the entity that one actually has. Self-report questionnaires such as those developed by Marcia (1966, 1967), Tan, Kendis, Fine, and Porac (1977), and Côté (1997) have all been used to assess identity attainment (or identity capital). Identity scores on these types of instruments have commonly been examined in relation to scores on other personality variables such as identity status (Marcia, 1967), interpersonal trust, locus of control, and dogmatism (Tan et. al., 1977), and identity style and continuity (Dunkel, 2005).

A third general approach to Erikson's construct of identity focuses on measuring different identity dimensions. Thus, for example, van Hoof and Raaijmakers (2002) have measured spatial-temporal aspects of identity, while Blasi and Milton (1991) have focused on one's subjective experiences of identity. Côté (1986) has assessed the identity crisis itself, while Berman, Montgomery, and Kurtines (2004) have developed a measure of identity distress. Markstrom, Xaioming, Blackshire & Wilfong (2005) have measured one's level of ego strength in relation to various psychosocial involvements during middle adolescence, while Bar-Joseph and Tzuriel (1990) have measured purposefulness, solidity, continuity, and social recognition in highlighting important dimensions of identity.

The most popular among dimensional approaches to assessing exploration and commitment elements of identity has been that of James Marcia. In Chapter 1 of this volume, Marcia has described his efforts to operationalize four qualitatively distinct types of identity resolutions. He examined the presence or absence of exploration and commitment variables in relation to the domains of vocational, ideological, and sexual/relational values that Erikson (1963) had suggested as central to the identity-formation process. Marcia's qualitatively different types of identity resolutions became known as the identity statuses. These identity statuses have now been examined in over 600 publications and doctoral dissertations dealing with identity issues over the past four decades (Kroger, Årseth, Martinussen, & Marcia, 2006). Additional measures of identity exploration and commitment variables exist, such as the Groningen Identity Development Scale (GIDS; Bosma, 1992), the Utrecht-Groningen Identity

Development Scale (U-GIDS; Meeus & Dekovic, 1995) and the Ego Identity Process Questionnaire (EIPQ; Balistreri, Busch-Rossnagel, & Geisinger, 1995). However, Marcia's (1966; Marcia et al., 1993) measure of identity status has been used far more extensively than other approaches. Of particular relevance for the present chapter are the types of quantitative and qualitative methods that have been used to investigate the identity formation process itself and the varied contributions these methods have made to the understanding of this process.

At least two dozen quantitative identity status studies have examined developmental features of identity during and beyond the years of adolescence. These quantitative studies have used longitudinal, cross-sectional, and retrospective methods to depict patterns of identity status movement and stability over time (e.g. Archer, 1982; Cramer, 1998, 2004; Fitch & Adams, 1983; Kroger, 1995; Kroger & Haslett, 1987; Marcia, 1976; Waterman, Geary, & Waterman, 1974; Waterman & Goldman, 1976). Additional quantitative studies of identity exploration and commitment factors have also been undertaken by Goossens and his colleagues, described in Chapter 8 of this volume, and by Meeus and his colleagues, described in Chapter 10.

Several interesting findings regarding identity development have emerged across these identity status investigations. For example, virtually all investigations have shown that only about half of the participants were rated identity achieved by time of entry into young adult life (about age 21-22 years). This result occurred whether identity was rated in overall terms or by individual identity domains (vocation, ideology, relationships). From these same investigations, the primary pattern of movement for those who did change identity status was from a less mature (foreclosure or diffusion) to a more mature (moratorium or achieved) identity position. This finding is in accordance with Erikson's description of the stages of ego growth in the identity formation process of adolescence. Empirical results suggest that identity moves from a configuration based on identifications with significant others (the foreclosure position) through a moratorium process to a new, more differentiated structure based on individual choice (the identity achieved position).

13.3 Assessing   identity   formation: Qualitative studies

Qualitative studies of the Erikson's identity formation process have been fewer in number but increasing in popularity over the past 15 years. These studies have often grown from Erikson's interests in psychobiography and life-span development. Such qualitative studies have generally also used a dimensional approach to identity and the identity formation process. Qualitative investigations have suggested results similar to quantitative investigations about the course of identity over time (e.g. Josselson, 1987; 1996; McLean & Pratt, in press). Yet, qualitative studies have frequently diverged in the types of insights offered about identity's formation and reformation processes over time. While quantitative methods have provided information about general patterns of development for large numbers of people, qualitative studies have more frequently probed the intricacies of the identity construction process via individual case studies or small groups of people. These differing approaches used in quantitative and qualitative studies are based upon different methodological assumptions and will be discussed in a subsequent section. However, qualitative and quantitative methodologies can, in my view, offer complimentary modes of understanding Erikson's identity formation process, both during and beyond adolescence.

The most long-term qualitative study of the identity formation process is by Ruthellen Josselson (1987, 1996), who has followed 10 individuals within each identity status over the course of early and middle adulthood, with a further follow-up in later mid-life currently in process. Josselson identified many patterns of change, but where development occurred, it was most commonly toward identity achievement. However, ongoing identity revision during adulthood was commonplace, and, as one grew older, it was often internal conflicts or new awarenesses, rather than external presses that were associated with identity changes. McLean and Pratt (in press) longitudinally examined turning point narratives told by late adolescents and young adults within different identity statuses over the course of six years; their work also showed less sophisticated forms of meaning making to be associated with diffusion and foreclosure identity statuses and more complex narratives and forms of meaning construction to be associated with an overall index of identity maturity. Kunnen and Wassnick (2003) investigated a single individual over the course of 13 months (with 49 data collection points) to examine the process of identity development in the face of conflict felt by a young man attempting to stop drug use. On a retrospective basis, I have used single case studies to explore internal, object relations issues that may be associated with various identity status changes (Kroger, 1993a; 2003). And Marcia (2002) has examined identity status changes in the identity formation process of Francesco Bernardone (later to become St. Francis of Assisi). Marcia's analysis vividly illustrates the interactional nature of parental generativity crises and late adolescent/young adult identity issues of the young Francesco, as he struggled to find meaning in his life and expression in the world around him.

Other dimensions of the identity formation process have also been assessed using qualitative methodologies. For example, phenomenological aspects of identity transformations via rites of passage have been undertaken by Iborra (this volume, Chapter 4) in his interviews with individuals who had experienced one of two rites of passage: a wedding or a competitive exam. The focus of this work was on the meanings that participants attributed to their experiences, in identity terms. Schachter (2002) has undertaken interviews with Jewish modern orthodox young adults to learn more about what their structural requirements for a "good" identity are (a sense of consistency, sameness and continuity; inclusion of all significant identifications, mutual recognition between individual and society, and feelings of authenticity and vitality). These requirements directly echo Erikson's (1968) earlier elaborations of the most crucial functions of ego identity. Schachter (2004) has also examined identity conflicts also through these same participants' narratives to find configurations of choice and suppression, assimilation and synthesis, a confederacy of identifications, and a configuration based on the thrill of dissonance to lie at the heart of ego identity conflicts. I have used narratives from younger and older late life New Zealand adults to examine how adolescent identity formation processes may be reawakened in old age (Kroger, 2002). A number of identity revision and maintenance processes of late adulthood held strong parallels to identity exploration and commitment processes undertaken many years earlier. Thus, qualitative studies of adolescent and adult identity development have examined ongoing identity formation processes of exploration and commitment alongside other, more varied, dimensions of identity.

13.4 Quantitative or qualitative approaches to identity? Differing underlying assumptions

The question now arises as to which research methodologies are most suited to investigating identity and its developmental course over time. And the answer must inevitably lie with the aspects of the identity formation process that one wishes to understand. Quantitative studies, in general, are based on a number of assumptions: 1) that there is an objective reality "out there", 2) that many of reality's dimensions are possible to assess through the rigors of traditional research design and statistical testing, and 3) that a position of "distance" from one's subject matter is the best stance from which a social scientist should attempt to view his or her subject material.

Quantitative studies of the identity formation process have frequently focused on the identity statuses (or other operalizations of exploration and commitment dimensions of Erikson's concept of identity) and their varied patterns of movement and stability over time. Quantitative studies have also examined events that are associated with particular identity status changes. Quantitative studies of identity formation have generally focused on one or two dimensions of the process, rather than investigating the multitude of interactions involved in the identity formation process. Furthermore, quantitative studies have examined those patterns of development most common to large numbers of individuals, often disregarding the patterns of individuals that depart from the norm. Predefined variables, such as one's identity status or one's breadth and depth of commitments, have been used in undertaking these types of investigations, and researcher distance in relation to the participants of an investigation have been assumed to be the best stance for ensuring "objectivity".

Qualitative methods, by contrast, are based on a number of different philosophical assumptions. Qualitative studies assume that there is no single "objective truth" that can be measured. Rather, qualitative researchers generally recognize that reality is a construction, and that there may be a multitude of realities that a study must consider. Qualitative researchers often seek to explore research participants' experiences from a more holistic point of view, at the same time recognizing that both participant and researcher interpretations are shaped by differing life experiences and understandings of life events. Rather than a stance of distance from research participants, qualitative researchers often seek close, personal contact with their interviewees in order to best understand their participants' perspectives. Qualitative researchers also attempt to understand the experiences of those who fall outside of the normative patterns of development that often preoccupy the quantitative researcher.

Qualitative studies of identity formation have often explored phenomenological aspects of the experience in a holistic manner and commonly from the perspective of participants themselves. Rather than aiming toward generalizations, qualitative researchers often seek to understand the identity formation circumstances of lone individuals. Additionally, the purpose of qualitative studies has often been to assess dimensions of identity that are not measurable via the operationalization of pre-defined constructs. While qualitative methods may, at times, be used to generate hypotheses for future testing via quantitative means, qualitative investigations of identity may also be used to examine complex, interactional and/or transformative elements of identity development that simply cannot be assessed through traditional quantitative means.

Whatever methods one chooses to investigate the identity formation process, it is important to bear in mind Honeychurch's (1996, p. 339) caution, cited at the beginning of this chapter, that "[a]ll theories and methods of research [. . .] pre-suppose a particular worldview [. . .]". In other words, there is no one, "best way" of undertaking identity development research, for all methods hold particular, underlying assumptions. Rather than letting available methodologies set limits to the types of identity questions that can be explored, one's research questions should always determine the methodologies best suited for one's own focus of inquiry into the identity formation process.

13.5 Quantitative and qualitative studies of identity: Integrating assumptions

Until this point, I have presented quantitative and qualitative methodologies as contrasting modes for studying the life-long identity formation process. However, I now consider how both quantitative and qualitative identity methodologies might be used with a single group of individuals in order to provide complementary insights into a complex developmental phenomenon. My comments come from experiences with a large investigation, "A Retrospective Study of

Identity Development by Midlife Adults" (Kroger & Haslett, 1987; Kroger & Haslett, 1991; Kroger & Green, 1996; Kroger, 1993a, 1993b; Kroger 2003).

The primary question guiding my interests in this investigation was how the ongoing, evolutionary process of identity formation takes place from the vantage point of men and women at midlife. A related interest was what types of events participants associated with periods of identity change and stability over time. Existing quantitative longitudinal research often had lengthy gaps between data collection points ranging from one to 10 years. So I adopted retrospective methods to learn from research participants themselves more about identity continuity and change processes over time –about the kinds of developments that might lie between the "time gaps" that previous quantitative longitudinal investigations had missed. I also wished to learn about the types of events that participants felt were crucial in bringing them to the roles and values they held at the time of interview.

To limit the scope of the study, I decided to select individuals who were unlikely to have been limited in their identity-defining choices by financial circumstances. So I used a "snowballing" technique to select 100 individuals from households in which at least one person held a professional or managerial work role. I also sought men and women who had made one of a variety of life-style choices regarding family/career balances. Participants ranged in age from 40 to 63 years. I used an adaptation of Marcia's (1966, 1967) identity status interview that was suitable for adults to explore the life courses of these individuals (40 men and 60 women) in the areas of vocational, political/social, religious, sex role and relationship decision-making.

I had asked participants to complete a "life history and marker event" questionnaire prior to interview so that it was possible to identify time periods more accurately in their lives. Participants were aware in advance of the interview domains that would be questioned during the interview, and while I began with questions of vocational decision-making, I let interviewees take the lead in identifying those domains that had been central to their own life courses. Interviews ranged from 1 ½ to 4 hours in duration and were conducted at a place of convenience to the participants. All were tape-recorded for later transcription, assessment, and reliability checks.

In the months following the interviews, research assistants and I assigned identity statuses to each participant for each year of age from 15 years to the present and developed a classification system of marker events that could be used to study the kinds of events that might be associated with identity status change and stability. My colleague Stephen Haslett and I used loglinear modeling procedures to assess constancy of transition pathways for all participants across all demographic variables of the study. We found that all demographic variables (gender, life-style choice, education level, age group, marital status, and parental status) were associated with statistically different identity status transition patterns. Markovian chains were then used to estimate the probability of being in a given identity status at any given age for all sample subgroups. Markovian chains were also used for estimating the probability of transition from one identity status to another for sample subgroups defined by initial analyses (Kroger & Haslett, 1987; 1991). Among the many findings from quantitative analyses were the following:

- collapsing over demographic variables, such as whether or not a woman returns to full or part-time employment following childrearing, may give a distorted picture of the identity formation process among adults
- the most common pathway of transition was from foreclosure to moratorium to achievement, where movement occurred
- length of time spent in the moratorium status differed markedly by age group and identity domains within most sample subgroups

Later, my colleague Kathy Green and I turned to the question of what types of events might be associated with identity status changes. Among findings were that exposure to new contexts was most likely to be associated with movement to the moratorium status during the youngest age group (15-24 years), while exposure to new contexts and internal change processes were most likely to be associated with movement to the moratorium position during the following years of adult life (Kroger & Green, 1996).

As I listened to participants describe the course of their lives through their many moving interviews, I was struck particularly by several issues that earlier quantitative analyses had not addressed: possible phases within the moratorium process, the relationship between identity development and context, and what I later came to call issues of identity structure as distinct from identity content. As I read through interview transcripts following the quantitative studies, my focus changed. No longer listening for one's likely identity status, I began to observe more dimensions of identity formation experiences from my participants.

One 53-year-old participant, Ellen, had been particularly articulate in describing her prolonged moratorium process. I used Ellen's life story to examine what may be involved in various phases of the movement from foreclosure to moratorium to identity achievement (Kroger, 1993a). Briefly, Ellen described her early married life with a sense of unreality. She lived in a tiny flat and "wondered who I was, and what I'd done, and why I'd done it. Because I had no role at all [. . .] I kept thinking I was in this funny play (Kroger, 1993a, p. 209)." She obtained employment for a short before her first child was due, but never regarded this work as anything but a game she was playing. Ellen had married a replication of her authoritarian father, and her Catholic religion had also provided her with an unquestioned framework for living. But gradually Ellen's feelings of unreality and conflict grew. "I began to feel that [my husband] and the church were the two things preventing me from being myself [. . .] that the attitudes of [these powerful men] in my life were the end of all my hopes of being – I needed to break away from both if I could ever be a person (Kroger, 1993a, p. 211)."

Over a period of several years and five children later, it was Ellen's physician that helped to serve as a bridging other in his prescription of the contraceptive pill. On the one hand, the physician was another male authority telling Ellen what she should do (an experience of the familiar), while at the same time he aligned himself with what Ellen really wanted to do for herself (take steps to control her own life). In Ellen's words, "I felt very much as if I'd suddenly taken my whole life into my hands with that decision [to take contraceptive measures], for I didn't think my husband would agree [. . .] a lot of things stemmed from that–the whole possibility of being able to make decisions for myself came from there [. . .] not to just feel angry at other people but to start doing things myself" (Kroger, 1993a, p. 212). Ellen continued to explore new vocational and family roles, initially battling feelings of guilt over taking a big slice from the family "that I really owed them." She also began to experience much conflict in her marriage.

Eventually, Ellen began to enjoy her more autonomous explorations, trying to "find out how the world was stuck together [. . .]. If I didn't go through this process of going to church and doing what others wanted, [. . .] would I self-destruct? Or had it just been a habit like cleaning your teeth? And I found there were many questions to ask in the world suddenly" (Kroger, 1993a, p. 213). Ellen's marriage did survive, albeit in a form of greater equality with her husband. From her eventual identity achieved perspective at age 53, she noted, "[I]n the long run it's better to be true to yourself than to other people's expectations of you." While Ellen sometimes found a good deal of loneliness in her new-found ownership of self, she concluded that "is a natural thing, and can, in fact, be quite peaceful" (Kroger, 1993a, p. 213).

I suggested the following series of phases and linked these to existing theoretical writings on the second separation-individuation process:

• Readiness to experience, rather than deny or distort conflict
• A focus on separation from internalized others, on escape and not being dependent
• A first step toward external action, and the role of a "bridging other"
• Ability to withstand guilt and fear of disintegration
• Repudiating childhood identifications; anger
• A focus on individuation
• The experience of differentiation and new forms of connection.

From Ellen's life story, I came to question the object relations theoretical stance that separation and individuation are two parallel tracks developing concurrently. Ellen's narrative suggested that issues of intrapsychic separation from internalized others occurs long before individuation developes and can be actualized.

I also was fascinated in my later reading of interviews to consider the question of whether one's existing identity status led one to contexts with certain features or whether one's contexts led one to make (or not) certain identity status changes. I selected two individuals, born two decades apart (with two vastly different historical ethoses) who were both born and raised in the same New Zealand capital city in order to contrast their identity developments and consider my guiding question (Kroger, 1993b). The woman, Elizabeth, experienced all the identity-defining constraints of her gender during the 1940's (only the boys in her family were supported through higher education), of living through World War II (and being restricted in her vocational options), and of adopting the guilt-laden ethos of the era (all must be saved to support New Zealand troops overseas). Yet despite these restrictions, Elizabeth carved out her own paid and voluntary pursuits to best meet her own identity needs. She engaged the attention of teachers and later her husband in supporting her interests of founding several organizations for children with special needs, and she later traveled internationally to further these causes. I contrasted Elizabeth's life story with that of Frank, a man growing up in the same capital city two decades later. At the time Frank left high school, the Viet Nam War was underway, and protest marches to the city's parliament steps were commonplace. Additionally, the Women's Liberation Movement was in full swing, and contextual support, or at least tolerance, for a wide range of identity-defining choices for both genders was in place. Yet despite such contextual supports for identity exploration, Frank entered the religious order of his childhood following graduation from school, without looking sideways. At 43, he interacted only with a small group of fellow priests and managed to narrow his world to such an extent that any potentially identity-disequilibrating events were unlikely to enter. I used further examples from additional narratives to write, "How the Identity Statuses Choose their Match" (Kroger, 1993b), a discussion of how, within broad contextual limits, individual personality factors led participants to select contexts that best suited their existing identity structures.

A third reading of interview transcripts engaged my curiosity about what actually changes in an identity status transition of adult life. From some of the interviews, there seemed to be clear evidence of what I later termed a "structural" change, a change involved in the actual form through which identity issues are resolved. In other interviews, adult life seemed to bring a change in the actual "contents" of one's identity commitments, without any underlying change of structural organization. I elaborated these ideas further in a paper, "What Transits in an Identity Status Transition?" (Kroger, 2003). I used Ellen's case, described earlier, as an example of an underlying structural change of identity, and compared her adult identity formation process with those of two men, whose adult lives suggested a revision of identity contents, one with and the other without, underlying structural change.

13.6 Identity in formation: A reflection on methods

These last three studies involved qualitative examinations of identity interview data that were originally collected for quantitative studies of identity development at midlife. The qualitative studies provided insights into a prolonged moratorium process, the relationship between identity and context, and the nature of identity status changes during adult life, issues that quantitative approaches to the data could not address. Many additional questions also arose from both quantitative and qualitative investigations described above. Are the phases of Ellen's prolonged moratorium crisis similar to phases that normatively occur in a late adolescent or young adult identity formation process? Is it not time to begin long-term studies of identity development with ongoing assessments at least at yearly intervals? Does one tend to undertake identity re-evaluations in a number of identity domains concurrently or consecutively? Answers to such questions may also help to clarify the direction of associations between identity status changes and significant life events. Are there further structural forms of identity in adult life beyond the committed (foreclosure and achievement) identity statuses described by Marcia et al. (1993)? Marcia's (1966) typology was, after all, based on interviews with late adolescents. Certainly the work of Kegan (1994) provides strong evidence of a new structural organization of the self that comes into being for some during midlife. This interindividual structure is characterized by a self coming into a new relationship with the very values and commitments that may have previously defined the self during early adulthood. Even Erikson (1974, cited in Hoare, 2002, p. 145) also has hinted at a further form of structural development that identity may take in adult life: "To have an identity combined with a sense of its own relativity, now that would be a *new* identity." These questions and directions for future identity research would not have arisen through the use of either the quantitative or qualitative studies in isolation.

The use of both quantitative and qualitative methodologies also provided me with insights into a number of additional identity dimensions. From this combination of methods, I gained a greater understanding of the relationship between identity domains and overall identity. After completion of the quantitative investigations, I concluded that because an individual's domains of identity varied so widely in identity status transition patterns, that identity should *not* be viewed as a global construct. However, upon later work with interview transcripts, I began to understand the very unique weightings of identity domains for each participant and the limitations that any study holds when domains alone are merely summed to provide a global identity index. For any understanding of identity structure, a sense of those domains in which the individual is actively engaged is vital to tap the form through which important identity commitments are organized. The identity status assessments of both individual interview domains as well as global identity status ratings for both quantitative and qualitative studies gave me a greater understanding of Erikson's (1968) statement that identity formation involves something more than the sum of its parts.

The combination of research methods also gave me a greater understanding of both group and individual processes in the act (or not) of identity formation. Through case studies, I gained an appreciation of the phenomenology of identity change, understanding that identity development involves more than just "telling a good story" (despite some claims to the contrary that one creates identity through the stories one tells). The kinds of life stories told by "story-tellers" in the different identity statuses differed greatly from one another. This informal observation has been examined more systematically by McLean and Pratt (in press), who found much less complex stories among foreclosure and diffuse adolescents than among those moratorium or achieved. A combination of quantitative and qualitative research methods in the study of Erikson's identity formation process offers the possibility for fascinating and complimentary insights into a phenomenon that neither methodology can capture alone.

13.7   In conclusion

Erikson (1963, 1968) has provided keen observations about the construct of ego identity. He stressed the importance of mutual interplay between individual and society in the identity formation process, and he has detailed some of identity's central properties. When functioning well, identity gives one a feeling of life continuity and self-sameness within. Identity is certainly central to one's sense of general well-being. As a subjective experience, identity is what gives one a reason move with direction in life. As a configuration, identity undergoes a change of structure through the identity formation process. Identity normatively becomes a central concern during adolescence, when the social milieu begins to press for engagement in various adult psychosocial roles, and one's biological and psychological features make responses to such processes both desirable and desired. Upon these varied identity descriptions, numerous instruments designed to tap some aspect of identity have been reviewed. Special attention has been given to the identity status approach of James Marcia (1966, 1967), which has become the most popular means to understand identity exploration and commitment factors during late adolescence and young adulthood.

I have reviewed a range of studies that have used quantitative and qualitative means to study identity status change as well as other dimensions of the identity formation experience. Differing assumptions generally underlie quantitative and qualitative approaches, and I have shown how each approach has the potential to contribute important insights into varied dimensions of the identity formation process. In conclusion, I have drawn from my own quantitative and qualitative investigations of the same participants to illustrate how differing focuses for the two methodologies can offer complimentary understandings of the complex phenomenon of identity development throughout adolescent and adulthood years. Ultimately it is the research problem that should determine a suitable methodology, rather than available methodologies determining the scope of the problem that can be addressed.

References

Archer, S.L. (1982). The lower age boundaries of identity development. *Child Development, 53*, 1551–1556.

Bar-Joseph, H., & Tzuriel, D. (1990). Suicidal tendencies and ego identity in adolescence. *Adolescence, 25*, 215–233.

Blasi, A., & Milton, K. (1991). The development of the sense of self in adolescence. *Journal of Personality, 59*, 217–242.

Berman, S.L., Montgomery, M.J., & Kurtines, W.M. (2004). The development and validation of a measure of identity distress. *Identity, 4*, 1–8.

Bosma, H.A. (1992). Identity in adolescence: Managing commitments. In G.R. Adams, T.P. Gullotta, & R. Montemayor (Eds.), *Adolescent identity formation* (pp. 91–121). Newbury Park, CA: Sage.

Constantinople, A. (1967). Perceived instrumentality of the college as a measure of attitudes toward college. *Journal of Personality and Social Psychology, 5*, 196–201.

Constantinople, A. (1969). An Eriksonian measure of personality development in college students. *Developmental Psychology, 1*, 357–372.

Côté, J.E. (1986). Identity crisis modality: A technique for assessing the structure of the identity crisis. *Journal of Adolescence, 9*, 321–335.

Côté, J.E. (1997). An empirical test of the identity capital model. *Journal of Adolescence, 20*, 557–597.

Cramer, P. (1998). Freshman to senior year: A follow-up study of identity, narcissism, and defense mechanisms. *Journal of Research in Personality, 32*, 156–172.

Cramer, P. (2004). Identity change in adulthood: The contribution of defense mechanisms and life experiences. *Journal of Research in Personality, 38*, 280–316.

Dunkel, C.S. (2005). The relation between self-continuity and measures of identity. *Identity, 5*, 21–34.

Erikson, E.H. (1963). *Childhood and society.* New York: Norton.

Erikson, E.H. (1968). *Identity, youth and crisis.* New York: Norton.

Erikson, E.H. (1975). *Life history and the historical moment.* New York: Norton.

Fitch, S.A., & Adams, G.R. (1983). Ego identity and intimacy status: Replication and extension. *Developmental Psychology, 19*, 839–845.

Honeychurch, K. (1996). Researching dissident subjectivities: Queering the grounds of theory and practice. *Harvard Educational Review, 66*, 339–355.

Josselson, R. (1987). *Finding herself: Pathways to identity development in women.* San Francisco: Jossey-Bass.

Josselson, R. (1996). *Revising herself: The story of women's identity from college to midlife.* New York: Oxford University Press.

Kegan, R. (1994). *In over our heads.* Cambridge, MA: Harvard University Press.

Kroger, J. (1993a). On the nature of structural transition in the identity formation process. In J. Kroger (Ed), *Discussions on ego identity* (pp. 205–234). Hillsdale, NJ: Lawrence Erlbaum Associates.

Kroger, J. (1993b). Identity and context: How the identity statuses choose their match. In R. Josselson, & A. Lieblich (Eds.), *The Narrative Study of Lives.* Newbury Park, CA: Sage.

Kroger, J. (1995). The differentiation of "firm" and "developmental" foreclosure identity statuses: A longitudinal study. *Journal of Research on Adolescence, 10*, 317–337.

Kroger, J. (2002). Identity in late adulthood. *Identity, 2*, 81–99.

Kroger, J. (2003). What transits in an identity status transition? *Identity, 3*, 291–304.

Kroger, J., Årseth, A., Martinussen, M., & Marcia, J.E. (2006, May). Patterns of identity development: A meta-analytic study of the ego identity statuses. In W. Beyers, & J. Kroger (Co-chairs), *The dynamics of identity formation during adolescence: Variations across time and domains.* Symposium conducted at the meeting of the European Association for Research on Adolescence, Antalya, Turkey.

Kroger, J., & Green, K. (1996). Events associated with identity status change. *Journal of Adolescence, 19*, 477–490.

Kroger, J., & Haslett, S.J. (1987). A retrospective study of ego identity status change from adolescence through middle adulthood. *Social and Behavioral Sciences Documents, 17* (Ms. no. 2797).

Kroger, J., & Haslett, S.J. (1991). A comparison of ego identity status transition pathways and change rates across five identity domains. *International Journal of Aging and Human Development, 32*, 303–330.

Kunnen, E.S., & Wassnick, M.E.K. (2003). An analysis of identity change in adulthood. *Identity, 3*, 347–366.

Marcia, J.E. (1966). Development and validation of ego identity status. *Journal of Personality and Social Psychology, 3*, 551–558.

Marcia, J.E. (1967). Ego identity status: Relationship to change in self-esteem, "general maladjustment," and authoritarianism". *Journal of Personality, 35*, 118–133.

Marcia, J.E. (1976). Identity six years after: A follow-up study. *Journal of Youth and Adolescence, 5*, 145–150.

Marcia, J.E. (2002). Adolescence, identity, and the Bernardone family. *Identity, 2*, 199–209.

Marcia, J.E., Waterman, A.S., Matteson, D.R., Archer, S.L., & Orlofsky, J.L. (1993). *Ego identity: A handbook for psychosocial research.* New York: Springer-Verlag.

Markstrom, C.A., Xaioming, L., Blackshire, S.L., & Wilfong, J.J. (2005). Ego strength development of adolescents involved in adult-sponsored structured activities. *Journal of Youth and Adolescence, 34*, 85–95.

McLean, K.C., & Pratt, M.W. (in press). Life's little (and big) lessons: Identity statuses and meaning-making in the turning point narratives of emerging adults. *Developmental Psychology.*

Meeus, W., & Dekovic, M. (1995). Identity development, parental and peer support in adolescence: Results of a national, Dutch survey. *Adolescence, 30*, 931–944.

Rosenthal, D.A., Gurney, R.M., & Moore, S.M. (1981). From trust to intimacy: A new inventory for examining Erikson's stages of psychosocial development. *Journal of Youth and Adolescence, 10*, 526–537.

Schachter, E.P. (2002). Identity constraints: The perceived structural requirements of a 'good' identity. *Human Development, 45*, 416–433.

Schachter, E.P. (2004). Identity configurations: A new perspective on identity formation in contemporary society. *Journal of Personality, 72*, 167–179.

Tan, A.L., Kendis, R.J., Fine, J.T., & Porac, J. (1977). A short measure of Eriksonian ego identity. *Journal of Personality Assessment, 41*, 279–284.

van Hoof, A., & Raaijmakers, A.W. (2002). The spatial integration of adolescent identity: Its relation to age, education and subjective well-being. *Scandinavian Journal of Psychology, 43*, 201–212.

Waterman, A.S., & Goldman, J.A. (1976). A longitudinal study of ego identity status development at a liberal arts college. *Journal of Youth and Adolescence, 5*, 361–369.

Waterman, A.S., Geary, P.S., & Waterman, C.K. (1974). Longitudinal study of changes in ego identity status from the freshman to the senior year at college. *Developmental Psychology, 10*, 387–392.

Epilogue:
No "final" remark / No "closing" words

This book should be completed by some final words. That was the intention of the editors. I would have liked to do them this favor, especially because they achieved what many skeptics thought would be impossible: to bring quantitative and qualitative approaches in identity research together and later unite them in a book. When the conference that led to the publication of this book ended, the mood in the Senate Hall of the TU Braunschweig was melancholy. Nobody wanted to go home straightaway. The conference had been much too short to conclude the dialogue about the respective possibilities and limitations of qualitative and quantitative methods in identity research. In the course of that weekend, competition and conflict had turned into a feeling of togetherness despite the acknowledgement of many differences between the qualitative and quantitative approaches. Under these circumstances I cannot and will not produce final words to end the discussion. In fact, I would rather see the dialogue continue and extend to other fields beyond identity research.

According to a quote of William Stern (1871–1938), purism in method selection leads to a dead-end street, pluralism in method selection, however, creates a productive research environment. Like no other psychologist of the 20th century, William Stern opened up areas of research and practical applications for the study of psychology. Following in the footsteps of William (and Clara) Stern, I myself have gained some very positive experience with a research strategy that combines qualitative and quantitative approaches. The results are certainly relevant to the research of identity development as well. On the basis of individual cases and later with the aid of specifically selected samples, we were able to show that the widely accepted conviction that every child refers to him or herself with his or her own name before beginning to use pronouns is in fact not empirically supportable. It depends indeed on the situation: children who give a statement refer to themselves by their own name, whereas children who want something apply a pronoun. The family situation also contributes to the speed with which children's utterances blend into the target language. Older siblings facilitate this transition for their younger brothers or sisters. It was only by means of meticulous qualitative analysis of the use of language in individual children that we came up with ideas that could later be confirmed by quantitative analysis as regularities in language development. This positive experience, using pluralism in method selection, does not lead to the conclusion "Anything goes!"'. That is untrue. What is decisive for failure or success is the combination of methods in an appropriate order. If the objective of your research is to identify not only correlations between variables but also processes within the person, it is absolutely essential that you begin by questioning individuals, not whole samples of subjects. The appropriate combination of research methods that replaces the rigid scheme of constructing and verifying hypotheses with a flexible strategy of a diverse phase of exploration and a theoretically directed phase of verification will point the way ahead. Both phases are equally necessary for and important to the research process. In this way, identity research will be open to new ideas and will have surprises in store for us for a long time. Final words are not yet in sight. Thus, I would like to leave you with the following words that may be interpreted literally: To be continued . . .

Werner Deutsch

Method Index